from Jackie with my 2009.
love –

Hope you enjoy – was
recommended.
—

Waiting for the Wave

TOM FLANAGAN

THE REFORM PARTY
AND THE
CONSERVATIVE MOVEMENT

McGill-Queen's University Press
Montreal & Kingston · London · Ithaca

© McGill-Queen's University Press 2009
ISBN 978-0-7735-3546-6 (cloth)
ISBN 978-0-7735-3568-8 (paper)

Legal deposit second quarter 2009
Bibliothèque nationale du Québec

Printed in Canada on acid-free paper.

McGill-Queen's University Press acknowledges the support of the
Canada Council for the Arts for our publishing program. We also
acknowledge the financial support of the Government of Canada
through the Book Publishing Industry Development Program (BPIDP)
for our publishing activities.

First edition published as *Waiting for the Wave: The Reform Party
and Preston Manning* by Stoddart Publishing Company, 1995.

Library and Archives Canada Cataloguing in Publication

Flanagan, Thomas, 1944–
Waiting for the wave: the Reform Party and the conservative movement /
Tom Flanagan.

Updated version of: Toronto: Stoddart, 1995, with subtitle: the Reform Party and
Preston Manning.
Includes bibliographical references and index.
ISBN 978-0-7735-3546-6 (bnd)
ISBN 978-0-7735-3568-8 (pbk)

1. Manning, Preston, 1942–. 2. Reform Party of Canada. 3. Canada –
Politics and government – 1984–1993. 4. Canada – Politics and government –
1993–2006. I. Title.

JL197.R34F5 2009   324.271'094   C2009-901382-7

To the reformers of all parties

Contents

Preface to the Second Edition

The last two decades have been a turbulent time in Canadian politics. When Brian Mulroney won a second majority government in 1988, he seemed to establish a Progressive Conservative dynasty. But only five years later his party lay in ruins, having elected only two members to the House of Commons in the 1993 election, partly because the Reform Party and the Bloc Québécois had siphoned off so much Progressive Conservative support. The Liberals then governed for thirteen years while the parties of the right tried to put Humpty Dumpty together again. First the Reform Party morphed into the Canadian Alliance (1999), then Stephen Harper and Peter MacKay merged the Alliance and the Progressive Conservatives to form the Conservative Party of Canada (2003). The new party led by Harper brought the Liberals down to a minority government in 2004, won its own minority government in 2006, and increased its margin, though still falling shy of a majority, in 2008. It's anyone's guess what will happen politically in the next few years as Canada struggles with the world recession that also began in 2008.

Having worked closely with Reform leader Preston Manning for two years (1991–92) and Conservative leader Stephen Harper for five (2001–06), I had an excellent view of what was happening on the conservative side of Canadian politics. I shared what I had seen by writing two books, *Waiting for the Wave: The Reform Party and Preston Manning* (1995) and *Harper's Team: Behind the Scenes in the Conservative Rise to Power*

(2007). Just to close the circle, Manning, through the Manning Centre for Building Democracy, gave me financial support for the second book, after Harper had given me a great deal of useful advice for writing the first one. Both were glad to have me write about the other, though each would have preferred it if I had not written about him!

The first edition of *Waiting for the Wave* became rare in bookstores and then virtually impossible to buy as Stoddart Publishers went out of business in 2002. At first, I thought the book could slip gracefully from political science to history as Reform turned into the Canadian Alliance, and the Alliance merged with the Progressive Conservatives. But, after the Conservative Party went on to win the election of 2006 and form the Government of Canada, it occurred to me, and Philp Cercone of McGill-Queen's University Press agreed, that contemporary readers interested in Harper as Conservative leader and prime minister might want to go back for another look at *Waiting for the Wave*.

Why? Because one of the main themes of the book is the tension between Preston Manning, the founding leader of Reform, and his protegé, Stephen Harper. Though the two collaborated fruitfully in the early years of Reform, Harper was never fully at ease with Manning's conception of a populist party; those differences are described at length in *Waiting for the Wave*. Anyone interested in better understanding Harper and the Conservative Party will learn much by going back over this earlier period in his life, when Manning was the leader and Harper the not-always-happy lieutenant.

Yet the Conservative Party is the legitimate heir of Reform, and the similarities are both obvious and deep-rooted: a Western Canadian base of members and activists; dependence on "mom and pop" grassroots fundraising rather than the deep pockets of the corporate elite; a philosophical commitment to property rights, open markets, and free trade; suspicion of political correctness and of new ideologies such as feminism and environmentalism; an emphasis on personal responsibility for individuals and punishment for lawbreakers; and an overt Canadian patriotism without anti-American denigration of the United States.

But the differences are significant, too. Harper has jettisoned the populism of Reform's early years, including Manning's theory of delegate representation based on the "consensus of the constituency"; the direct-democratic institutions of referendum, initiative, and recall; and a xenophobic mentality (which Preston never shared but which sometimes cropped up among Reform members) towards the claims of Québécois, ethnic groups, and native peoples. Many of these differences are highlighted in the debates between Manning and Harper chronicled in *Waiting for the Wave.*

Even apart from its later evolution into the Conservative Party of Canada, the Reform story is one of the most interesting episodes in Canadian political history. Seemingly from nowhere, a new party is launched in 1987 that gathers up almost all the Progressive Conservative support in Western Canada and much in rural Ontario. That, along with the defection of francophone nationalists to Lucien Bouchard's Bloc Québécois, helps reduce the previously governing Progressive Conservatives to two seats in the 1993 election. The PCs never recover from that blow, limping along until they finally have to merge with Reform's Canadian Alliance progeny in 2003.

Reform came to Ottawa in 1993 and became the official opposition in 1997 determined to change the way the political system worked, installing an elected Senate and direct democracy, and making room for the West by breaking the stranglehold on power exercised by elites in Ontario and Quebec. In the end, Reform didn't succeed in changing the system, but it did bring new leadership to the system, with the rise to power of Harper and the Conservatives.

The narrative of the first edition of *Waiting for the Wave* ended in 1994. For this edition, I have added an update chapter sketching Reform's progress in the 1990s, its transformation into the Canadian Alliance through Preston Manning's United Alternative movement, and the merger with the Progressive Conservatives. For the full story of how the new Conservative Party came to power under Stephen Harper, see *Harper's Team,* where I offer an inside view based on the privilege I had of serving as Harper's campaign manager.

Apart from the update, I haven't tried to rewrite *Waiting for the Wave* for this second edition. The book was widely read by Reformers in the 1990s and exercised some influence in the incessant internal debates about Reform's future. Although I wouldn't write it in exactly the same way today, it should stand as it is as part of the Reform story. But, if I were to rewrite it now, I would be more sympathetic with Preston's attempts to turn Reform into a national governing party. I was quite critical in the first edition of what I then saw as opportunistic departures from basic Reform principles, but I later cheerfully accepted the far greater departures that Stephen Harper made after he assumed the mantle of leadership. When I worked with Preston in the early 1990s and wrote *Waiting for the Wave,* I was still thinking of the Reform Party as a vehicle for a doctrine. Now fifteen additional years of living, including five years of managing campaigns, have given me more experience of practical politics and made me less concerned about doctrine.

A change in the political environment is also involved. The creation of the Reform Party was a response to the political crisis of the late 1980s and early 1990s. Federal deficits had been rising for fifteen years, and neither the Liberals nor the Conservatives seemed to be able to bring them under control. First Trudeau and then Mulroney had opened the Pandora's Box of constitutional change, and the debates over the Meech Lake Accord made the separation of Quebec from Canada seem like a real possibility. As Preston often told me in those days, Canada was caught in a triple crisis: a constitutional crisis involving the position of Quebec in the Canadian state, a fiscal crisis of uncontrolled deficit spending, and a political crisis over the seeming inability of the "old-line parties" to deal with the constitutional and fiscal challenges. Hence the need for a new party with a new worldview to come to power. In that intense atmosphere, the integrity of political doctrine seemed crucial because we were arguing for a new approach to Canadian politics.

By 2001, when Stephen Harper began his rise to power, the triple crisis was largely past. With considerable pushing from Reformers, Jean Chrétien's Liberal Government had balanced the budget, reduced the personal income tax, and passed the Clarity Act to counter the separatist threat. The fiscal crisis was over, at least for the time being; the constitutional crisis seemed to be in abeyance (though the threat of Quebec separatism never totally goes away); and the political crisis was fading as voters became less worried that their representatives were unable to cope with issues threatening the very existence of Canada.

Against that backdrop, Harper could pursue not a politics of radical new ideas but a more conventional politics of coalition formation. The goal was to build a political party that could provide some alternation in power by challenging the Liberals for government. It was a much more conventional form of politics than Manning's, presenting the voters with a new choice of governing teams, not a whole new approach to politics.

It could be said that Harper succeeded where Manning had failed, because Manning's goal had also included creation of a new governing party. But even though Manning never became prime minister while Harper did, Manning probably had a greater effect on Canadian public policy. With his prophetic personal style and his politics of ideas, he pushed the whole system in the direction of fiscal responsibility, lower taxes, and stiffer resistance to Quebec separatism. Harper won elections and became prime minister, but as the leader of a minority government, and also lacking control of the Senate, he was engaged in an almost constant struggle for political survival, which severely limited the scope for transformational initiatives of public policy.

Future historians, therefore, will have to look at Manning and Harper as a team. They will probably credit Manning with greater originality and vision, and Harper with greater tactical shrewdness and command of *realpolitik*. Manning and Harper together, they will conclude, made Canadian politics in 2009 very different from what it had been in 1989.

Preface to the First Edition

When an author has been personally involved with his subject, he has to explain the connection so readers can be aware of any biases in the work. This is particularly important in books about contemporary politics, a field in which all of us, authors and readers alike, have a stake and where no one can boast of Olympian objectivity.

I was not among the early members or supporters of the Reform Party, and in fact I paid relatively little attention to it in its first few years because I was deeply involved in historical research on Métis land claims in Manitoba. I joined the party in early 1990 after I read some Reform literature. I filled out the membership application and gave some money to the party but did not otherwise get involved. Later that year, I met Preston Manning when he came up to the University of Calgary several times for "egghead lunches" with faculty members. I enjoyed these discussions but still had no connection with Reform except for membership.

Early in 1991, Manning called to ask if I would work for the party in the newly created position of director of Policy, Strategy, and Communications. I had not applied for the job, and no one was more surprised than I when the appointment was offered. Nonetheless, I went to work on May 1, 1991, on a two-thirds basis, devoting the other third of my time to my continuing position as a political science professor at the University of Calgary.

Almost from the beginning, I was not entirely happy working at the national office. I felt trapped in a confused organization that had no clear lines of authority. At first, I attributed this situation to Manning's personal characteristics. Sometimes he does not delegate, gets immersed in minute details, ignores advice, and pursues personal whims. Although he has found ways to compensate for these weaknesses and has succeeded in spite of them, they create difficulties known to all who have worked closely with him.

After 12 months, I requested a less pretentious title, director of research, and reduced my commitment to the party to half-time. During the referendum campaign, I became further disillusioned with Manning's managerial style and also began to doubt his commitment to some of the policies that had drawn me into the party in the first place. But more importantly, I began to realize that my problems with Manning were more philosophical than personal, and that what I had initially perceived as managerial weaknesses were actually products of his worldview. I therefore resigned my position effective the end of 1992, although at Manning's request I retained the title of policy adviser. He fired me from that position on July 27, 1993, when I disagreed vehemently with his choice of campaign director for the coming federal election and told him I would not refrain from public criticism.

Since my departure, I have not held any position in the Reform organization, although I am still a member of the party. As this book will show, I have some serious disagreements with Preston Manning. Even though I admire his remarkable political achievements, there are elements in his worldview, leadership style, and political strategy that I cannot support. But I am as strong a supporter as I ever was of the Reform policies contained in the Blue Book, the party's policy manual. I rejoiced at the party's breakthrough in the 1993 election, and I hope it will do even better in the future.

I started this book in early 1993, almost as soon as I left the party's employment, and finished the manuscript in July 1994, after Parliament recessed for the summer. Writing it was a psychological necessity for me — I had to make sense of my time working for Manning, and particularly of the experiences that led to my resignation. However, it is meant to be a work of scholarship, not a "kiss-and-tell" personal account. Here and there I draw on personal observations, but the book is mainly based on the documents cited in the Notes, supplemented by hundreds of hours of conversations with Reformers at all levels: MPs, executive councillors, party staffers, and ordinary members. For obvious reasons, I cannot name all these people here; but I want to acknowledge my indebtedness and gratitude. Without their willingness to share their experiences and documents with me, this book could never have been written.

My greatest debt is to my dear wife, Marianne Stanford Flanagan. A native Albertan who grew up under Ernest Manning's government, she became a Reform supporter before I did. She gave me her support during the hectic months of working for the party; and she has spent untold hours talking with me and helping me interpret what I found in my research. Finally, I would like to thank the people at Stoddart, especially Donald G. Bastian, Lynne Missen, and Deborah Viets, who did so much to improve the manuscript.

Waiting for the Wave

Introduction

On October 25, 1993, the Reform Party of Canada, led by Preston Manning, carried off a remarkable electoral triumph. It received 18.7% of the popular vote and elected 52 members to the House of Commons, who represented ridings in five different provinces. Five years before, in the election of 1988, the Reform Party had collected only 2% of the vote and had not elected anyone at all. The party's success was all the more striking because the Bloc Québécois, which had not even existed in 1988, elected 54 MPs from Quebec on the same night. Together, the Reform Party and the Bloc Québécois effected an unparalleled transformation of the Canadian party system. Once before a new party had entered in a big way (the Progressives with 65 seats in 1921), and once before two new parties had made a simultaneous entry (the CCF and Social Credit in 1935, with seven and 17 seats, respectively); but never had two new parties broken into the House of Commons on such a scale in a single election. Observers wondered whether the change was permanent, and suggested that the NDP, reduced to nine seats, and especially the Progressive Conservatives, with only two MPs, might be fated to disappear.

This book attempts to explain the success of the Reform Party in breaking into the political system. It focuses on strategy, although many factors in addition to strategy have been involved in the party's success. To speak only of the leader, Preston Manning has demonstrated certain essential attributes, such as intelligence, patient attention to detail, the capacity for hard work, the ability to communicate with ordinary people, and quiet confidence in the face of long odds. Whether you like or dislike Manning and the Reform Party, it is an extraordinary achievement to have built a party that could sign up over 100,000 members and elect 52 MPs. Manning certainly didn't do it all by himself, but he motivated and led the people who did the work. He also brought the Manning name, which, based on his father's 26 years as premier of Alberta, conferred a degree of respectability upon the party, without which it might have been relegated to the political fringe, where almost all new parties find themselves.

But even taking all of this into account, there is still a sense in which strategy is indispensable to political success. Just as the most advanced weapons will be useless unless they are aimed in the right direction, so all the intelligence and effort in the world will not lead to success unless it is mobilized to take advantage of other parties' weaknesses. Proper strategy is necessary, even if not sufficient, for success.

However, this emphasis on strategy must be properly understood. The word *strategy* conjures up images of rational calculation, of making deliberate choices between well-considered alternatives; but it can also refer to a pattern of behaviour, of actions undertaken for all sorts of reasons that we would not usually call rational — emotional, intuitive, or spiritual reasons. A pattern of actions can amount to a strategic choice even if it is not the product of strategic calculation. Of course, much of what Manning does is calculated; but at the deepest level his political career is motivated by a unique personal sense of mission — not, as is often thought, to impose a right-wing fundamentalist agenda on Canadian politics, but to act as a mediator, to bring together the warring factions into which Canadian society has become divided. As a careful student of Canadian politics, Manning is convinced that he can "sell" his message of mediation, that there is a political "market" for what he has to offer; otherwise, he would not have ventured into politics. But the message itself originated as a moral imperative that grew out of his religious experience. In comparison to most politicians, this makes Manning more confusing and frustrating, but also more interesting. He is the most recent in a series of Canadian leaders, including men such as Louis Riel, J.S. Woodsworth, William Lyon Mackenzie King, and William Aberhart, whose participation in politics was fundamentally guided by a religious vision of the world and a personal sense of mission based on that vision.

Manning's religiously grounded mission expresses itself politically in what he calls populism, the attempt to base politics on "the common sense of the common people." This populism is, according to Manning, not an ideology but a methodology, not a doctrine or a set of positions but a process for discovering the "will of the people" and thereby overcoming superficial divisions among the people. As in the medieval expression *vox populi, vox dei*, Manning has brought together the voice of the people, expressed in a populist political party, with the voice of God, expressed in his personal mission as leader of that party.

The leader of a political party, like the coach of an athletic team, is always judged by results, and by that test Manning has succeeded brilliantly thus far. He is now in the select company of J.S. Woodsworth, William Aberhart, W.A.C. Bennett, René Lévesque, and the few others who have led new Canadian political parties to a breakthrough. Whatever his weaknesses, he has managed to succeed on the strength of real and great abilities. In particular, he has three unusual assets:

• He is a human barometer of political dissatisfaction lying beneath the surface. Time and again, he has brought issues to the surface that other politicians were ignoring. He expresses what his audiences have been feeling but have not heard from any other Canadian political leader. Filling voids and representing the unrepresented is, at bottom, the secret of the Reform Party's success.

• He has a flair for what Murray Dobbin has called "calculated ambiguity."[1] He is able to express politically incorrect sentiments, such as opposition to official bilingualism and multiculturalism, with carefully crafted statements that, while radically opposed to the conventional wisdom, steer clear of extremism. This skill distinguishes him from other would-be political leaders who get consigned to the political fringes when they try to express views that the mainstream parties consider inadmissible. Without this ability, he could never have prospered as he has.

• Perhaps most importantly, he is working from a well-thought-out, long-term plan. Before the Reform Party was launched, he had already developed a distinctive theory of what the new party should become and a definite strategy for bringing the party to power. As we will see, there are serious problems in both the philosophy and the strategy. Nonetheless, the very fact of having this compass in his mind is an enormous advantage for Manning. Events sometimes force him to take wide detours, but he never loses his bearings.

But whether or not he is ultimately successful in the game of politics, questions remain about the substance of his political project. Much of this book will be devoted to examining Manning's methodology of populism, which is the political vehicle for his religiously grounded sense of mission. Using this methodology, he has managed in a short time to transform the Canadian party system, even though few appreciate what he is really trying to do. It is not that he has concealed his intentions; on the contrary, he has been extraordinarily candid about them. But people do not pay close attention to what he says when it varies from what they expect to hear. This book pays Preston Manning the ultimate compliment; it tries to understand exactly what he is saying and doing. As a genuinely original political thinker who aspires to become prime minister, he deserves to be understood by the Canadian public.

But as much as this book is about Preston Manning, it is also about the Reform Party; and the two are not identical. The party that Manning has built has a dual identity. It is partly the trans-ideological populist movement portrayed in his rhetoric, but it is even more a new conservative party formed by a mass migration of voters deserted by the centrist leaders of the Progressive Conservative Party. Perhaps the most interesting story in this book lies in the complicated interplay between the leader's unique mystical populism and the quite ordinary conservatism of most Reform supporters. At the time of writing, the identity of the party remains suspended between these two poles, but that is unlikely to go on indefinitely. Manning has always emphasized that his populist project, by its very nature, must be accomplished quickly. He now defines fulfillment of the project as forming a Reform government by the end of this century. If that does not happen — if the waves on which his political strategy is based do not carry him to power in the next election — the populist impulse will disintegrate and the party will be left with the conservatism of its members. Thus the course of events over the rest of this decade will arbitrate among three possible outcomes:

• The waves raised by a political crisis (the separation of Quebec, a fiscal collapse, or both) will carry Manning's project to completion, and he will contend for power in the next election as the head of a large, broadly based, and essentially non-ideological party-movement.

• Ideological conservatism will prevail, and the Reform Party will locate itself definitively on the right, perhaps as a sort of "NDP of the right," setting an agenda for other parties to enact, perhaps as a replacement for the Progressive Conservatives. In either case, Manning will probably not remain the leader.

• Torn by internal contradictions, the party will split apart. If there is a separation crisis, some Reformers may join elements of other parties in a grand coalition government of national unity. If there is no crisis, the party may simply disintegrate as the Progressives did in the 1920s.

Political science is retrodiction of the past, not prediction of the future. This book cannot say what will happen to the Reform Party, but it will help readers understand what happens as events unfold.

1

The Real Manning

To a remarkable degree, the Reform Party is the personal project of Preston Manning. Throughout the party's brief history, Manning has been its only leader and its only authoritative spokesman. He contributed the party's name, most of its Statement of Principles, and many of its policies. He does not control everything that goes on in the party; indeed, he pays surprisingly little attention to some important activities. But if he is interested in the issue, he will try to arrange matters so that he can make all important decisions. As I was told by insiders when I went to work for the party, "Preston is either in or out. There is no in-between." Hence, any analysis of the Reform Party must begin with a detailed consideration of Manning's thinking.

That task is obstructed by two misconceptions about Manning that have come to dominate public perceptions. The first is that his political philosophy is directly derived from his religious convictions, and the second is that he is an extreme right-wing conservative. Both of these judgments contain a grain of truth — Manning is indeed a devout Christian, and some of his political opinions could fairly be called conservative. However, as usually purveyed, these stereotypes are so exaggerated as to amount to misconceptions.

The first is the central theme of Sydney Sharpe and Don Braid in *Storming Babylon*. The authors say of Manning: "Every one of his policies, from his views on capitalism to privatization, can be traced in a straight line back to his vision of the proper Christian society."[1] Without drawing any distinctions, Sharpe and Braid present a collage of views attributed to William

Aberhart, the founder of Alberta Social Credit; Preston's father, Ernest Manning; the Christian and Missionary Alliance, the church that Preston Manning now attends; and Preston Manning himself. But it is a parody of scholarship to assume that what William Aberhart believed in 1935, or Ernest Manning said in 1943, is what Preston Manning believes in 1994; nor is it safe to assume that the doctrines of the church to which Manning gives *personal* credence determine his *political* thinking. The personal is not always the political.

Manning, partly as a response to Sharpe and Braid, presented a subtle discussion of his religious faith in his book, *The New Canada*. The chapter devoted to this subject was obviously the one he cared about the most when he was writing the book; it was the one chapter, apart from the policy section of the work, that he pressed me to read and comment on.

Although "raised in the evangelical Christian tradition," Manning writes in *The New Canada* that he now prefers to describe himself simply as a "practising Christian."[2] He equates this statement of faith with his "most deeply held values," a phrase quite far from an assertion of the literal truth of the Scriptures. He does not refer anywhere to the inerrancy of the Bible or other themes of Protestant fundamentalism; there is nothing in this chapter that one could not hear from the pulpit of any mainstream Christian church in Canada. Indeed, Manning is almost coy in *The New Canada* about the exact nature of his religious beliefs. He writes that he could respond to a question about this subject "by reciting the Apostles' Creed or the statement of faith of any of the various churches (Baptist, and Christian and Missionary Alliance)" that he has attended; but since that would not be meaningful to non-Christians, he says he will discuss his religion "in terms that will be intelligible to non-religious people as well as to those of other faiths."[3] He thus leaves it unclear whether he regards the creedal aspect of religion as having literal or merely metaphorical significance.

This is particularly striking when one considers the religious views Manning expressed a quarter of a century ago. In 1967, in a "Back to the Bible Hour" radio address entitled "National Spiritual Revival: A Centennial Project for Canadian Christians," he sounded very fundamentalist, speaking to born-again Christians about the "infallible Scriptures"; the "spiritual bankruptcy" of modern society as evidenced in the increase of "juvenile delinquency, adult crime, drug addiction, drunkenness, adultery, divorce, prostitution, homosexuality and general moral laxity"; and the need for spiritual revival through prayer.[4]

In contrast, Manning's religion as described in *The New Canada* seems contemporary, almost psychological in character. He writes that "the most important thing in life is relationships" and that "strained and broken relationships are the principal sources of frustration, pain, and despair in our modern world."[5] He sees reconciliation, that is, the restoration of broken relationships, as the major theme of religion, and the mission of Jesus Christ as a "mediation initiative" to restore the relationship between God and man as well as among men. As the example of Jesus shows, mediation of serious conflicts may well require sacrifice on the part of the mediator.[6] Inspired by this insight, Manning says, he made mediation, or conflict resolution, the main theme of his management consulting practice.[7]

He once wrote a long article, entitled "The Reconciliation of Parties in Conflict: The Theory and Application of a Model of Last Resort," in which he expressed the Christian theology of redemption in the modern language of conflict resolution.[8] The first column below contains the terms Manning used; the second column contains their obvious scriptural counterparts:

The Initiator	God
The Alienated Community	Mankind
The Mediator	Christ
The Agent of the Initiator	Holy Spirit
The Advance Man	John the Baptist
The New Order and Its Members	Christians
The Opposition	Satan
The Agents of the Opposition	Devils and Sinful Men
The Traitor	Judas Iscariot
The Organizer	Paul

In this "model of last resort," the sacrificial work of Jesus Christ can be a guide for resolving those "'hopeless disputes' where reconciliation has been previously attempted but not achieved."[9] The key is for the mediator to be ready to sacrifice his own interests to bring the parties together.

In *The New Canada*, Manning explains how he sent a copy of this work to "a number of eminent practitioners of the art of conflict resolution," including Charles Malik, a Lebanese diplomat and former president of the United Nations General Assembly. Malik's reply, according to Manning, encouraged him to take his conflict-resolution model into the "concrete arena of politics by running for office or seeking some important political appointment."[10] Although Manning does not say so explicitly, he invites the conclusion that, in leading the Reform Party, he is offering himself as a mediator, perhaps even a sacrificial victim, to the entire Canadian community.

This theme was evident in his thought even before the founding of the Reform Party. "Do we feel led of the Spirit to become involved in the politics of our country or province or city?" he wrote some years earlier. "Then let us go and be involved in politics but . . . let us be sure that our real motive is to give ourselves sacrificially to others and for others as God directs and not simply a desire to advance our own interests and convictions, even our own religious interests and convictions."[11] Mediation and self-sacrifice, which are the main themes of Manning's mission as he presents it, do not mean trying to "storm Babylon" in an attempt to create a Christian society or impose Christian morality on others. Manning wants to work within the political system from a Christian perspective, participating in a democratic dialogue where the will of the majority ultimately prevails. "As a populist political party," he writes, "the Reform Party accepts a political agenda that comes from its consultations with Canadians. Since most Canadians do not have a strong or explicit Christian commitment, that agenda will not be a specifically Christian agenda."[12] Religious faith, therefore, is the personal motivation for Manning's political career but does not determine his political positions.[13]

The one exception to this generalization concerns a matter not of substance but of process, namely the question of how elected representatives should approach "moral decision making in the political arena."[14] Even before the founding of the Reform Party, Manning had arrived via religious reasoning at something like what political scientists call the delegate theory of representation — that MPs should vote according to the majority view in their constituencies. In Manning's words:

1. Respect and represent majority opinion.
2. Faithfully represent your personal convictions concerning the will of God.
3. Speak the truth in love.[15]

Manning has kept this position at the core of Reform Party thinking about representation.[16]

His stance on abortion and assisted suicide illustrates his theory of representation. While his personal view is pro-life, his political view is that these questions should ideally be settled by popular referendum. In the absence of that procedure, he and other Reform MPs should state their personal convictions to the voters, debate the issue with them, and vote according to the consensus in their constituencies, if one exists. Only if no consensus exists in the riding should the MP vote according to his personal conscience.[17] This position may be criticized on various grounds, but it is far from the theocratic view portrayed by Sharpe and Braid. Indeed, based on consultations in his Calgary Southwest riding, Manning has announced that he will probably vote for a bill legalizing assisted suicide under certain conditions, even though he is personally opposed to it.[18]

Manning's stance on other moral issues involving religious faith is similar. Although he doubtless has strong personal convictions on divorce, homosexuality, contraception, drugs, and pornography, he has never imposed them on the Reform Party and indeed has deterred the party from tackling some of these issues, which many members feel strongly about and would love to see on the agenda. Having participated in policy discussions at the national office for two years, I can report that religion never played a role in considering the merits of policy positions.

However, Manning does have an increasing tendency to surround himself with evangelical Christians, not for policy reasons but because a common approach to religion encourages rapport and loyalty. Strikingly, all five officers in the first Reform caucus (nominated personally by Manning) were evangelical Christians. Yet non-evangelicals such as Cliff Fryers, Gordon Shaw, Stephen Harper, and Rick Anderson have also played key roles as party organizers and advisers. There is certainly a potential faultline between evangelicals and others, but it has little to do with public policy. It manifests itself more in issues of style, such as the ill-fated code of ethics for members of the Reform caucus. The evangelicals wanted this code to include certain aspects of personal life, while the others wanted to keep it more narrowly focused on political conduct. The way this conflict spilled over into the media showed that Manning can get into trouble if he overindulges the sense of comfort he feels with other evangelical Christians.

The second misconception about Manning is represented by Murray Dobbin's central thesis in his book *Preston Manning and the Reform Party*. Dobbin interprets Manning's every move as part of a long-term plan to "creat[e] an ideologically consistent conservative party."[19] Dobbin marshals more evidence than Sharpe and Braid, but his interpretation of it is peculiar. Everything that Manning has said and done that seems conservative is presented as indicating his true self, while anything that does not fit the pattern is dismissed as "calculated ambiguity,"[20] to cite that infamous phrase again.

Anything non-socialist would look right-wing to Dobbin, whose leftist views are well known and whose book was financially supported by the Douglas-Coldwell Foundation, an offshoot of the NDP.[21] But even a more neutral observer might easily fall into Dobbin's trap of assuming that Manning's views are the same as those of other party spokesmen who are indeed ideological conservatives, such as Stephen Harper and the late Senator Stan Waters. However, the truth is more complex. Those representing a political party in public go to great lengths to appear to be singing from the same hymnbook. They emphasize their areas of agreement and gloss over possible contradictions to preserve the useful fiction that the party has a single view. Reform Party policy is actually an amalgamation of Manning's populism with the conservatism espoused by most Reformers. It has been convenient for Manning to reach a rapprochement with this conservatism, and he undoubtedly agrees with large parts of it; but his own thinking flows in different channels — an essential fact, but difficult to discover without peeking behind the façade of party unity.

Manning never refers to himself simply as a conservative; he prefers to say that old distinctions of left and right no longer apply to the emerging politics of the 21st century. He said as much in his speech at the Vancouver Assembly of May 1987, when he called on those in attendance to found an "ideologically balanced" new party with "a strong social conscience and program as well as a strong commitment to market principles and freedom of enterprise," a party of "hard heads and soft hearts, able to attract supporters away from the Liberals and NDP as well as the Conservatives."[22] He repeated these sentiments in the "Hockey Analogy" mailed to all party members in January 1990. There he compared the party to a hockey line of three forwards playing right (marketplace), centre (populism), and left (social concern). Although he did not say so explicitly, he came close to identifying his own social concern as representing the left of the party. But in any case, the crucial thing was to integrate these ideological perspectives; for "it is a virtual certainty that the politics of the 21st century will not be oriented on a right-left-centre basis."[23] Although he dropped the hockey analogy after encountering some resistance to it from party members, he continues to make the same basic point in both public and private statements.

Hostile observers, such as Murray Dobbin, have discounted this as camouflage designed to conceal his hard-right conservative agenda, but that was not my impression while working with Manning. On a two-week trip to Latvia, Russia, Ukraine, and Czechoslovakia in May 1992, I personally saw him raise this point in meetings with numerous politicians. He could not possibly have been posturing; he had nothing to gain by advancing this view in private discussions with East European politicians who considered themselves right-wing. The fact that none of them agreed with him never stopped him from raising it the next time; it was an idée fixe in his mind.

Although he prefers to position himself beyond ideology, Manning will accept the label of *social conservative*, a term that appears in Ernest Manning's 1967 book *Political Realignment*, which Preston helped write.[24] Social conservatism is described there as a synthesis that "will harness the energies of a free enterprise–private economic sector to the task of attaining many of the social goals which humanitarian socialists have long advocated."[25] This was not an original idea; similar terms, such as the German concept of *soziale Marktwirtschaft* (social market economy), were commonly used in post-war Christian Democratic parties to signal acceptance of publicly financed programs of health care, pensions, and child benefits. Like Manning's notion of the obsolescence of left, right, and centre, social conservatism was part of the convergent political climate of the 1950s and early 1960s, described in Daniel Bell's famous essay on the end of ideology: "In the Western world, therefore, there is today a rough consensus among intellectuals on political issues: the acceptance of a Welfare State; the desirability of decentralized power; a system of mixed economy and of political pluralism."[26]

Although Manning's use of the term social conservatism can be traced to the intellectual climate of the 1960s, it also reveals something about his own penchant for dialectical verbal formulas that appear to reconcile opposing ideas. Social conservatism purports to unite two contradictory impulses: the economic efficiency of conservatism and the humanitarian concern of socialism. But in asserting that the two can be made compatible, Manning tends to overlook the dependency-creating effect of government welfare initiatives. If, for example, you promise to pay people unemployment insurance compensation when they are not working, you must expect the rate of unemployment to be higher than it otherwise would be because the cost of unemployment is lowered. This is "moral hazard" at work — a principle long understood in the private insurance industry. In other words, there is a choice to be made in the real world: you have to be either conservative or social(ist); you cannot be both at the same time. Yet Manning often resorts to dialectical verbal formulas to paper over real-world conflicts of interest or principle.

Manning shows little interest in the revival of conservative thinking in Britain and the United States in the 1980s. Although he is an intellectual man who reads widely, he makes no reference in his own writings and conversation to leading neo-conservative authors such as Friedrich Hayek, Milton Friedman, Thomas Sowell, Irving Kristol, Nathan Glazer, Michael Novak, or the public-choice school.[27] Neither in public nor in private does he ever refer to Margaret Thatcher or Ronald Reagan as models for what he would do if he became prime minister of Canada. He is fascinated with Václav

Havel, who, like himself, claims to transcend ideology, but oddly uninterested in Václav Klaus, the prime minister of the Czech Republic and a self-professed conservative intellectual now leading a government.

Reinforcing Manning's removal from conventional ideology is a mild but definite technocratic bent. This helps to explain his early fascination with systems theory, which coloured *The White Paper on Human Resources Development* that he and Erick Schmidt, a sociology graduate student at the University of Alberta, drafted for Ernest Manning in 1967. "The Government," they wrote, "believes that the time has come for the people of Alberta, through their representatives, to declare explicitly their intention to make human resources development a supreme provincial concern."[28] Human resources is a managerial-technocratic idea, not a conservative one. Thinking of human ability as a resource to be developed by public policy is at bottom a statist idea alien to philosophical conservatism.

Under Manning's leadership, the policies espoused by the Reform Party are far from consistently conservative. The strongest conservative commitment is to balance the federal budget, but even that is not, in itself, conservative; budget-balancing has been embraced by governments of all ideological stripes, from Ralph Klein's free-enterprise conservatives in Alberta to Roy Romanow's social democrats in Saskatchewan. It only becomes a conservative position when a commitment to balance the budget without tax increases leads to a reduction in the scale of government activity. Manning has embraced the combination of balanced budgets and no tax increases, and he accepts the consequent downsizing of government; but he normally presents this downsizing as a means to the end of fiscal responsibility, not as something desirable in itself. Would he be a critic of government programs if there were enough money to pay for them?

There is little in the Blue Book (the Reform Party's policy manual) on deregulation; and support for market processes, though mentioned in several places, is far from unqualified. For example, one reading of Reform's agriculture policy is that farm subsidies will continue as long as other countries maintain them, which could be forever. Nor does the agricultural policy call for an end to marketing boards. At the 1992 Winnipeg Assembly, Manning intervened from the chair to support withdrawal of a resolution "to reform supply management at home to make it more consumer sensitive," and to replace it with a motion to "reform supply management at home in the long-term interests of both our domestic producers and our consumers" — another example of dialectical verbal compromise.[29] In 1993, he accepted an agricultural task-force proposal for replacement of import quotas with tariffs on price-controlled commodities,[30] thus aligning the party with the emerging

GATT regime; but this is still a long way from pledging to dismantle supply management altogether, which would be the objective if one were consistent about basing economic policy on the market.

The party's environmental policy, very much Manning's personal production, is based on the non-market concept of sustainable development rather than on the market concept of profit maximization over time. The Reform Party, according to the Blue Book, "supports the federal government taking leadership in developing a new discipline integrating economics and the environment."[31] This sentence is almost a trademarked example of Manning's thought, exemplifying trust in intellectual solutions and belief that current thinking is inadequate and needs to be replaced by a new but as yet undefined synthesis.

The Blue Book is particularly non-conservative in its approach to social programs. It wants them to be "financially sustainable," but does not offer a coherent critique of the fundamental flaws in Canada's monopolistic state programs, except for an analysis of unemployment insurance stemming from Stephen Harper. Manning has repeatedly described himself as wanting to save medicare and pensions by making them financially sustainable; but he does not advocate privatizing them, or even introducing an element of competition through quasi-markets backed by public funding. In his televised debate with Audrey McLaughlin during the Charlottetown referendum campaign, he said, "I like the programmes — all I say is you better figure out how to pay for them."[32] In practice, his conception of financial sustainability involves removing benefits from, or imposing charges upon, recipients at the upper end of the income scale.[33] This is perhaps the most politically expedient way to approach this ticklish subject, and it fits his religiously inspired ideas about leading through sacrifice; but it is not philosophically conservative because it makes the state even more redistributive. The Blue Book is silent on the ethics of redistribution, and I have never heard Manning discuss that subject, even though it is a central issue for conservative philosophers.

Outside the economic sphere, Manning's conservatism is even harder to pin down. The Blue Book is silent about the Crown, and Manning evinces no interest in the subject, even though it is prominent in conservative thought in the British tradition. The military policy in the Blue Book amounts to a continuation of present activities (NATO, NORAD, peacekeeping) but at lower cost, even though Canada is already something of a joke among NATO nations for the low level of its defence spending. Manning startled his supporters during the 1993 election campaign by musing aloud about withdrawing from NATO[34] — perhaps not a bad idea, but certainly not one typically held by conservatives.

One item in the party's Statement of Principles affirms "the importance of strengthening and protecting the family unit,"[35] but beyond that the Blue Book gives a wide berth to all the contemporary issues of sexual politics, such as pornography, sexual harassment, reproductive rights, employment equity and pay equity, and homosexuality. In 1990, a task force headed by Manning's wife, Sandra, concluded that there were no "women's issues," only social issues or family issues.[36] In itself, that could be a conservative sentiment, but in practice it has mainly served as a pretext to avoid taking positions.

Manning's difficulty in coming to grips with social issues is vividly illustrated by his statements on the rights of gays and lesbians. After the *Haig and Birch* decision of the Ontario Court of Appeal read sexual orientation into the federal Human Rights Act,[37] I sent a memo to Reform candidates advising them to accept the presence of homosexuals in the Armed Forces but, if they wished to have a position on sexual orientation, to draw a line at legalized marriage for same-sex couples. After receiving some critical comments, Manning countermanded the memo and started saying in public that the party had no position on the rights of homosexuals.[38] However, in response to a question at a public meeting in Victoria, he stated a personal view that the ban on gays in the military should be reinstated because their presence threatened the solidarity of fighting units.[39] Then, after a vitriolic editorial in the Vancouver *Sun*, entitled "Bigoted Is as Bigoted Says," he sent this apology to the newspaper:

> I regret that my comments regarding gays in the military . . . may have left the impression that I believe gays should be treated in any way other than as full and equal citizens of Canada. That is not the case.
>
> As I told Canadian Press, the Reform Party has no position on this issue, nor is any position on this issue being contemplated. I was expressing a personal opinion that the presence of known gays in military combat units may unnecessarily endanger such soldiers and damage unit solidarity — not because gays are any less capable as soldiers, but because of the prevailing hostility toward gays among rank-and-file personnel.
>
> Whether there should be a "ban" on gays is a moot point, since the Supreme Court would likely declare such restrictions unconstitutional.[40]

Subsequently, Manning speculated that his definition of a family might "one day encompass homosexual couples raising children."[41] He also said that, while he favours amending the Canadian Human Rights Act to include gays and lesbians, he dislikes use of the term *sexual orientation* because it might be interpreted to include other sexual practices such as pedophilia. He also seems to oppose legislation conferring spousal bene-fits upon same-sex couples, although it is difficult to be certain because, as is so often the case, he has attributed this position not directly to himself but to the grassroots of the party.[42] These various statements regarding homosexuality may represent confusion or tacking in the wind, but they certainly are not the utterances of a leader imposing a hard-right agenda on the party.

There are, of course, issues on which the Reform Party is known for assuming conservative positions, but even here there are complicating fac-tors. For example, Manning started to speak about criminal justice in the spring of 1992, calling for measures such as a referendum on capital pun-ishment, restriction of parole, and tightening of the Young Offenders Act.[43] However, his sudden interest seems to have been largely motivated by a desire to substitute something for the party's constitutional agenda, from which he was preparing to distance himself. On multiculturalism, Manning's critique is only partial. He does not want the federal government to fund ethnic groups, but he does not object to provincial or local govern-ments doing so. He even likes to use the mosaic analogy so dear to the hearts of multiculturalists:

> If Canadians wish to preserve and develop a Canadian mosaic, Reformers advocate a new division of responsibility for doing so. It should be the responsibility of individuals, private organizations, and if necessary, local levels of government to provide and polish the pieces of the mosaic. The federal government should be responsible for providing the common back-ground and glue which keeps the mosaic together by upholding personal freedoms and enforcing common values.[44]

Of course, Manning holds many opinions that most people would call con-servative, but they are not supported by an overall conservative philosophy. He is not consistently and strongly conservative in the sense of writers such as William Gairdner, Peter Brimelow, and Barbara Amiel, or of organizations such as the National Citizens' Coalition and the Fraser Institute. Rather, he is eclectic in his thinking, and has a tendency to embrace contradictory positions in the belief that they will be reconciled in some future synthesis. He is cer-tainly not a socialist or even a liberal, but in ideological terms he could lead a centrist party with a favourable orientation to business. He could be a Democrat like Bill Clinton, talking about productivity, economic growth, international competitiveness, level playing fields, the knowledge economy, and job retraining.

The real Manning appears with particular clarity in a document he drafted in May 1993 entitled "The Reformer's Guide to the New Economy," which at one time he expected to use as a major speech or pamphlet in the 1993 election. He wrote this to counter what he called the "slash and burn" tone of the Zero in Three deficit reduction package, which had been the party's main policy initiative in the first part of 1993.[45] This vision of the New Economy was based on the book by management consultant Nuala Beck, *Shifting Gears*, which emphasizes the transition from resource extraction and manufacturing to a service-oriented, information-based economy.[46] Manning listed a number of things that the federal government must do "to make the transition from the Old Economy to the New Economy":

- job creation through deficit reduction
- job creation through improving Canada's international competitiveness ("making free trade work better for Canada")
- increasing the employability of Canadians through a new federal commitment to education, national education standards, worker training, and re-training
- stimulating economic activity by eliminating inter-provincial barriers to trade
- increasing the disposable income of Canadians through income tax reform
- improving productivity through the reform of federal infrastructure investments
- improving productivity through increased support of scientific research and development
- improving productivity through reform of the federal public service
- commitment to improved environmental conservation and development of green industries.[47]

The most interesting thing about this list is how eclectic it is. It includes a couple of conservative, market-oriented ideas, such as deficit reduction and tax reform (here Manning has in mind changing the personal income tax from a progressive or graduated schedule to a flat or single-rate structure). But these are offset by other ideas that imply greater government intervention in the economy, such as spending more on research and development and encouraging "green industries." Still other ideas are mainly managerial-technocratic in character, such as national education standards and better job training.

Not just the content but the rhetoric of the speech is vintage Manning, strongly reminiscent of *The New Canada*. The Old Economy is "literally dying" while the New Economy is "struggling to be born." What is needed are "maps and guides" to show us where we are going. Although not explicitly articulated, a kind of historical determinism underlies the rhetoric.

Manning rarely condemns ideas or ideologies as being false or harmful in their own right. Rather, he associates them with the Old Canada or the Old Economy as being an outdated part of the past. Again we see the dialectical character of his thinking, in which the goal of the politician is to do what is appropriate to the time, not to know what is true or false in any absolute sense.

He also has a dialectical view of the role of ideology in the Reform Party. Although he initially attracted support from the conservative side of the spectrum, he does not see that as determining the long-term identity of the party. Rather, he envisions a dynamic process in which he will recruit centrist or even leftist members, whose presence will change the party's ideological centre of gravity, which in turn will make it more hospitable for centrists and leftists, and so on.[48] Eventually, he wants the Reform Party to embrace the whole ideological spectrum, just as he wants it to become a demographic microcosm of the whole Canadian society.

This dynamic helps to explain why much of Reform's policy in controversial areas so important to conservatives remains undeveloped. Manning has postponed policy development on topics such as aboriginal rights and social programs because he feels the party, populated as it now is by conservative-minded members, would commit itself to policies that would block its future growth.[49] In Manning's mind, the Reform Party in its present conservative state is a step on the path towards a broader, all-inclusive movement. If that means leaving behind some of the party's current supporters, so be it.

This quest for a future synthesis in which present conflicts will be suspended has personal as well as religious roots. Manning is, above all, highly averse to overt personal conflict. A gentle, soft-spoken man, he likes to be surrounded by calm. He is not bothered by an abstract discussion of intellectual differences; in fact, he greatly enjoys such discussions. However, he does not like a heated debate that confronts differences head-on. After working for Manning for a few weeks, I realized that he starts to stutter slightly when the stress level rises, so I tried to use that as a signal not to overdo my disagreements with him. His aversion to open conflict is so strong that he made the following statement under the heading of Health and Fitness on his candidate questionnaire when he filed for the nomination in Calgary Southwest:

> I would say that I am used to long hours of work, travel, and the standard
> stresses and strains of political life. I would add, however, that I find internal

bickering and quarrelling among our own Reform Party people, usually over minor issues and personality conflicts, to be far more stressful to myself than any attacks or stress caused by external opposition or the challenge of meeting contemporary political issues.

I am pleased to know that internal dissension is not a problem in Calgary Southwest. By maintaining this situation and subjecting unavoidable disputes to internal resolution, the Constituency association can make a major contribution to maintaining my personal health and well-being.[50]

This may seem like a remarkable confession for the leader of a political party to make, for what is politics if not a series of conflicts? However, the paradox is not as great as it appears; for, while Manning shies away from open conflict, he is skilled in conducting covert battles. Using his talent for agenda manipulation, he will work patiently and carefully for months at a time to undermine those who are obstructing him, or to put into power those willing to carry out his wishes.

Manning professes to see political leadership as mediation through personal sacrifice, but that formula does not describe his actual behaviour, which in practice amounts to conflict avoidance. When conflict arises within the Reform Party, he typically ignores it as it continues to grow or asks someone else to settle it. Then, when it becomes so intractable that something has to be done, he acts unilaterally to remove the troublemakers. The result is not mediation through self-sacrifice, as portrayed in *The New Canada*, but suppression of differences through deference to the leader's judgment.

A good example of this is his handling of the dissident problem in Winnipeg, where four local activists, whose followers controlled several constituency associations, found themselves increasingly at loggerheads with the national office. Manning allowed the situation to fester for a long time, then asked Cliff Fryers and Don Leier to resolve it. When they were unsuccessful, he dealt with the problem in early 1992 through a one-sided poll of the Manitoba membership in which he threatened to refuse to visit constituencies that did not follow his recommendation to get rid of the dissidents.[51] In the end, he eliminated his opponents, but at substantial cost to the party. The Winnipeg organization was shattered by the sudden expulsions that came after a long period of neglect, and Reform elected no one in that city in 1993. In the run-up to the 1993 election, Manning again resorted to the threat of avoidance; he sent out a memo to all constituencies saying that they could not expect visits from him unless they avoided "friendly fire," that is, criticism.[52] Based on the evidence, Manning's description of mediation through self-sacrifice is more of an idealized self-image than a realistic self-portrait, at least in the context of his political career.

This desire to avoid open conflict, and the urge to settle it by expulsion and suppression, seem to be part of a larger complex of traits in Manning's character centring on the quest for personal autonomy. This includes his preference for doing things himself rather than assigning them to others, his cultivation of individual advisers as opposed to advisory groups in which his opinion might be outweighed, his general aloofness from committees, and his tendency to slip out of communication with his own staff. There is nothing pathological about any of these tendencies; in fact, they would be highly appropriate in careers such as researcher, writer, or consultant. But they are unusual and sometimes counterproductive for a national party leader whose task is to assemble and lead a team into sustained conflict with other teams.

Typically, when a leader creates a new political party or takes over an existing one, he brings with him a circle of trusted associates. Pierre Trudeau had associates from *Cité libre*, Brian Mulroney had college friends from St. Francis Xavier University and the Laval law school, Peter Lougheed had business and football friends, and Jean Chrétien had his Montreal circle. Manning, however, did not bring an inner circle with him to help build the Reform Party; he came as an almost solitary figure, accompanied only by David Berger, an employee of his consulting firm, and his father, who remained in the background. Of course, some old friends, such as Ray Speaker and Werner Schmidt, have been elected as Reform MPs or played other important roles in the party, but not as part of an operational team working day to day with the leader.

Starting from scratch, Manning has gradually built up around himself a group of operatives — team would not be the right word — who are willing to follow his political judgment implicitly. The biggest exception, Stephen Harper, ultimately proved the rule; although he made a major contribution in the early years, he did not remain in the inner circle past 1992. Looking at where Manning is now, one cannot say this essentially solitary style of leadership has failed. In less than 10 years, it has carried him from obscurity to the head of a large political movement with 52 MPs in the House of Commons. But as the size of the enterprise increases, and as more people of talent and independent mind get drawn in, this leadership style becomes more problematic. Manning is encountering serious difficulties in caucus; and it is hard to see how he can ever succeed in leading a cabinet unless he develops a more collegial, team-building approach.

2

The Common Sense of the Common People

If neither fundamentalism nor conservatism is the driving force of Manning's political career, what is? His own, often-repeated answer is populism. He opens *The New Canada* with a chapter entitled "Prairie Populism," in which he explains what it meant to be the son of Ernest Manning: "From the day I was born to the day I left home to attend university, I lived in an environment shaped by the consequences of that political explosion on August 22, 1935 [the date of the first Social Credit victory in Alberta]."[1] After the defeat of Alberta Social Credit in 1971, Manning writes,

> I came to the conclusion that if I was ever to be personally involved in politics, I wanted to be involved in a genuine populist movement rather than a traditional political party. I also decided that, rather than getting in on the tail end of the populist movements produced on the Canadian prairies during the Depression, I would wait for the next one.[2]

The word *populist* is not in the constitution of the Reform Party and Manning did not use it in his founding speech at Vancouver; but he did talk at length there about the "reform tradition," which in his vocabulary means essentially the same thing as populism, and he inserted the reform tradition into the party's constitution:

> Whereas there is a reform tradition in Canadian politics whereby farsighted and courageous men and women have sought to correct such injustices and

inequities and to achieve more responsible and representative government in Canada, this reform tradition being represented by such persons as:

- Joseph Howe in Nova Scotia, Louis Lafontaine in Lower Canada, and Robert Baldwin and Egerton Ryerson in Upper Canada;
- The Fathers of Confederation, in particular Georges [sic] Cartier, John A. Macdonald, and George Brown;
- The Western Reformers including Louis Riel, F.W.G. Haultain and the Independent members of the old Territorial Legislature, and the leaders and supporters of the Progressive Party, the Cooperative Commonwealth Federation (CCF), and the Social Credit Movement;
- The leaders and supporters of the Quiet Revolution in the Province of Quebec;
- The leaders and supporters of such Western protest groups, parties, and interest groups as the Confederation of Regions Party, Canadians for One Canada, the Western Canada Concept, the Canada West Foundation, and the Committee for a Triple E Senate; and,
- The leaders and supporters of political parties and interest groups working for the attainment of Provincial Status for Yukon and the Northwest Territories, and,

Whereas there is a need for a contemporary expression of the reform tradition in Canadian federal politics in the form of a new, broadly-based federal political party . . .[3]

In *The New Canada*, Manning describes the reform tradition in these words:

Canada's reform tradition did not begin in the West. It originated with the early reform parties of Nova Scotia, Upper Canada, and Lower Canada — the parties that fought colonial elites such as the Family Compact and the Château Clique and sought to replace them with more representative and responsible institutions of government. These reform parties prepared the way for Canadian Confederation.

During the present century, the two Canadian regions that have shown a consistent tendency to generate and support reform movements have been Quebec and western Canada.

Quebec has a long tradition of third-party movements outside the traditional parties, namely, the Bloc Populaire Canadien, the Union Nationale, the Ralliement des Créditistes, the Parti Québécois, and the Bloc Québécois. While not all of the movements have been populist, the majority have been so. And in each case, with the exception of the Union Nationale, these movements have been dedicated to radical changes, including fundamental changes in relations between French Canada and the rest of the country.[4]

There is some elasticity in Manning's concept of the reform tradition, and he tailors it to suit the occasion. For example, when he spoke on the reform tradition at the 1992 Winnipeg Assembly, he failed to mention Louis Riel, perhaps because he thought Riel might be too controversial in that city. However, there is one element in the reform tradition that Manning never omits, namely, the three successful new parties created in western Canada in this century: the Progressives, the CCF, and Social Credit. This is the bottom line of Manning's reform tradition: the creation of a populist movement to challenge the hegemony of the existing parties.

Curiously, Manning has never laid down a concise definition of populism, even though it is the central concept in his political thought; but the essential features appear in passing in various statements he has made. One is that populism is neither left nor right; rather, it relies on "the common sense of the common people": "There is such a thing as 'the common sense of the common people,' and if a politician, a party or a government can tap into it and harness that power to the formulation and implementation of public policy, there is no more potent political force on the face of the earth."[5] Political reforms to give effect to "the common sense of the common people" will "allow the public to have more say in the development of public policy through direct consultation, constitutional conventions, constituent assemblies, national referenda, and citizens' initiatives."[6] Correspondingly, populist parties must be grassroots movements with "bottom-up decision-making processes";[7] hence their style and internal organization must be quite unlike that of the traditional parties. Moreover, they aim not just at governing within the prevailing system but at changing the system itself — creating new institutions and new modes of popular participation. Thus Manning closes the first chapter of *The New Canada* with this rhetorical question:

> Given the need for fundamental changes in the Canadian federal system in the 1990s — in particular, major changes in our constitutional, economic, fiscal, and parliamentary systems — it is highly appropriate to challenge Canadians to answer the following question: "Should we revive our own reform traditions and harness them to the task of getting our constitutional, economic, and parliamentary houses in order during the 1990s?"[8]

Finally, populist parties arise as temporary movements to challenge the traditional parties; they may govern for a time, but they die out when their work is done, only to be reborn in a later generation: "These Western populist parties have a more natural life cycle than the traditional parties. They live, they die, the seeds go into the ground and then they come up again, perhaps in a different form."[9]

The temporary nature of a Manning-style populist party is reflected in the Reform Party's constitution: "This Constitution shall become null and void, and the Party shall cease to exist, on November 1st, 2000 A.D., unless this Constitution is re-enacted in its present or amended form by a two-thirds majority of the delegates to a Party Assembly held before that date."[10] Manning has said that this clause was included "because so many of the delegates had belonged to political parties that had outlived their usefulness,"[11] but this is a typical example of the populist convention of attributing the leader's own ideas to the wisdom of his followers; according to a contemporary report, the provision "was included at the request of Mr. Manning."[12] This sunset clause reflects Manning's own conception of a populist party arising at a time of crisis and sweeping to power on a wave of discontent. It also tends to make the party a personal vehicle for the leader, so identified with him that it could not exist without him.

Strikingly, Manning conceives populism as content-free; he believes that it does not prescribe any particular ideology, or indeed any ideology at all. In conversation with him, I once said that I saw Reform as a populist conservative party, and that he was in it more for populism and I was in it more for conservatism. He replied that I did not have it quite right; populism, he said, was a methodology, not an ideology in conflict with conservatism. This helps to explain, among other things, why Manning always lists the CCF as one of his predecessors in the reform tradition. Since his populism is a methodology, not an ideology, he can embrace the CCF as an effective political vehicle and a forebear of Reform.[13]

However, Manning has also insisted ever since *Political Realignment* appeared in 1967 that a party should have "a clearly defined set of meaningful political ideals and principles."[14] That book contains a list of 20 Social Conservative principles to guide the party that Ernest and Preston Manning hoped to found.[15] When the Reform Party was organized at Winnipeg 20 years later, Preston himself drafted not only the preamble to the constitution, which described the reform tradition, but also a Statement of Principles, using, as he put it, "materials I had been collecting for the past twenty years."[16] Of the 20 items in this Statement of Principles, about six are similar to items in the Social Conservative principles of 20 years earlier. Of particular interest is the first item, which also corresponds to the first in the older list: "We affirm that political parties should be guided by stated values and principles which are shared by their members and rooted in the political beliefs of Canadians."[17]

This exemplifies a fundamental tension within the Reform Party and within Manning's thinking. He interprets the party as an exercise in populism, a neutral methodology for bringing about fundamental change as defined by "the common sense of the common people." Yet he has equipped that party from the outset with a statement of principles which, though broadly worded, are not meaningless. They commit the party to Manning-style social conservatism by endorsing his characteristic ideas, such as a "responsible, broadly based, free-enterprise economy," the "personal and collective responsibility to care and provide for the basic needs of people who are unable to care and provide for themselves," the necessity of fiscal responsibility, and the importance of Canada's human resources.[18] These and other items in the Statement of Principles may now be shared by the Reform Party's members but were not developed by them; they were written by Manning and then approved as part of the party's constitution, making it very difficult for subsequent generations of members to change them. Manning portrays his populism as a methodology for discovering "the common sense of the common people," but it is equally a methodology for getting people to accept the leader's views.

Generations of scholarship have identified certain common features of populist movements that also recur in the Reform Party.[19] Populism, according to the Marxist sociologist Peter R. Sinclair, "demands the reform of capitalist structures rather than social revolution."[20] This is undoubtedly as true of the Reform Party as of its populist predecessors, but it is of interest only to Marxists like Sinclair, who are always wishing for revolutionary movements. His other points are more significant: that "populist ideology stresses the worth of the common people and advocates their political supremacy"; that populist organizations reject "intermediate associations" between the members and their leader; and that there is a "tendency for populist protest to be directed against some group which lies outside the local society."[21]

How well do these characteristics apply to the Reform Party?

1. *The common people.* This trait is omnipresent in Manning's thought and rhetoric; he claims to have founded his populist movement on "the common sense of the common people." But the matter is not so simple. Manning himself is hardly typical of the "common people." He successfully studied physics and economics at the University of Alberta, and is well-read. For decades he worked closely with his father, a leading statesman of 20th-century Canada. Although he lives modestly and has not acquired great wealth, he has met many wealthy and powerful people in business and political life.

Unlike many so-called populists, he has never engaged in elite-bashing, even at the time of the 1992 referendum, when commentators were predicting the collapse of elitism in Canada. In fact, Manning swam against the current by going to Ottawa shortly after the referendum and saying:

> The Reform Party is not anti-elite. We are not interested in pitting one group of Canadians . . . against another.
>
> We believe that there is a need for a new type of political movement that mediates between public opinion and expert opinion, between national interests and regional interests, between people who make decisions and those who are affected by them.[22]

This was, in fact, a reference to one of his favourite ideas. In the years I worked for him, he repeatedly mentioned to me a sentence he attributed to Václav Havel: "The function of the political party is to mediate between expert and public opinion." He could never give me the source of the quotation, and I have searched in vain for it in Havel's books.[23] But the source is irrelevant. The fact that Manning attributes this sentence to Havel, for whom he has so much respect, shows how important it is in his thinking.

On a less elevated level, Manning is wont to lapse into the language of management consulting. "They'll never be able to sell that," he would say about some Conservative policy idea, such as Michael Wilson's "prosperity initiative." The implication was that he, using populism as a methodology, would be able to "sell" policies, such as balanced budgets and adjustment to the competitive global economy, over which the Tories had run into stiff political resistance. Manning's populism as methodology, therefore, is quite far from simply letting "the common sense of the common people" run public affairs. It is better understood as a specific form of leadership.

A closer look at the direct democracy espoused by the Reform Party confirms this. Manning advocates the introduction of binding referendums, citizen initiatives, and recall, but all of these policies are carefully qualified in party policy documents:

• Referendums are for "moral issues such as capital punishment and abortion, and on matters that alter the basic social fabric such as immigration, language, and measurement."[24] Manning does not envision a lengthy, California-style ballot filled with dozens of propositions. "We are not calling for some extreme form of 'government by referendum'. . . . We are not saying that a nation that has averaged one national referendum per century should suddenly start to have one every second Tuesday. . . . We advocate these measures as a necessary complement to parliamentary democracy."[25]

• Initiatives will require the signature of 3% of eligible voters.[26] This would mean the collection of about 600,000 signatures in contemporary Canada, not an easy task. As with the referendum, the initiative would clearly be a supplement, not a replacement, for representative government. In fact, the initiative proposal in the Blue Book was formulated in terms of a non-binding plebiscite, rather than a binding referendum, until the Winnipeg Assembly in 1992.

• Manning delayed quite a while before bringing out a detailed recall policy; and, perhaps influenced by my own lack of enthusiasm for recall in a parliamentary setting,[27] he even expressed some doubts about it in *The New Canada*.[28] He did not move to develop a specific policy until unrest developed in the party over the issue, and when he did he amended the draft policy to require the recall petition to bear the signatures of 50% of eligible voters — an onerous threshold ensuring that recalls would be rare.[29]

Even in their qualified form, these are significant reforms, but they do not amount to what Sinclair calls the "political supremacy" of the common people.[30] They are at best modest supplements to the tradition of parliamentary democracy. The evidence is overwhelming that Manning's populism does not imply the abolition of leadership; and this should not be surprising, for populism without leadership would be completely ineffective. The supposed authority of "the common sense of the common people" masks at least two major internal contradictions.

First, except perhaps in a small, homogeneous society, the people, even the common people, are always diverse. The common people will contain farmers, tradesmen, labourers, white-collar workers, small businessmen, retired people, students, and so on, whose objective interests may be quite opposed to each other. Those economic divisions, moreover, will be cross-cut by cleavages of language, ethnicity, and religion. Upon closer inspection, "the common sense of the common people" dissolves into the opinions of many diverse groups separated by conflicts of objective interest. There may be some overarching interests shared by almost everyone, but these are more the exception than the rule.

Second, even if the people were not divided by such objective factors, there is good reason to think that widespread agreement — the "consensus" of which Manning likes to speak — will be rare. It is now well understood in political science that decisions are a function of the procedures used to arrive at them. Only if the agenda is controlled so that people are presented with bipolar alternatives one at a time will there necessarily be majorities in favour of particular alternatives. If more than two alternatives to an issue exist, there is no inevitable majority, and the results depend on the decision rules used to winnow out alternatives.

The populist dream of consensus about policy matters is both empirically impossible and logically incoherent. "The common sense of the common people" does not have any independent existence; it is an artifact of agenda control. Who decides what questions will be asked? Who posits the alternative courses of action? Who decides on voting rules? The answers determine what the will of the people shall be. As a political leader Manning operates with an intuitive grasp of the importance of agenda control, and within the Reform Party he tries to reserve that control for himself.

But, regardless of how things look to a skeptical political scientist, Manning systematically creates the impression that he is merely the spokesman of the popular will. An interesting example is the Reform Party's policy on moral questions such as abortion and euthanasia, which requires the MP "to faithfully vote the consensus of the constituency in the appropriate divisions of the House of Commons if such a consensus exists."[31] But it is doubtful whether the dictionary definition of *consensus* ("unanimity, agreement, concord") can ever describe constituency opinion on controversial moral questions. If 80% of the voters are pro-choice and 20% pro-life, that means there is a strong majority on one side, but not that everyone agrees. The 20% pro-lifers are not part of a pro-choice consensus; they are a dissenting minority. At a practical level, Manning understands this and will use the term *clear majority* interchangeably with consensus.[32] But if all he means is clear majority, why does he persist in speaking of consensus? Precisely because the latter term's connotations of universal agreement imply that there is a singular popular will — and that is the essence of populism.

2. *Weakness of intermediate associations.* There are forms of populism, such as Ross Perot's movement in the United States, in which there is not even a political party to mediate between leader and followers. In contrast, Manning wanted from the very beginning to build a political party; but the party he has built reveals its populist character through the weakness of its internal structures and procedures, which leave him as leader remarkably free to do what he wants.

Superficially, the party's executive council, elected at the biennial assemblies, appears to be a powerful body. The party's constitution provides for the election of the members of the executive council, who then select from among themselves their officers, including a chairman, who is chief operating officer of the party; they also appoint members to whatever committees they desire to have.[33] These procedures appear ultra-democratic, but they actually strengthen Manning's position. He, as leader of the party, is an ex officio member of executive council; the practice has been for him to nominate the chairman and other officers of council as well as the chairmen and members of all committees, after which council votes to ratify the appointments. Manning has used this prerogative to ensure that all key positions are filled by reliable loyalists and to isolate mavericks on the council.[34]

Once he fills the positions, the system is almost invulnerable because the handpicked chairmen of all the committees, led by the chairman of the party, constitute the management and planning committee, which is the truly active part of executive council. The full council meets every two or three months, whereas the M & P committee, as it is called, meets every two weeks, and more frequently if required. Inevitably, executive council tends to function as a ratification body for M & P.

In other parties, the party president or chairman is elected by members or their delegates at a convention, thus giving this officer a mandate similar to the leader's. In times of crisis, a party president may even oppose the leader, as when Dalton Camp worked to bring down John Diefenbaker.[35] It is hard to imagine anything like this happening in the Reform Party as long as the chairman is in effect the leader's handpicked lieutenant.

Another key feature of the Reform Party's organization is its remarkable degree of centralization. That, unlike the other parties, Reform maintains no special wings for youth, women, or aboriginals is understandable in terms of the party's ideology. But centralization goes far beyond that; there are also no geographical organizational units — no regional, provincial, or local organizations, caucuses, or campaign committees. There is the executive council, assisted by the national office, on the one hand, and the 200-odd constituency associations, on the other, with nothing in between. There were early experiments in establishing regional area councils, but they were terminated when they began to challenge executive council.

Again, none of the three traditional parties is so highly centralized; they all have regional and provincial machinery of various types. Reform has had to pay a price for its ultra-centralization, for when the national office has to communicate directly with 200 constituencies, many things fall between the cracks. In particular, the repeated embarrassments that the party has suffered because of racist and other extremist elements are largely due to the weakness of administrative supervision over local constituency organizations. Why then does Manning persist in the policy of extreme centralization?

Because he fears fragmentation in a new party, and because he has a keen sense of personal power.

Power, however, is not quite the right word; it suggests that Manning is interested in controlling the actions of others, and that is not in fact the case. He is about as far from an authoritarian personality as can be imagined. For Manning, power really means autonomy, his personal ability to follow his own inclinations as leader, to say what he wants to the public without being contradicted or impeded by party structures. He takes little pleasure in managing others; in fact, he is sometimes even reluctant to give the directions to staff that are necessary to carry on efficient management. Much of the time, he would rather do something himself than tell someone else to do it.

When his autonomy is threatened or frustrated by others, Manning reacts, not by confronting and dominating them directly, but by getting them out of the way. He uses his central role as leader to keep "problem" people out of key positions, to frustrate their endeavours so that they eventually quit, or, if necessary, to have them fired or expelled from the party. And, of course, he influences nomination and election processes within the party to ensure that he is surrounded by people who will not interfere with his autonomy.

This distinction between power as control and power as autonomy is essential to understanding the style of Manning's leadership. He certainly strives to maintain unchallenged leadership, but for the purpose of preserving his own independence, not for exercising effective command over others. Those, like Murray Dobbin, who paint him as a virtual dictator hiding behind a mask of populism, misread what is happening. Manning is not carefully "managing the membership" of the party, as Dobbin puts it;[36] he is often content to ignore it as long as he is free to go his own way.

Superficially, the members appear to have control over party policy. The Statement of Principles is part of the constitution, and policy resolutions require a vote of approval at assemblies by a double majority of votes and provinces.[37] At the Saskatoon Assembly, a further constraint was added: "Between assemblies, interim policies and objectives of the Party shall be those determined by the Leader in consultation with and approved by the Executive Council. . . . Such interim policies and objectives shall be placed before the next assembly for approval by delegates."[38] But despite these constitutional provisions, the reality is that Manning exercises virtually complete control over party policy.

To begin with, he appointed Stephen Harper as chief policy officer but discouraged him from seeking a seat on executive council. This meant that policy matters could be decided between Manning and Harper without involving the council, except in the rare cases where formal ratification was sought.

Constitutionally, the assembly is supreme over policy in the sense that it votes on the policy resolutions comprising the Blue Book, but the contents of the latter have never tightly constrained what Manning chooses to talk about in public. Some of his favourite subjects — for example, manpower retraining and higher education — are scarcely covered in the Blue Book.[39] In January 1992, Manning unveiled a proposal for voucher funding of university education,[40] which was not subsequently brought before the executive council or the Winnipeg Assembly, yet he continued to refer to it. On the other hand, there are many subjects in the Blue Book, such as a more competitive banking system or an integration of social programs into the tax system, which he never talks about.

Dobbin portrays Manning as carefully managing, even manipulating, Reform assemblies to ensure that the right policies are approved. But in fact, because Manning does not feel closely bound by the results of assemblies, he has often taken a remarkably laissez-faire attitude towards their proceedings.

Consider the 1992 Winnipeg Assembly. Manning did carefully manage the preparations; together with Harper, he drafted a platform to be submitted for approval at Winnipeg and to be used in the upcoming federal election. It was sent out in draft form for commentary by all riding associations, and the resulting comments and suggestions were organized into alternative resolutions by a resolutions committee with which he kept in touch through Harper. Thus what came to the floor in Winnipeg was carefully designed to produce the desired results.

At that point, however, management lapsed. Manning did not intervene to stop Cliff Fryers, who chaired the assembly, from allowing new resolutions to be introduced from the floor when this was requested by some of those in attendance, even though this violated the announced rules of procedure. He did nothing to stop the defeat of a multiculturalism plank incorporating his own wording ("a Reform Government will assign the protection of cultural identity to individuals, groups, and lower levels of government").[41] He was not even there when a radical motion affirming "the right of law-abiding citizens to own and use firearms" was introduced from the floor and debated (Harper intervened on his own initiative to get it tabled).[42] Manning intervened only once, to support a meaningless verbal compromise when a spirited debate broke out on supply management.[43]

This relative lack of concern with assembly proceedings and decisions stems from Manning's feeling that he is not bound by them. For instance, in his main speech at Winnipeg, he used his own wording on multiculturalism, even though it had earlier been repudiated by the assembly (no one seemed to notice).[44] It is not that Manning would ignore or oppose the Blue Book, rather he uses it selectively and interprets it as he wishes.

Between assemblies, Manning remains essentially unconstrained (or at least he was until he had to start dealing with a Reform caucus in the House of Commons). Approval of policy initiatives by executive council, if requested, is a foregone conclusion; but it is seldom requested, and Manning, or an assistant, judges whether it needs to be requested. This would be unsurprising in other parties; their party leaders do not feel compelled to clear policy matters with their national executive bodies, but those other parties do not have constitutions requiring their leaders to do this. Other leaders, moreover, operate under the constraint of having to carry their caucus with them, something that Manning did not need to worry about before entering the House of Commons (he held teleconference "caucus" calls with Deborah Grey when she was the lone Reform MP, but she rarely wanted to edit policy statements). Nor does Manning let himself get tied down by a chief of staff and policy advisers. In my time in the national office, he generally met with me and other policy advisers individually, thus ensuring that a committee dynamic would not develop. The one time such a dynamic did develop, namely, at the start of the referendum campaign, he dissolved the group almost immediately. Manning would also not infrequently make policy announcements while travelling, without having consulted with national office staff beforehand. When I complained about this, he responded not by consulting more systematically with staff but by making extra efforts to circulate transcripts of his remarks, so that we would know what positions he was taking.

As if to counter the impression that he is a one-man show, Manning hardly ever uses the pronoun *I* when he discusses policy; he prefers rather to speak in the populist *we*. And this is not just a pretence; there is normally a high degree of consultation underlying his pronouncements. But no regularized process for consultation exists. Instead, Manning relies on a wide variety of processes, which he employs at his own discretion. For example, he has at different times justified his positions with reference to one or more of the following:

- Questionnaires mailed to all Reform Party members
- Straw polls printed in *The Reformer* with request for reply
- Letters sent to constituency presidents requesting reply
- Letters to nominated Reform candidates or meetings with them
- "Caucus" meetings with Deborah Grey (used to approve issue statements for inclusion in the Green Book)
- Leader's task forces on particular issues

• Advice of so-called experts
• "What we [read Manning] hear in our public meetings."

Now these are all valuable sources of information, and one of Manning's great strengths as a politician is his ability to listen to such a multiplicity of sources. As many observers have noted, he is often a reliable barometer of emerging public concerns that have not yet registered on politicians in other parties. But where decision making is concerned, the crucial fact is that Manning himself controls all the consultative processes and arbitrates between them. He drafts, or at least edits before approving, any questionnaires, letters, issue statements, or other such documents. He chooses the experts and the personnel of task forces. He decides what is relevant and important in the question-and-answer sessions following his speeches.

Significantly, Manning does not usually defend his positions as mere deductions from the Blue Book, which would have the effect of tying him to a fixed body of propositions. And his consultative processes rest upon diverse sets of people: all Reform members; special groups within the party, such as candidates or local activists; and sources that are not even necessarily within the party, such as experts or the audiences who happen to attend his speeches. Even more problematic, he maintains that on certain issues, for instance, native self-government, Reform policy has to be made in consultation with the interest group affected by it, that is, native people themselves. I have also heard him say with regard to national defence policy, about which Reform members tend to be quite hawkish, that he would treat the party as only one interest group whose views would affect but not determine the ultimate policy. Manning's populism is fluid. He speaks in the name of "the common sense of the common people," but he is the only one who is authorized to express it, and he has various and not necessarily compatible ways for discovering that elusive wisdom.

3. *External enemies.* It is here that Manning departs most from Sinclair's paradigm of western Canadian populism, which in its various incarnations has had a colourful rogues' gallery of external enemies: financial interests, capitalists, the "50 big shots," communists, Jews, and so on. Manning criticizes only the "old system," or lack of vision. His post-referendum statement that the Reform Party "is not interested in pitting one group of Canadians against another" constitutes a fundamental aspect of his thinking.

This point is easily missed if one assumes that all Reform Party statements represent Manning's own ideas. David Laycock, an authority on western Canadian populism, has written: "For the Reform Party, the people are all those who are not members of or represented by 'the special interests.' A recent RPC pamphlet states on its cover that 'In Ottawa, every special interest group counts except one: Canadians.' The Reform Party presents itself as the representative of the unrepresented."[45] The pamphlet in question was prepared in early winter 1992 by Laurie Watson when she first became the party's manager of communications. Manning let it go out, but these were not words he himself would have chosen. The critique of "special interests" does appeal powerfully to the conservatives in the party and is essential to the thinking of such conservative writers as Milton Friedman, Friedrich Hayek, and the public choice school; but it does not form a major part of Manning's own thinking.

Manning not only appears to posit no opponents (not even any opposing ideologies), he is frank about the danger that populism will degenerate into xenophobia or racism.[46] He has been willing to expel racists from the party, but this policy has not always been implemented effectively and has led to major public embarrassments, such as the near-nomination of Doug Collins in 1988 and the Heritage Front episode in Toronto in 1992. These embarrassments have been partly due to the administrative problems that accompany populism. Because the party hovers between grassroots populism and ultra-centralization, the over-loaded leader — overburdened by his own choice — is sometimes surprised by local situations. These embarrassments also owe something to Manning's preference for acting on his own autonomy as opposed to seeking control over others. He would expel racists or extremists when they became a public nuisance or embarrassment, but he would not go looking for them in the first place.

Far from whipping up animosity against external enemies, Manning's populism goes to the other extreme of overlooking or even denying the existence of basic political cleavages. Mainstream politicians in a liberal democracy tend to speak in universal terms. They claim that their policies are in the general interest, and they welcome supporters from any sector of society. Racists, extreme nationalists, and others who openly identify enemies beyond the pale are rightly suspected of incipient totalitarianism. But while liberal democracy does not tolerate the naming of enemies, it takes for granted that all politicians will encounter opposition and that opposition is legitimate and necessary. Because any set of policies will help some people and hurt others (or at least help some more than others), opposition is bound to arise in the normal course of politics.

But this open acceptance of opposition is muted in Manning's version of populism. Because groups have opposing economic interests, ideological conflict over the economy occurs in all democracies; yet Manning denies the relevance of ideology in our time. Conflict between English and French has always been central to Canadian politics, yet Manning argues that ordinary people in both linguistic communities "want more or less the same things for themselves and their children — a safe environment, good jobs with good incomes, high-quality education and health services, respect for their personal values and cultural heritages, and the freedom to live their lives in peace and dignity."[47] This is undoubtedly true as far as it goes; but it blurs the reality that francophones and anglophones constitute distinct linguistic communities whose interests are often in conflict. Likewise, Manning believes that there are, or should be, no fundamental distinctions between aboriginals and racial minorities and other Canadians, and that there are no distinctive women's issues. A similar pattern is evident in his view of labour-management relations: "The Reform Party supports the harmoniza-tion of labour-management relations, and rejects the view that labour and management must constitute warring camps."[48] Manning tends to see con-flict not as the inevitable clash of different interests but as an abnormal con-dition to be overcome by applying a new model of "systemic reform."

It is not that any of these opinions are necessarily false; indeed, there is much to be said for each of them as statements of intention. But taken together they evidence a particular style of thinking about politics, which could be called monism, that is, a philosophy of oneness. Such monism is certainly preferable to a Manichean dualism, which divides society into friend and foe, victim and oppressor, and then tries to mobilize a campaign against the forces of evil. Populism in a dualistic mode can lead to intoler-ance, terrorism, and civil war; and it is to Manning's great credit that he has no taste for dualism. But monism and dualism are not the only choices. The third and most realistic one from the standpoint of political science is plu-ralism, the frank recognition that all societies are internally divided in com-plex patterns of cleavage, and that the art of politics consists of building coalitions based on overlapping interests and opinions. In the pluralist view, a coalition of the entire "people," even of the "common people," is extremely rare, emerging only in times of war or another grave crisis. Under more nor-mal conditions, politicians have to be selective, brokering certain interests into a coalition capable of exercising influence and ultimately power.

Manning simply does not think in these terms. A revealing episode occurred when I first went to work for the party and he asked me to carry out a survey of party members. His expectation was that a populist party should be a demographic representation, almost a microcosm, of the larger society. Of course, the Reform Party is no such thing; its membership is highly skewed geographically (90% of members live in the three provinces of Alberta, British Columbia, and Ontario) as well as demographically (referred to internally as the "4 Ms" — married, middle-aged, middle-class men).[49] There is nothing surprising or sinister about this; all parties are skewed in various ways. The interesting point is that Manning hoped for something different.

Around the same time, we also received a large batch of data from an Angus Reid poll of the western provinces, commissioned Frank Luntz to do a national survey for us, and started to subscribe to the Environics *Focus Canada* quarterly reports. Manning's interest in this wealth of data never went much beyond the "horse race" aspect of how we stood in relation to other parties. He showed no interest in using the data to identify and target the geographic, demographic, and psychographic groups that might be expected to respond to our policies. If anything, he seemed to reverse the logic and was more concerned with addressing the groups (youth, women, non-white) where we were weakest and had the worst prospects. But in any event he soon cancelled our polling program altogether, saying there was no way we could use the data, which was true enough within a monistic frame of reference.

This monism surfaced again in the Reform Party's expansion plan, announced shortly after the 1993 election. Manning's list of targets for expansion efforts amounted to an inventory of Canadian society: "Quebec, the four Atlantic provinces, some parts of Ontario, young people, women, visible minorities and former supporters of the Progressive Conservative Party and New Democratic Party."[50] Rather than building on strength to produce an electoral coalition tied together by specific ideas about public policy, this list exemplifies Manning's belief in a movement-party that can represent all facets of society simultaneously.

This monistic populism seems to stem from Manning's evangelical Christianity. His conception of bringing Reform to everyone mirrors the strategy of evangelism described in St. Paul's First Epistle to the Corinthians: "And unto the Jews, I became as a Jew, that I might gain the Jews. . . . To them that are without law, as without law . . . that I might gain them that are without law. To the weak became I as weak, that I might gain the weak: I am made all things to all men, that I might by all means save some."[51]

Manning's populism also reflects the political experience of his native Alberta. At least prior to the 1990s, there was never a prolonged period of two-party competition there. Each time that a provincial government was replaced, a newly founded or re-established party swept into power on a wave of discontent, completely destroying its predecessor. The Liberals formed the first government in 1905, the UFA replaced the Liberals in 1921, Social Credit replaced the Liberals in 1935, and the resurgent Lougheed Conservatives replaced Social Credit in 1971. In the Alberta pattern of politics, one party has always functioned as the representative microcosm of the provincial society. This is a fascinating phenomenon, but it is not typical of Canadian politics.

Manning thinks in terms of a new party sweeping to power on a tidal wave of popular discontent, as Social Credit did in 1935 in the depths of the Depression. He sees the new party as being able to encompass virtually all of the interests within society and thus able to suppress conventional ideological polarities of left and right. Again, this was true of Social Credit throughout much of its 36 years in power. It consistently won about 50% of the popular vote and most of the seats in the legislature. Although it was generally perceived as ideologically conservative, anyone with realistic political objectives had to work with, if not through, the party because it was so firmly entrenched in power.

Finally, Manning as leader dominates the populist party. He controls the entire agenda, including the appointment of key personnel and the formulation of policy. Ernest Manning ran the Social Credit party in the same way. To round off the comparison, both have avoided personal aggrandizement, maintained a simple personal and political style, and kept in close touch with the grassroots. Ernest Manning had a listed telephone number and answered much of his own mail while he was premier of Alberta. The scope and intensity of contemporary politics have demanded some adjustments from Preston, but he still sees himself in that mode. It is his personal contact with "the common sense of the common people" that gives the Reform Party its populist character and, paradoxically, makes him so dominant over it.

Yet another irony exists. Manning is an original thinker, and both his personal mission of mediation and his populist theory are far removed from the pluralistic assumptions of most politicians; nonetheless, at an operational level his approach to politics can be quite conventional, almost opportunistic. His ultimate, visionary objective is universal reconciliation; and he has come to believe that he must achieve political power, and indeed become prime minister, in order to reach that goal. Ideology, therefore, is lower down in his scale of priorities. The point is not to implement any particular agenda but to reach a position where today's democratic processes can be reformed, to let the will of the people become politically effective. This in turn leads to a conception of strategy as timing. The key is to sense the popular mood, to move with it, to ride the wave into office.

3

Strategy

Manning's populism, underpinned by his religious sense of mission, is not strategic in the usual coalition-building sense. In politics, strategy normally means offering rewards (policies and patronage in all their many forms) in exchange for the support of particular individuals and groups, thereby cementing a coalition to exercise influence and take power. Politicians might not express it this way, but this is what they do in practice. Manning, in contrast, is led by his populism to think in universal rather than coalitional terms. For him, politics is a kind of evangelism, proclaiming the "good news" of Reform to all. Whence his desire, discussed in the last chapter, to make the Reform Party a microcosm of Canadian society.

What substitutes for strategy in Manning's thought is timing. This does not mean timing in the micro sense of being quick with a riposte, or of knowing on what day to issue a statement to the media. In fact, Manning's micro-timing is not very crisp; he often misses opportunities to score points in debate or in the media. His strength, rather, is macro-timing — the ability to divine major political trends, coupled with the patience to wait for them to develop and the audacity to assume positions that are considered politically incorrect by conventional politicians. In the following statement, Manning is particularly clear about his sense of macro-timing:

> I was a student of Western political history and I tended to identify with what
> I considered to be the Western reform movements — Riel, Haultain and the
> movement to establish Saskatchewan and Alberta, the Progressives, the CCF,

and Social Credit. I had gotten the view in the early '70s that there was something in the dynamics of Western Canada that produces these things every once in a while and that it would produce another one. I think I vaguely made up my own mind that I would rather be involved in the next time the West does that than get involved in one of the traditional parties. . . . These Western populist parties have a more natural life cycle than the traditional parties. They live, they die, the seeds go into the ground and then they come up again, perhaps in a different form.[1]

Not surprisingly, in view of this emphasis on timing, Manning's conception of strategy amounts to "waiting for the wave."[2] As he once put it, he sees a populist party as a sailing ship that can't generate its own power and must wait for the wind and waves. Thus, we "keep positioning ourselves so that when the next wave comes along, we can ride it higher and longer."[3]

This wave conception of strategy helps to explain an otherwise puzzling aspect of Manning's leadership style — his relative lack of interest in many areas of public policy. As leader of the Reform Party, he has been content to operate with virtually non-existent foreign and defence policies, and policies in some other areas that consist of little more than catchwords. In fact, the only three Reform policy areas that have been thoroughly elaborated over the years are the Triple-E Senate, balanced budgets, and criminal justice. If Manning saw himself as the leader of an ideological conservative party, this would make no sense; but it is perfectly consistent for the leader of a populist movement waiting for the wave. If you are going sailing, too much baggage will only hold you down.

Manning's occasional inconsistencies, such as his confusing statements on the rights of gays and lesbians, his reversals on the GST, or his demand for a constitutional moratorium after years of arguing that constitutional change was essential, can also be understood in this light. Sometimes he is sending up trial balloons to see if they fly; other times he believes that the wind has changed and he has to tack accordingly. What remains constant is that he ultimately takes his bearings from the popular mood as he perceives it.

Manning has made three attempts to found a new political movement, each at a time when, to continue the sailing metaphor, the wind seemed to be blowing up waves. First was the 1967 attempt to launch social conservatism, which got no further than the book *Political Realignment* and a small Social Conservative Society. This attempt was made at an opportune time when there was widespread dissatisfaction with politics. The old warriors Diefenbaker and Pearson were retiring from the leadership of their parties, and the federal Social Credit party was visibly played out. But ultimately Pierre Trudeau, not Manning, caught the wave.

The second attempt came in 1978, when Manning founded the Movement for National Political Change, which never got beyond the stage of compiling a mailing list.[4] Again there seemed to be an opening. Trudeau was unpopular (and, indeed, did lose the 1979 election). Many doubted the competence of the new Conservative leader, Manning's old adversary Joe Clark. And the election of a separatist government in Quebec in 1976, followed by Trudeau's attempts at constitutional reform, foreshadowed a crisis. But the opening disappeared when Clark caught the wave in the election of 1979, then fell out of the boat and allowed Trudeau to return with a large majority. The defeat of the separatists in the Quebec referendum of 1980 closed off that opening for good.

The third attempt came in 1986 with the CF-18 affair, when the federal cabinet decided "in the national interest" to give a major airplane maintenance contract to Canadair, Ltd., located in Montreal, even though the bid from Bristol Aerospace of Winnipeg was cheaper and adjudged technically superior by the government's own team of evaluators.[5] The CF-18 came to symbolize the general disappointment of western expectations in the Mulroney government. This time Manning found in western regionalism a wave he could ride, or, to use another of his metaphors, a kite he could fly.[6] The result was the Reform Party, ostensibly launched as a western regional party but defined by its constitution as a potential national party, which had always been Manning's goal.

Machiavelli wrote in *The Prince*: "I believe that it is probably true that fortune is the arbiter of half the things we do, leaving the other half or so to be controlled by ourselves."[7] A sense of timing is an indispensable part of practical statecraft; to forge ahead regardless of circumstances betokens ideological blindness or arrogant folly. But he also wrote that "those princes who are utterly dependent on fortune come to grief when their fortune changes."[8] Recognizing in the spirit of Machiavelli that a sense of timing is not the same as fatalism, Manning has used a portfolio of positioning strategies to keep the party afloat and paddling in the troughs between the waves. I have identified five such strategies employed in the party's brief history, which I call:

• The Party of the Right
• The Party of English Canada
• The Party of the West
• The Party of the Hinterland
• The Party of the People.

Each is discussed below. Readers wishing a more technical analysis grounded in the literature of political science should refer to the Appendix.

THE PARTY OF THE RIGHT

Under the leadership of Brian Mulroney, Joe Clark, and Robert Stanfield, the Progressive Conservatives never occupied a consistently conservative position. There was, to be sure, a right-wing element within the party (its members often referred to disparagingly as rednecks and dinosaurs) which sometimes exercised influence, but it seldom dictated policy. To speak only of the Mulroney years when the Conservatives were in power, they:

• expanded federal bilingualism by amending the Official Languages Act and leaned on several western provinces to increase French services at the provincial level
• passed a new Multiculturalism Act and established a Department of Multiculturalism
• failed to bring back capital punishment
• promised to amend the Canadian Human Rights Act to include sexual orientation
• brought in the Employment Equity Act (affirmative action)
• increased immigration to new heights of 250,000 a year
• ran budget deficits averaging over $30 billion a year from 1984 through 1993
• raised taxes repeatedly.

Of course, they also did some things that conservatives had wanted. They:

• reduced inflation to virtually zero
• privatized some major Crown corporations
• partially deregulated certain industries (finance, transportation, communications)
• negotiated free trade agreements with the United States and Mexico
• used the tax system to begin transforming several social programs from universality to a needs basis.

However, this last initiative was only undertaken in Mulroney's second term when Reform had become a serious threat to Conservative support in western Canada. Before Reform existed, social programs were a "sacred trust," to use Mulroney's phrase. But the point is not that the Mulroney Conservatives were not conservative; they certainly were in some ways. However, they were not conservative across the board; and the conservative actions they did take often required them to reverse prior commitments (they sold Air Canada after promising not to and introduced tax clawbacks on unemployment benefits, old age security, and family allowances after declaring social programs sacred).[9]

In effect, the Conservatives in the 1980s adopted a number of positions shared by the Liberals and New Democrats: official bilingualism, multiculturalism, deficit spending, medicare and other social policies, and several waves of constitutional change (the Charter, Meech Lake, Charlottetown) that incorporated theories of group rights. This led to the virtual non-representation of strongly conservative voters, who began to feel that the Conservative Party had drifted away from its conservative moorings. It is not surprising, therefore, that the 1980s saw several attempts to found a federal party to the right of the Conservatives. Viewed from this perspective, the foundation of the Reform Party in 1987 was the third act of a drama that began with the formation of the Confederation of Regions Party in 1983 and carried on with the establishment of the Christian Heritage Party in 1986.

This view of the Reform Party has a certain straightforward appeal and can be supported with empirical evidence. A questionnaire administered to delegates at the Reform Party's Winnipeg Assembly in October 1992 showed that they considered themselves well to the right of the Conservatives. On a seven-point scale ranging from 1 (extreme left) through 4 (centre) to 7 (extreme right), they scored themselves on average as 5.3 (strongly right of centre) and the Conservatives as 3.8 (slightly left of centre).[10] These are the volunteers and donors without whom the party would quickly collapse.

The conservatism of party members is also reflected among Reform voters in general.[11] During the 1993 election, Richard Johnston and his colleagues found that Reform supporters were to the right of other voters, and in particular to the right of Progressive Conservative voters, on most issues. Reform voters were more opposed to bilingualism, immigration, multiculturalism, aboriginal self-government, abortion, and homosexual marriage; they were more supportive of capital punishment, women with children staying at home, and cuts to welfare and unemployment insurance.[12] The difference between Reform and Conservative voters is similar in size to the difference between NDP and Liberal voters. In effect, Reform voters represent the former right wing of the federal Conservatives. In various polls taken in the early 1990s, anywhere from 40% to 60% of those who claimed to support Reform said they used to vote Conservative; and another unmeasured but not insignificant fraction previously voted Confederation of Regions, Christian Heritage, or Social Credit.[13] About three-quarters of Reform Party members have never belonged to another federal party, but of those who have, 73% used to belong to the Conservatives and 7% to Social Credit.[14]

There is, however, one great problem in viewing the Reform Party as a would-be Party of the Right: as demonstrated in the previous chapter,

Manning does not see it this way. Thus, although the Reform Party has undoubtedly invaded the political system from the right, it has never pursued that strategy single-mindedly because the leader does not accept it, at least as a sole strategy.

THE PARTY OF ENGLISH CANADA

Canadian politics is always about ideology, but it can never be exclusively about ideology. As long as Quebec is part of Canada, politics must also manage the tension between two large linguistic groups whose interests often diverge. This creates a conflict that cuts across the standard ideological lines of left, centre, and right.

At the beginning of the 1980s, the Liberals could still count on the French-Canadian vote, as had been true since the election of 1896; but Pierre Trudeau's patriation of the Constitution in 1982 over the objections of both provincial parties in Quebec created resentment upon which the Conservatives could capitalize. Brian Mulroney won over a majority of the francophone vote in Quebec in 1984 partly by promising to redress the constitutional grievances inflicted by Trudeau. In other words, by outbidding the Liberals on the constitutional (ethno-linguistic) issue, he broke up the coalition of French and English voters that had kept the Liberals in power during most of the 20th century.

This strategic manoeuvre led directly to Meech Lake; Mulroney had to deliver on the promise made in his Sept-Isles speech of August 6, 1984, to bring Quebec into the constitutional family "with honour and enthusiasm."[15] It also led to a peculiar positioning of the three major parties in the election of 1988. Each for its own reasons was led to suppress the ethnic dimension in that campaign. The Conservatives did not want to jeopardize their hard-won coalition between francophone voters in Quebec and their traditional anglophone supporters in rural Ontario and western Canada. The Liberals also realized that their much older coalition between English and French was jeopardized by Meech Lake and thus preferred not to talk about it. The NDP, buoyed by positive polls, thought they were finally going to make inroads into Quebec, so it was not the time for them to ask awkward questions about Meech Lake. The result was the alignment visible in Figure 3-1, constructed by Richard Johnston and his colleagues from 1988 survey data.

The axes of this figure are derived from survey questions known as "feeling thermometers," which ask respondents to score their feelings about various individuals and groups on a scale of 0 to 100, with 50 representing neutrality. In the context of the 1988 election, in which free trade with the U.S. was the major issue, calling oneself pro-U.S. was a good proxy for holding conservative or rightist ideological views, and calling oneself anti-U.S. for liberal/socialist or leftist views. The most striking aspect of the figure is that

Figure 3-1

Voters and Parties in the Ties to U.S.-French Canada Space

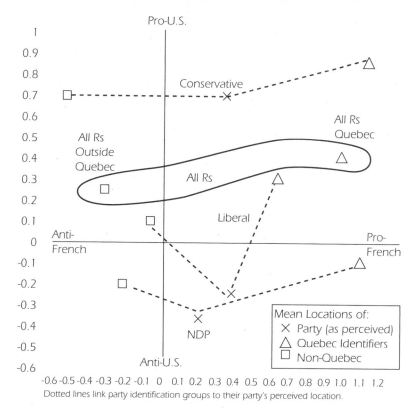

Dotted lines link party identification groups to their party's perceived location.

SOURCE: Richard Johnston et al., LETTING THE PEOPLE DECIDE: DYNAMICS OF A CANADIAN ELECTION (Montreal and Kingston: McGill-Queen's University Press, 1992), 103.

respondents saw the parties as differentiating themselves along the ideological (vertical) axis but not along the ethno-linguistic (horizontal) axis. Respondents perceived the Liberal and Conservative parties at almost exactly the same point (0.4) on the horizontal axis and the NDP not far away (0.2). Yet the Quebec and non-Quebec identifiers (partisans) of all three parties were demonstrably polarized on this dimension, least in the case of the Liberals, most in the case of the Conservatives. The Conservatives, as the new majority party, were highly vulnerable to being outbid on both ends of the ethnic dimension, causing their coalition to fall apart.

This process had already begun with the formation of the Reform Party in 1987, but at the time of the 1988 campaign there were not enough Reformers to affect the picture painted by Figure 3-1. However, the cracks in the Conservative coalition later turned into outright fractures. Anglophone Conservatives in western Canada defected in droves to the Reform Party, which was the only national party to oppose Meech Lake. Then from the other side Lucien Bouchard led a defection of Quebec francophone Conservatives to found the Bloc Québécois.

In strategic terms, Reform and the Bloc have some important similarities. Each has positioned itself farther out on the ethno-linguistic dimension. Each, moreover, has tried to draw supporters from all parties by adopting a broad-gauge ideological stance. Until after the 1993 election, the BQ had no real policies other than the sovereignty of Quebec, and its supporters ranged from Marxists and trade unionists on the left to reactionary nationalists and former Créditistes on the right. The Reform Party, in contrast, has always had an identifiable ideological position on the right; but that position has been widened by Manning's attempts to blur left, right, and centre in order to appeal to dissatisfied Liberal and NDP voters.

It is tempting to see The Party of English Canada as the key to the Reform Party's success or failure. With the three old parties supporting Meech Lake and the Charlottetown Accord, Reform was positioned to attract support from all sorts of people opposed to Quebec's constitutional demands. There are, however, problems in applying this model if we seek to study the party in detail, and once again Manning is the source of the perplexity. On the one hand, he deliberately sought polarization on the linguistic dimension. He did this in a dramatic way at Reform's Edmonton Assembly in November 1989, when he said, "If we continue to make unacceptable constitutional, economic, and linguistic concessions to Quebec at the expense of the rest of Canada, it is those concessions themselves which will tear the country apart. . . . A house divided against itself cannot stand." Following Manning's lead, the assembly voted to adopt a hard-line position towards constitutional demands from Quebec:

> The Reform Party supports the position that Confederation should be maintained, but that it can only be maintained by a clear commitment to Canada as one nation, in which the demands and aspirations of all regions are entitled to equal status in constitutional negotiations and political debate, and in which freedom of expression is fully accepted as the basis for language policy across the country. Should these principles of Confederation be rejected, Quebec and the rest of Canada should consider whether there exists a better political arrangement which will enrich our friendship, respect our common defence requirements, and ensure a free interchange of commerce and people, by mutual consent and for our mutual benefit.[16]

This "love it or leave it" ultimatum to Quebec was not an aberration; Manning repeated these sentiments periodically in the following years. Even during the run-up to the Charlottetown Accord, he deliberately generated newspaper stories about being able to "live with the loss of Quebec."[17]

All of this sounds very polarizing, but it is only part of the story. Although Manning may be able to contemplate the departure of Quebec from Canada, that is not what he wants. He sees himself as ultimately becoming the leader of a pan-Canadian Reform Party including a strong contingent of francophones from Quebec. A major unstated reason for not contesting the 1993 election in Quebec was the virtual certainty that any expansion effort at that time would have become an English-rights movement forever precluding francophone support. The long-term goal of securing support in Quebec ties together many facts that seem strange when viewed in isolation:

• In 1991–1992, Manning spent, by Reform standards, an appreciable amount of money to translate the Blue Book, the *56 Reasons* pamphlet, and several of his speeches into French. Supposedly the French texts would help francophones inform themselves better about the Reform Party, but their real importance was symbolic, to signal the party's interest in an eventual rapprochement with Quebec.

• Manning agrees that the prime minister of Canada should be bilingual and says he will learn French when he gets closer to that position (he began to take French lessons in the spring of 1994).[18]

• Although he has few contacts in Quebec, he visits the province regularly and holds consultative meetings on a small scale; he has also tried to maintain mailing and information lists. The first draft of *The New Canada* contained a promise to carry out a grand fact-finding tour of Quebec in the summer of 1992 (others thought the idea untimely and dissuaded Manning from doing so).

• Although he adhered to the rationale for staying out of Quebec prior to the 1993 election, he wished that he were involved in the province. He stunned many Reformers by musing in public in February 1993 about nominating candidates in Quebec in time for the next election.[19] This was not an isolated occurrence; he once asked rhetorically in a meeting in 1992, "Wouldn't it be something if we produced 75 candidates in Quebec just before the next election?" During the 1993 campaign, he promised that Reform would be in Quebec for the next election.[20]

• As described in detail in Chapter 6, Manning moved away from the Reform Party's constitutional position during 1992. Because of sentiment in the party, he eventually had to lead a No campaign, but he would have preferred to stay out of the fight. During the campaign, he deliberately said little about the concessions to Quebec that had enraged so many anglophones (the distinct society clause and the guarantee that 25% of Commons seats would be reserved for Quebec in perpetuity).

• Shortly after the 1993 election, Manning announced his Countdown to Victory plan for the Reform Party, the centrepiece of which is expansion into Quebec and nomination of a full slate of 75 candidates in that province in the next federal election.[21] Underlying the plan is the goal of winning enough seats to form a majority government. Long gone are the days when Manning's objective was simply to elect enough Reform MPs to hold "the balance of power for the West and the North."[22] His new goal (undoubtedly always his real one) is to be the next prime minister of Canada. He can count as well as anyone, and so he realizes that he is unlikely to fulfill that ambition without winning some seats in Quebec as long as Quebec remains in Canada with 75 of 295 seats in the House of Commons.

All in all, the same conclusion applies to The Party of English Canada as to The Party of the Right: both models describe aspects of Reform's positioning at certain times, but the leader of the party has not pursued either of them consistently.

THE PARTY OF THE WEST AND THE PARTY OF THE HINTERLAND

Neither the Progressives nor Social Credit nor the CCF were based on regional ideologies, but regionalism was certainly a vital subtext in their statements. Their critique of eastern bankers and other financial interests was an essential part of their appeal to western voters. Manning, of course, comes out of a Social Credit background, and he has a well-thumbed copy of W.L. Morton's *The Progressive Party in Canada* on his bookshelf. He also realizes that territorial concentration of one's supporters is the fastest and surest way to elect MPs in the Canadian system of plurality voting. He has referred more than once to the inglorious end of H.H. Stevens's Reconstruction Party, which got a respectable 8.7% of the popular vote in the 1935 election but elected only one member. The Reconstruction vote "was spread as thin as butter on a slice of bread," as Manning likes to put it, and hence failed to achieve electoral success.

In this light, it was a logical move to create the Reform Party as a purely western party, thereby actualizing the latent political dimension of region-alism that was not part of the overt positioning of the other parties. Ever since Diefenbaker, the Conservatives had been the de facto party of western Canada, but those credentials were severely tarnished by Mulroney's coali-tion with Quebec nationalists. In many western eyes, the West seemed to lose out every time a choice had to be made.

Manning and the Reform Party followed a regional strategy from 1987 to 1991. News that the CF-18 maintenance contract had been awarded to a Montreal firm — the epitome of western grievances — catalyzed formation of the party.[23] Ted Byfield's inspired slogan "The West Wants In" was regional without being separatist. Reform's original split-maple-leaf logo never received an official interpretation but seemed to imply that Canada was incomplete without western equality. The party adopted the Triple-E Senate, based on a theory of regionalism, as its most distinctive policy. And it ran candidates only in western ridings in the 1988 election. Although it did not elect any candidates then, it soon elected Deborah Grey in a by-election and Stan Waters in Alberta's unique advisory senatorial election. In one large poll of the four western provinces taken in April 1991, the Reform Party was tied with the Liberals for the lead among committed voters (Reform 29%, Liberals 29%, NDP 27%, PC 13%).[24] In short, The Party of the West promised to be a viable strategy for breaking into the system.

The adoption of a regional strategy at the outset helps explain why Manning has never proposed proportional representation (PR) as an electoral reform. In view of the well-known effects of first-past-the-post voting, to advocate PR is usually a rational proposition for a new, small party trying to gain a niche in the system; not surprisingly, Mel Hurtig advocated PR on behalf of his National Party.[25] But a party pursuing a regional strategy can rationally hope to come first in a significant number of ridings within the region it claims to represent; in fact, it may well do better with plurality voting than with PR.

Ironically, however, the Reform Party abandoned the western strategy at the height of its success when it decided to go national in the spring of 1991. This may seem like a major shift in course, but it was only the next stage of Manning's long-term plan. He had made it clear in his founding speech at Vancouver that "a new federal political party representing the West should have 'room to grow' into a truly national party."[26] The party's constitution established it as a national party with a temporary regional base; it would run candidates only in the western provinces and territories until two-thirds of the membership approved national expansion in a party referendum.[27] Manning began to tour Ontario in March 1990, and the first Ontario

Reform constituency association was established in Simcoe North in August of that year.[28] These efforts were part of an expansion program directed by Gordon Shaw, vice-chairman of the party's executive council; that plan culminated in the pro-expansion vote at the Saskatoon Assembly of April 1991 and the subsequent party referendum. Although there was a show of being dragged into Ontario by popular demand (Ontario delegates to Saskatoon wore buttons saying "The East Wants In"), the expansion was a calculated move. It was not forced upon Manning by public pressure, nor was it a hasty reaction to a couple of favourable polls.

How, then, did Manning intend to replace the western strategy? In his Vancouver speech, he had suggested that the new party, when it did go national, might attract support in the "resource-producing regions" of Ontario, Quebec, and Atlantic Canada.[29] This sounds like a Party of the Hinterland, appealing to farmers, fishermen, miners, oil and gas producers, loggers, and other producers of primary products, as well as to those who earn their living supplying and serving primary industries. Manning sometimes acts as if he were pursuing such a strategy — he is never so much at home as when visiting remote rural ridings — but in fact neither the Blue Book nor the party's general orientation caters to the special situation of primary producers.

Even though going national fulfilled Manning's original intention, it resulted in a sharp discontinuity. The blue and red split-maple-leaf logo was replaced with a green "R," and "The West Wants In" disappeared in favour of "The New Canada." The Triple-E Senate retained pride of place among Reform policies; but other distinctively western policies, such as the $7-billion buyout of the Crow rate, negotiation of a common market among western provinces, regional fairness tests for federal expenditures, and regional banking institutions, effectively vanished, even if some of them remained in the Blue Book. The Reform Party cannot be fully defined as The Party of the West or The Party of the Hinterland any more than it can be fully defined as The Party of the Right or The Party of English Canada.

THE PARTY OF THE PEOPLE

As we saw in the preceding chapter, Manning's deepest commitment is to populism. Although he did not use that word in his Vancouver speech, it has increasingly become his talisman. One political scientist describes populism in these words:

> The notion that "the people" are one; that divisions among them are not
> genuine conflicts of interest but are manufactured by a few men of ill will;
> that parties are merely self-serving factions; and that the people will be best

looked after by a single unpolitical leadership that will put their interest first — these ideas are *anti*political, but they are nevertheless essential elements in a political strategy that has often been used to gain power.[30]

As practised, for example, by the self-styled populist Jimmy Carter, this is "the technique of populist unification across as much as possible of the political spectrum."[31] It is a way of breaking up existing electoral coalitions and enticing voters into new groupings not based on traditional definitions of class or ethnicity. Manning's populism, and his rejection of established ideologies, can be comfortably situated in this perspective. As he said in his founding speech, he wanted to attract voters from all parties. What better way than to encourage them to think in terms of an all-encompassing "people" transcending divisions of class and race?

Populism however, is highly problematic as a political strategy. An appeal, as Manning puts it, to "the common sense of the common people"[32] includes almost everyone. If so, then whom do you target? Whom do you expect to become your core voters? What will you offer them that other parties do not? Populism is vague as a positioning strategy because it does not advise any particular location for the party. An appeal to "the common sense of the common people" can be made from an infinite number of locations. Thus, there have been populist movements of the right (Social Credit), centre (Progressives), and left (CCF).

Populism has a natural affinity with timing strategies. Particularly in times of crisis, there is a tendency for "the people" to close ranks, to emphasize what unites rather than divides them. The formation of grand coalition governments of national unity during wartime (for example, the Union government in Canada during World War I) is an often-remarked example of this phenomenon. The spectacular rise to power of Social Credit in Alberta during the Depression illustrates how a crisis atmosphere can lead voters to turn en masse to a new alternative.

The distinction between a positioning and a timing strategy is crucial. Positioning is inherently active; it requires the leader and the party to stake out territory and defend it consistently. Timing, in contrast, is much more passive; it requires waiting for the right moment in the hope of being carried along by powerful forces unleashed by events outside the party's control. A new party trying to break into the system may make use of both. To follow a positioning strategy oblivious of the tide of current events might condemn the party to irrelevance; but to emphasize timing to the exclusion of positioning might degenerate into opportunism, leaving the party completely dependent upon the vicissitudes of fortune.

Another way to understand Manning's populism is to think about what results the other strategies might yield. The Party of the Right and The Party of the West would both put Reform into a particular niche in the political system, where it might be secure and influential but probably would not be able to win enough seats to govern. With luck, Reform as The Party of the Right might eventually displace the Progressive Conservative Party and form a government, but it would likely be a long march; the NDP has been trying to accomplish a similar trick from the left for 60 years. The Party of English Canada would likely lead to national polarization, in which the Reform Party might form a government in a deeply divided polity, which is abhorrent to Manning's monistic worldview. In contrast, "waiting for the wave" as The Party of the People might lead to dominance: a single party could sweep to power on a tidal wave of discontent and govern without hindrance in the face of a fractured opposition. Although Manning has never explicitly said that this is his preferred model, this is the one that best explains his actual behaviour as leader of the Reform Party, as we will see in the rest of this book.

4

Positioning the Party

In a broad sense, the rise of the Reform Party in western Canada[1] was due to a loss of confidence in the two major parties. The Liberals, who had been weak ever since Diefenbaker swept the West in 1958, were further damaged by Trudeau's National Energy Program. And the Conservatives, who elected 58 western MPs in 1984, soon began to disappoint their western voters, who perceived Brian Mulroney as tilting to the side of the equally large Quebec caucus. The flashpoint of discontent became the government's decision in October 1986 to award to the CF-18 maintenance contract to Canadair Ltd. in Montreal rather than Bristol Aerospace in Winnipeg; but even before this decision, *Alberta Report* had called for the formation of a western party, and quiet discussions were already under way.

Two different networks of people came together to found the Reform Party. One was a group in British Columbia, whose central figures were Francis Winspear, a retired millionaire from Edmonton, and Stan Roberts, a former Liberal MP from Manitoba and president of the Canada West Foundation. The B.C. people were mainly of Liberal background. The other group was composed of Calgary oilmen whose political history was mainly Conservative; they quickly adopted Preston Manning as their chief thinker and organizer. With Winspear putting up much of the money, and Ted Byfield promoting the cause in the pages of *Alberta Report*, the two groups came together to create the Reform Association of Canada and sponsor the Western Assembly on Canada's Economic and Political Future, held in Vancouver May 29 to 31, 1987.[2]

Manning's address to the Vancouver Assembly, entitled "Choosing a Political Vehicle to Represent the West," deserves to become known as one of the great political speeches of Canadian history. A judicious mix of careful analysis, plausible casuistry, and occasional eloquence, it brought public confirmation of the leadership he was already exercising behind the scenes in the Reform Association. Many of those who heard him that day underwent something like a conversion experience that made them tireless workers and dedicated loyalists in his cause.

To reflect the fact that the audience contained Liberals as well as Conservatives (and even a few New Democrats), Manning proposed to create a trans-ideological western party:

> Obviously, if the West were to choose a new political vehicle to advance its Agenda, we would be careful to position that vehicle ideologically and policy-wise so that it would have equal potential for drawing the support of Western Canadians from both the Liberals and the NDP, as well as the Conservatives. In fact, one could go so far as to say that if a new federal political party cannot be positioned in this way, it should not be initiated.

And at greater length:

> In order to ensure that we could draw support from the disaffected members of the Liberals and the NDP as well as the Conservatives, it is important that a new Western political party have a strong social conscience and program as well as a strong commitment to market principles and freedom of enterprise.
>
> A new federal party which embodies the principal political values of the West will transcend some of the old categories of left and right. It will provide a home for the socially responsible businessman and the economy conscious social activist. It should be a party whose members and leaders are characterized as people with "hard heads and soft hearts," i.e., people who attach high importance to wealth creation and freedom of economic activity on the one hand, but who are also genuinely concerned and motivated to action on behalf of the victims of the many injustices and imperfections in our economic and social systems.[3]

This was the social conservative theme of *Political Realignment*, now attached not to a new party of the moderate right but to a non-ideological populist movement. Manning was emphatic that he did not want to found "some extreme 'right-wing splinter group' which would only garner votes, if at all, from the Conservative side of the house."[4] In strategic terms, he was proposing not a Party of the Right but a Party of the West.

But these seemingly straightforward statements contained a degree of ambiguity. The assembly had been advertised by *Alberta Report*, a magazine known for its conservatism as well as its western regionalism. And to the extent that Manning touched upon policy issues in his speech, he played on conservative themes. He excoriated the National Energy Program as an "unmitigated disaster" and criticized the NDP for having focused "exclusively on the re-distribution of wealth" as well as for standing "idly by while a few dockworkers inflict millions of dollars of damage on Western producers by stopping the flow of Western resources to the seaboard through untimely strikes."[5] Ideological conservatives, who undoubtedly made up the majority of the audience, would easily have assumed that Manning was truly a conservative on practical issues and was merely indulging in rhetorical flourishes to attract refugees from other parties.

Even while advocating creation of a western regional party, Manning said he wanted to found a "truly national party"[6] — the political equivalent of squaring the circle. How can a party be regional and national at the same time? Manning's answer was that the new party could be "a truly national party with its roots in the resource-producing regions."[7] It might operate only in the West at the outset, but it had to have "room to grow from [a] regionally based party to a truly national party capable of forming a national government."[8] The concept of "resource-producing regions" provided the link. As he expressed it when he started to speak in Ontario in 1990, there was plenty of "regional alienation" elsewhere in Canada — "in northern and rural Ontario, in northern and rural Quebec, and in every Atlantic province."[9] Although he never discussed it at great length, Manning's original idea of a national party assumed that he could construct a Party of the Hinterland, a political coalition of primary producers — farmers, fishermen, loggers, miners, and so on — that would oppose the administrative and financial centres of power in Ottawa, Toronto, and Montreal.

This desire to leave "room to grow" perhaps explains the scarcity of references to the French language and Quebec in Manning's speech. Neither official bilingualism nor Meech Lake appeared, even though the tentative form of that agreement was already in the public domain. And when he was implicitly critical of Quebec, as when he referred to the CF-18 affair, he paired that province with Ontario and spoke of central Canada. This was certainly not a speech to launch a Party of English Canada. Nor was the assembly in an anti-Quebec mood; the delegates rejected a motion "urging the Western provincial legislatures to withhold support for Meech Lake until Triple-E provisions should be included in the accord."[10] (The Meech Lake Accord, it must be remembered, had just been negotiated in April 1987 and would not be formally accepted by the first ministers until June; it was still largely unknown in May, when the Vancouver Assembly took place, and opposition to it had not yet started to coalesce.)

Although Manning's original conception of the Reform Party was clear and, in its own way, consistent, parties inevitably become vectors that also carry the thinking of members other than the leader. Two developments in Reform's early history were particularly significant in this connection. One was Manning's triumph over Stan Roberts for the position of leader. The departure of the Liberal Roberts and his circle of followers deprived the party of the ideological balance that Manning had claimed to seek. Most of those who were left in the Reform Party had been Conservative (or Social Credit) in politics and were conservative in their thinking.

Second was the role played by Stephen Harper, whom Manning named chief policy officer after the 1987 Winnipeg Assembly. Harper, a one-time Conservative activist, had been executive assistant to Calgary West MP Jim Hawkes before breaking with the Tories. Now a graduate student in economics at the University of Calgary, he had not been part of the original Reform Association but came to Vancouver more or less as an observer. He brought with him a short paper, co-authored with his fellow student John Weissenberger, entitled "Political Reform and the Taxpayer," which he did not deliver at the assembly but which he gave to Manning to read. It denounced the "liberal-socialist philosophy" as "an economic disaster for Canada" and called for "a genuine conservative option, a Taxpayers Party," which would represent "the public interest of the taxpayer" against "the expenditure demands of special interest groups." The Progressive Conservative Party, said Harper, was no longer a viable option because its red Tory leadership had moved it "to the Center." The new Taxpayers Party would be based on a clear set of conservative principles, and "the N.D.P. has shown that a clear viewpoint can be made effective with even a small representation."[11]

Harper's conception of the Taxpayers Party approximates the strategy of The Party of the Right. Although he agreed with Manning on many policy matters, Harper differed fundamentally on Manning's conception of a non-ideological regional party, which would eventually grow into a non-ideological national party large enough to govern the country. Indeed, the difference is almost like night and day. Nonetheless, Manning was impressed by Harper and asked him to prepare an address for the Winnipeg Assembly, where the new party was to be established in October 1987.

For that event, Harper wrote a major speech called "Achieving Economic Justice in Confederation,"[12] in which he tried to marry the theme of western regional protest that had dominated the Vancouver Assembly to his own conservative outlook and desire for a Taxpayers Party. His economic analysis sketched a pattern of disadvantage for the West traceable to the market distortions of Sir John A. Macdonald's National Policy of protective tariffs, east-west transportation links, and territorial administration for the benefit of central Canada. He then called for a new National Policy to rectify a century of intentional discrimination against the West. This much fit with Manning's non-ideological regionalism, but Harper also added other elements associated with Canadian conservatism and with resistance to demands from Quebec. He criticized "the special treatment accorded the province of Quebec"[13] and pointed to the role played by official bilingualism in keeping westerners out of positions of power in Ottawa.[14] He also criticized the welfare state as being not so much government's "sacred trust" (borrowing Mulroney's famous phrase) as "the taxpayers' burden — a burden which has been borne disproportionately by Western Canadians"[15] because of the fiscal transfer effects of Confederation. Harper's speech was a significant step towards creating a conservative western party, rather than the non-ideological party that Manning had said he wanted; yet Manning was quite taken with the speech,[16] and he appointed Harper chief policy officer. Again, Manning was sending a message that, whatever he might say about ideology, he was really a conservative at heart.

The delegates at Winnipeg adopted Manning's 20-point Statement of Principles, which in some respects was crafted to be trans-ideological. For example, it balanced its commitment to free enterprise ("we believe that the creation of wealth and productive jobs for Canadians is best achieved through the operations of a responsible, broadly based, free-enterprise economy in which private property, freedom of contract, and the operations of free markets are encouraged and respected") with a commitment to humanitarian charity ("we believe that Canadians have a personal and collective responsibility to care and provide for the basic needs of people who are unable to care and provide for themselves"). But what exactly did this mean? Did a "collective responsibility" imply the government should care for others, or could this responsibility be satisfied by private philanthropy? Even the most rock-hard conservative could accept the words if they were interpreted in the latter sense.

The delegates also held non-binding ballots on 29 policy resolutions. Some of these, like Stephen Harper's speech, illustrated the conservative outlook that most members brought to the party. They included proposals to balance the federal budget in three years, to eliminate grants and subsidies to business, and to develop an immigration policy. Others, such as opposition to the Meech Lake Accord and to the extension of bilingualism, were not only conservative but had the potential to position the Reform Party as The Party of English Canada. It must have been clear to Manning that the new party was quickly taking on a strongly conservative and English-rights flavour, yet he did not try to restore the balance he had spoken of at Vancouver.

Harper melded all these elements into a manifesto adopted in Calgary on August 14, 1988, as the party's Platform and Statement of Principles. This document served as Reform's platform in the 1988 election and was subsequently edited, at which point it became the Blue Book. The main difference between the 1988 document and the Blue Book is stylistic; the platform is a sort of extended essay with subject headings, whereas the Blue Book is in a more concise point format.

The platform could be compared to a mosaic put together from three colours of tiles. There is a definite overall pattern; but the observer can still detect the original colours, and in some cases the pieces don't fit together snugly, leaving gaps visible to the eye. The most striking colour, although it does not occupy the most space, is western regionalism, expressed in policies such as the Triple-E Senate, regional fairness tests for federal expenditure, opposition to the Meech Lake Accord, a $7-billion payment to western farmers to buy out the Crow rate, the privatization of Petro-Canada, economic union among the western provinces, opposition to the tight money policy of the Bank of Canada, and support for regional banking. The second colour is Manning-style populism, the search for "the common sense of the common people," expressed in the demand for more free votes in the House of Commons, publication of votes in caucus, and the introduction of direct democracy (including referendums and plebiscites, but not recall). The third colour is conservatism, expressed in economic policies such as balanced budgets, an end to agricultural and business subsidies, and an end to the postal monopoly; and in social policies such as reform of the welfare state to make it less bureaucratic, opposition to state-run day care, the return of unemployment insurance to genuine insurance principles, opposition to official bilingualism, and reorientation of immigration towards economically productive migrants and away from family reunification and refugees.

With some ingenuity, the different colours can be made to match and the tiles to fit together, at least up to a point. The populist assault on party discipline was especially plausible in the West because western MPs had gone along with their national parties on regionally unpopular issues such as the National Energy Program and the CF-18 maintenance contract. And while public opinion in the West is not monolithically conservative, it certainly contains a large conservative element that a regional party must regard. This is especially true in Alberta, and at this stage the Reform Party was for all practical purposes an Alberta party. The headquarters were in Alberta, most of the key activists were Albertans, and the Manning name resonated in that province far more than it did elsewhere.

Nonetheless, there were still some gaps and jarring contrasts in the picture. For example, regionalism and fiscal conservatism do not always point in the same direction. How does one reconcile a plan to balance the budget in three years with a demand for $7 billion to compensate western farmers for loss of the Crow rate? And there is nothing intrinsically regional about the demand for political reform (free votes in the Commons, referendums, and plebiscites). In fact, direct democracy might work against the interests of a less populated region. It is entirely possible that a referendum on the National Energy Program might have produced large majorities in favour in all provinces except Alberta, British Columbia, and Saskatchewan.

Sometimes the gaps were closed through strategic emphasis. For example, there was a general call for privatization ("We urge that ownership and control of corporations be placed in the sector that can perform them most cost-effectively, with greatest accountability to owners, and the least likelihood of incurring public debt. We believe that there is overwhelming evidence that this would be the private sector in the vast majority of cases"); but the only Crown corporation specifically mentioned as headed for the auction block was Petro-Canada.[17] This emphasis turned privatization into a western issue. Sometimes, however, the gaps were papered over with verbal formulas. For example, the section on social reform in the platform bore the subheading "Completing the Western Agenda."[18] But there is nothing specifically western about opposition to bilingualism and state-run child care.

Manning did nothing to change the obvious conservative orientation of the platform, but he wrote in his foreword that "we reject political debate defined in the narrow terminology of the Left, Right, and Centre. This vestige of the French and Industrial Revolutions may continue to delineate our old-line parties, but it is increasingly out of place in the complex and multidimensional world that we live in today."[19] The foreword typifies Manning's approach: allow the party members to adopt a conservative, occasionally even hard-right, agenda, but insist in public that it is not conservative.

The party's first platform represented a compromise between Manning's non-ideological populism and the ideological conservatism of most of the western adherents of the new party. Regionalism was the glue holding everything together. It was a non-ideological element that Manning could use as the first stage in trying to build a new national party, and it also appealed to the western conservatives who saw the socialist interventionism of the old-line parties as the root of their grievances. Compromises are not bad or surprising in them-selves — all party platforms are compromise documents. But compromises tend to come unstuck, and this has happened to Reform in the course of time. After national expansion removed the glue of regionalism holding the mosaic together, the gap between non-ideological populism and ideological conser-vatism gradually became more obvious. Manning closed the gap temporarily by making a turn to the right in the 1993 election campaign, but it reappeared immediately afterward as he launched upon his national expansion campaign to make the Reform Party a demographic reflection of the entire country.

The Reform Party could not mount a coordinated campaign in the 1988 elec-tion. There was no money for paid advertising, Manning was busy in Yellowhead riding running against Joe Clark and received only sporadic media coverage, and local candidates pretty much went their own way. But even if Manning was effectively unable to position the party because of lack of resources, he attempted to do so by sending out circulars to Reform can-didates, and these provide a glimpse into his thinking at that stage. Initially, he presented Reform as a western party. In a memorandum sent out on August 29, 1988, enclosing the platform, Manning related virtually every-thing to the West. For example, he called for:

> A sensible approach to official languages. Our opposition to legislated bilingualism should be noted and our desire for a languages policy that reflects the needs of Western Canada should be underlined.
>
> An immigration policy that is fair, humane, and consistent with the needs of the West.[20]

Briefly Manning set out the objective for the Party and the West:

- Economic Fairness (Jobs for the West)
- Political Equality (A Voice for the West)
- Responsive Government (MPs who reflect the West).[21]

Towards the end of the campaign, Manning wrote that he had tried to offer the voters in Yellowhead:

> 1. *Real Representation in the Next Parliament.* A Reform Member will speak and vote in the next Parliament — on issues like Senate reform, official languages, immigration, federal spending, etc. — exactly the way

Westerners would like him or her to speak and vote. This is a promise which traditional party politicians cannot truthfully make or keep.

2. *Fair Representation of the West's Interests in Freer Trade.* A Reform Member will represent *both* the historic desire of Westerners for lower tariffs and more secure access to the U.S. market, *and* the concern and doubts of Westerners about the current Free Trade Agreement, which all of the traditional parties have badly misrepresented.[22]

Free trade was unquestionably a major problem for Reform in 1988. Many westerners who were sympathetic to what they had heard about Reform nevertheless voted Conservative because they did not want the Liberals to win an election that had become a virtual referendum on free trade. Any Reform leader would have had trouble with the issue, but the way Manning tried to handle it smacked of calculated ambiguity and foreshadowed later strategic problems. While supporting the Free Trade Agreement philosophically, he tried to oppose it politically, arguing that "the problem with the current Free Trade Agreement and the debate surrounding it is that it has not been honestly communicated."[23] This statement exemplifies his tendency to redefine political problems as communication problems and his view of himself as the political leader able to persuade the public to take bad-tasting economic medicine. While refusing to give unambiguous support to the FTA, he also wrote an "Open Letter to Free Trade Liberals," inviting them "to make the Reform Party of Canada your new political home" and to accept Reform's commitment to "free and fair trade honestly communicated."[24] The phrase "free and fair trade" typifies Manning's inclination to unify opposites, since "fair trade" is the rallying cry of those who actually oppose free trade. All in all, it was a confusing performance that presaged Manning's tendency to defend his positions with rhetoric borrowed from opposing viewpoints (for example, "saving" social programs by reducing federal support for them). But perhaps the most troubling aspect of it was his inability to get beyond his opponents' agenda and articulate his own. Free trade was self-evidently a Conservative issue, and Reform had nothing to gain by talking about it, yet by the end of the campaign it had become, by Manning's own admission, one of two issues he was spending the most time on. Would he not have been better off to say something like this: "Yes, we support the Free Trade Agreement; the Conservatives have at least done one thing right. But its impact on the West will be marginal, and the real issues are a, b, and c," then move on to Reform's strongest talking points?

*

Although it was disappointing not to have elected anyone in 1988, the next 12 months were the most exhilarating in the Reform Party's history prior to the 1993 electoral success. Deborah Grey's victory in the Beaver River by-election of March 1989 was followed by Stan Waters' triumph in the Alberta senatorial election of October. Suddenly Reform had a presence in Ottawa, and both its opponents and the media were starting to take it seriously.

Senior party members did some serious rethinking during 1989. Both Preston Manning and Stephen Harper believed some change was necessary, but their views were very different, and the difference between them illustrates the internal tension between populism and conservatism that has marked the party's history. In March 1989, Harper sent Manning a memo containing a root-and-branch critique of what he saw as Manning's strategy, namely, "that the Party should emphasize its geographic nature while downplaying its ideological content. It should [in Manning's view] become a 'Hinterland-Grassroots' Party, a populist coalition of the 'thinly-populated resource-producing regions,' overwhelmingly concerned with rectifying imbalances between Central Canada and the vast Canadian Hinterland."[25] Harper's criticism was trenchant. He pointed out that the rural resource-producing regions did not have a large enough population or enough parliamentary seats to achieve Manning's goal of some day forming a government. Moreover, the objective interests of the so-called hinterland were highly diverse and could not easily be assimilated into a common cause against central Canada. Consequently, grassroots populism based on a hinterland strategy could never produce a "coherent political agenda."

As an alternative Harper proposed that the Reform Party could and should become "a modern Canadian version of the Thatcher-Reagan phenomenon." It should seek its core supporters in the private-sector middle class of Canada's urban areas, offering these voters a market-oriented ideology. Building on that economic base, it "should tailor its broader, 'social' agenda to gain a sizeable chunk of the urban working class and rural sector 'swing' vote, without alienating its urban private sector middle-class 'core.' The key is to emphasize moderate, conservative social values consistent with the traditional family, the market economy, and patriotism."[26] The goal should be to bring together those parts of the urban middle class, urban working class, and rural population that can agree on an agenda of market economics and traditional values. The older model of a conservative party based largely on the middle and upper classes is no longer viable because so much of the urban middle class (for example, teachers, nurses, social workers, public-sector administrators) is now part of the "new class," or "knowledge class," as it is sometimes called, and is thus a political class dependent on tax-supported government programs.[27] Political coalitions now divide less along class lines than on the question of public-sector dependence.

Realignment along these lines had already taken place in American politics. Between 1950 and the mid 1970s, the Republicans ceased by a considerable margin to be the preferred party of business executives and the university-educated,[28] and Ronald Reagan won the presidency in 1980 and 1984 with the support of a large fraction of traditional "lunch-bucket" Democratic voters. In simple terms, Reagan's formula consisted of depicting the struggle as smaller government and traditional values pitted against big government and social engineering directed by liberal elites.

Ideology is necessary to hold such a coalition together. Directly challenging Manning's belief in the obsolescence of ideology, Harper argued: "The Reform Party must continue to be moderate in tone, but it is pointless to attempt to avoid the 'Right' label. Instead, the Party should shape the term and stress what it wants the term to mean, i.e., the 'Economic Right,' 'Moderate Right,' 'Principled Right.'"[29] Ironically, Harper noted that *Political Realignment*, the book that Preston and Ernest Manning had written together, had called for merging Social Credit and the Progressive Conservatives into a party of the moderate right. Although he did not press the point, he was obviously raising the question of why Preston had now become so allergic to ideological labels.

In the strategic terms used in this book, Harper was fundamentally advocating The Party of the Right, but his comments about Quebec also recall the model of The Party of English Canada. Following the many analysts who have argued that the national unity issue has inhibited the ideological polarization of Canadian politics, he suggested that "a modern Party of the Economic Right must be prepared to effectively ignore the National Unity issue, neglect organizational effort in Quebec, and ultimately risk calling the separatist bluff."[30]

Like Harper, Manning at this time sought ways to broaden the appeal of the party, but in other respects his thinking was on a different track from that of his chief policy officer. In the spring of 1989, he became particularly interested in making the environment a major Reform issue, so he appointed a task force to prepare policy resolutions for the Edmonton Assembly scheduled for October. "In one sense," he wrote, "the environmental issue is one of the few with the potential to cut completely across the traditional left-right-centre spectrum. The Reform Party should be well positioned to deal with an issue of this nature."[31] Further, "as a new party, we start with a clean slate and can move beyond the obsolete models and clichés which currently characterize so much of the [discussion]." This last remark provides more evidence of Manning's belief that he can create a synthesis that has eluded other thinkers up to the present moment. Note also that the environment is not in any way a distinctively western issue.

That Manning would turn to it illustrates the eclectic nature of his thinking as well as his tendency to be reactive (this was the period when Lucien Bouchard, as federal minister of the Environment, was pushing hard for the so-called Green Plan). It also illustrates his tendency to follow personal enthusiasms with little connection to the party's established agenda.

Prodded by Harper's March memo, Manning undertook a more in-depth examination of where the party should stand. There were some fascinating changes between Manning's first draft, written in March, and the final draft, which appeared in June. Whereas the first draft called for a positioning statement and defined the Reform Party as a "national, democratic, conservative and caring federal political party," the final draft spoke of multiple positioning statements, deleted the word *conservative*, and defined Reform as "a national party dedicated to producing a system of government which is truly representative of and responsible to the people."[32] These were not trivial editorial emendations. The language in the first draft was designed to absorb at least part of Harper's idea of a party with a coherent conservative ideology, whereas the final draft was much less ideological and more populist in inspiration.

In the end, Manning continued to use calculated ambiguity in his positioning statements. To the extent that they directly addressed policy issues, they were always susceptible of a conservative interpretation, but were not limited to it (my comments are in brackets):

- Senate Reform and other measures to secure fair and equal treatment for the West and all other regions of Canada within Confederation [not conservative as such, but contrary to the prevailing notions of Canada's political class].
- Balancing the federal budget, and advancing market-based solutions to economic and environmental problems [overtly conservative, certainly not leftist].
- More direct representation of the views of all Canadians in federal policy making and decision making through referenda and parliamentary reform [not conservative as such, but contrary to the tradition of the Canadian left of pursuing social change through Parliament].[33]

Uncharacteristically (probably driven by Harper's contrary proposals), Manning listed specific target groups for these positioning statements. Not surprisingly, the list was ambiguous. At one level, it seemed to include almost everyone; at another level, it looked like Harper's anglophone suburban-rural conservative coalition built around free-market economics and traditional social values:

1. *Grassroots democracy:* Grassroots democrats (primarily in rural areas) interested in more direct participation.

2. *Regional fairness for all*: Regionally alienated in West, North, Northern Ontario/Quebec, Atlantic Canada. Those who reject "special status" for Quebec.

3. *Social responsibility:* Conservative New Democrats. Youth with social concerns. Ethnic voters. Volunteer sector. Church people. Moderate pro-family and "law and order" people.

4. *Economic growth & financial responsibility:* Small-c conservatives. Right-wing libs. Small business, farmers. Middle-class taxpayers. Urban, young with pocket-book concerns.

5. *Environmental conservation:* Conservative environmentalists. Farm people. Fish and game people. Youth with environmental concerns. Owners, workers in new environmental industries.[34]

Again, there was a significant change from the first to the final draft. The first draft put "economy" first and "grassroots democracy" fifth, whereas in the final draft "grassroots democracy" came first and "economic growth & financial responsibility" was fourth. Manning's lists are always implicitly prioritized, and what he sees as most important usually comes first. Putting "grassroots democracy" at the top reflected his decision to emphasize this as the main theme of the party.

Of course, these internal debates were invisible to the public; people only saw the party's pronouncements on the issues of the day. At this level, a major development was Reform's opposition to the Goods and Services Tax, which, although not an issue in the 1988 election, became a major factor in the Beaver River by-election and the Alberta senatorial election. Opposition to the GST undoubtedly proved a great short-run success for the Reform Party, but it also paved the way for future difficulties. The underlying problem was a lack of consistency in the party's stance.

Manning's position appeared straightforward — "a commitment *not* to introduce taxing measures such as the 9% Goods and Services Tax *until* the Federal Government has clearly demonstrated its ability to control spending."[35] However, major problems lurked beneath the surface. The GST was not really "a new taxing measure" but a replacement for the Manufacturers Sales Tax, which all economists believed to be a bad tax because its incidence was so capricious. It was also the second stage of the Conservatives' tax reform policy that had begun in 1987 with a reduction in the highest marginal rate of the personal income tax. The revenue generated by the GST would replace revenue lost from abolition of the MST and changes to the income tax. The government's claim that it would be "revenue neutral," that is, that it would not impose a net increase in overall taxation, has proven to be correct.

Reform's 1988 platform contained the pledge: "We will work toward a simple and visible system of taxation including the possibility of a flat tax."[36] To be consistent with that position, the party should have supported reductions in the marginal rate of personal income tax and the abolition of the MST. The GST, moreover, was a flat tax — the kind of tax that Reform claimed to support. Manning has repeatedly emphasized that "Reformers are in the business of providing constructive alternatives to government policies,"[37] and that has sometimes been true; but on this issue he fell into the usual pattern of opposing a new measure without clearly explaining to the public what Reform intended to do about taxation. The public could hardly be blamed if it assumed that the Reform Party opposed the GST outright and without qualifications. In effect, Manning let the Axe the Tax movement set the Reform Party's agenda, just as he had done in 1988 when he let the Triple-E movement determine the party's policy on Senate reform.

After the GST became law, Manning invoked fiscal responsibility to argue that it could not be repealed immediately because to do so would increase the deficit.[38] He had to pay dearly for this inconsistency, which made him appear to be reversing himself and thus drove away members who had joined the party under the impression that it was an anti-GST crusade. The whole thing became an embarrassment that had to be settled by a membership poll in the spring of 1992, which led to a new position ratified at the Winnipeg Assembly: a Reform government would abolish the GST in stages *after* it had succeeded in balancing the budget.[39]

The GST posed a major challenge, as had free trade. A small party is inevitably put on the spot when a much larger competitor announces a policy overlapping with its own. There may have been no way for Reform to benefit from the short-term opportunity without paying a price for it in the long term. But a deeper anchoring of Reform's GST policy — not just opposing the GST but explaining what a Reform-inspired tax regime would be — would have been helpful in preventing a slide into opportunism.

Manning's other big positioning adventure in 1989 was to enunciate a much stronger policy concerning Quebec. The 1988 platform contained a comprehensive critique of the Meech Lake Accord, but in practice Reform's opposition to the accord was mainly on grounds that it would permanently frustrate western aspirations. Manning was still thinking in these terms in early 1989 when he considered reviving the party's constitutional task force "in order to help us arrive at a more definitive position on the Meech Lake Accord and the appropriate way to link the passage of a modified Meech Lake Accord with a Senate Amendment."[40] (Note that his opposition to the Meech Lake Accord, as to the Charlottetown Accord, was never more than partial and always open to compromise.) But at the Edmonton Assembly in October 1989, he unveiled a qualitatively different and much more controversial approach to Quebec. Using Abraham Lincoln's metaphor of the "house divided," which of course has deeper roots in the New Testament, Manning said:

> If Canada is to be maintained as one undivided house, the government of Canada must ask the people of Quebec to commit to three foundational principles of Confederation:
>
> • That the demands and aspirations of all regions of the country are entitled to equal status in constitutional and political negotiations.
> • That freedom of expression is fully accepted as the basis of any language policy.
> • That every citizen is entitled to equality of treatment by governments, without regard to race, language, or culture.
>
> If these principles are accepted, our goal of one united Canada is achievable. But if these principles of Confederation are rejected by Quebec, if the house cannot be united on such a basis, then Quebec and the rest of Canada should openly examine the feasibility of establishing a better but more separate relationship between them, on equitable and mutually acceptable terms.[41]

Stephen Harper, Stan Waters, and others had been urging Manning to put more emphasis on Quebec; now he had done so, but in a way fraught with potential difficulties. His first principle, that the aspirations of all regions of the country deserved equal political consideration, was the essential point, but the other two were gratuitous. The official languages policy of the Reform Party's 1988 platform called for "a recognition of French in Quebec and English elsewhere as the predominant language of work and society."[42] To bring in freedom of expression looked like a statement of support for Quebec's anglophone minority, which had been conspicuously absent from the 1988 platform. To support the language rights of English Quebeckers might not be a bad policy in itself, but it is at cross purposes with the "territorial bilingualism" that Manning says he advocates, and it is a definite barrier to attracting francophone supporters for the Reform Party in Quebec. Manning will have to sort out these problems if he ever hopes to expand into Quebec. And referring to "equality of treatment by governments, without regard to race, language, or culture" further compounded the mischief by linking language policy to issues of racial discrimination and multiculturalism, which are in fact distinct from language.

"Manning Calls Quebec's Bluff," read the headline in *Alberta Report*,[43] and he had done so in a highly provocative way with his reference to Lincoln, which carried overtones of secession and civil war. His speech electrified party members; and, with its confrontational positioning on the ethnic dimension of Canadian politics, it laid the foundations for Reform's rise to national prominence in 1990. By positioning Reform as The Party of English Canada, Manning effectively tapped into the unease about Meech Lake that was building in the country. Three provinces had now announced varying degrees of opposition, Pierre Trudeau had come out against it, and Robert Bourassa had aroused the country by using the notwithstanding clause to immunize Quebec's language legislation against Charter challenge. However, the Mulroney government still insisted that everything was fine and the accord would pass. Deborah Grey had raised the issue in April 1989 in her maiden speech in the House of Commons.[44] Now, Manning was stating obvious truths in the face of official denials — a powerful position for Reform.

The party's month-by-month standing during 1990 is shown in Figure 4-1. Its steady climb from about 4%, which left it on the fringe, to 7% to 9%, where it might begin to count as a player on the national stage, was obviously correlated with the collapse of the Meech Lake Accord. Manning's positioning made it plausible for the party to present itself as a systemic alternative to the three traditional parties, all of whom had rushed to support Meech Lake. In this instance, Manning superbly executed his populist strategy of waiting for the wave and then riding it as far as it would take him.

The process by which the Reform Party expanded into Ontario and Atlantic Canada was typical of Preston Manning's methodical approach to politics. At Vancouver, he had called for a national party with a western base, and emphasized the need to leave "room to grow." At Winnipeg, a constitution had been adopted that limited the party to running candidates in the West for the time being, but did not prevent it from "conducting educational and promotional campaigns in other parts of Canada."[45] In June of 1989, he appointed a task force, chaired by Edmonton lawyer Bob Matheson, to investigate expansion and prepare a report for the upcoming assembly. At that event, the delegates moved ahead cautiously, as Manning wanted. They rejected a motion to limit the party to the West; reaffirmed its "long-term goal . . . to be a National Party, based on political values, born in the West"; and endorsed the establishment of "a permanent committee . . . to deal with the question of expansion, which

Figure 4-1
Reform Support 1990

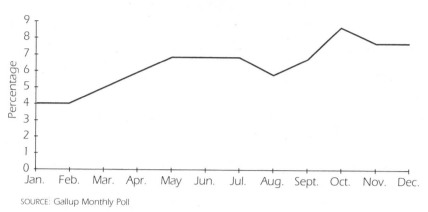

SOURCE: Gallup Monthly Poll

will continue to look for opportunities and to assess the dangers of expansion on an ongoing basis."[46]

After Edmonton, the pace picked up. A new expansion task force was appointed, chaired by Gordon Shaw, who was also vice-chairman of executive council. Manning made his first speaking trip to Ontario in March 1990 and went back again in September, at which time he dined with luminaries such as Hal Jackman and Conrad Black and spoke to the Canadian Club in Ottawa.[47] For a time, Stephen Harper oversaw the Ontario expansion from Deborah Grey's office. He, his brother Robert, Gordon Shaw, and others combed Ontario to find reliable organizers. In spite of a nasty internal squabble among the Ontario pioneers, which led to the departure of several, the movement grew quickly. After much careful thinking the task force prepared a package of resolutions and constitutional amendments for the Saskatoon Assembly in April 1991, while a large squad of Ontario Reformers, and a much smaller number from Atlantic Canada, proclaimed, "The East Wants In!" The delegates at Saskatoon passed everything by a huge majority, and the result was given final effect by a mail referendum of Reform's membership, in which 42.4% of Reformers returned their ballots and 92% of those voted for expansion.[48]

The internal debates surrounding expansion — not only what was discussed but, even more significantly, what was not discussed — give valuable insights into strategic thinking within the party. One set of fears about expansion was practical in character: Was the party ready? Did enough latent support exist in Ontario? Could the party find the money and technical expertise required to do the job? Such fears seemed realistic at the outset but diminished as Reform grew rapidly throughout 1990.

Bob Matheson underlined another widespread fear when he wrote, "How should we respond to the concerns of some of our own members that unless the Reform Party is very careful in its approach to expansion it could be swallowed up by Central Canadian interests just like the CCF/NDP?"[49] These entirely valid concerns were ultimately assuaged through amendments to the party's constitution, which "federalized" its governing structures and decision-making processes. After expansion, the executive council would be composed of a maximum of three directors from each province, and one from each territory.[50] Ontario's large population might allow it to dominate assemblies in the future, but the executive council would have a provincial character, somewhat like the Triple-E Senate. The deliberative processes of assemblies were also changed. In future, changes to party policy and the constitution would require not only a majority of votes cast (two-thirds in the case of constitutional amendments) but also "a majority vote of the delegates from a majority of the Provinces," again limiting the power of populous Ontario.[51] Finally, the delegates voted to entrench the Triple-E Senate in the party's Statement of Principles. These constitutional changes were afterwards complemented by other measures such as requiring all new constituency associations to endorse a short list of essential Reform principles before they could be officially recognized by executive council. Thus far, the approach has proven successful in that there has been no concerted attempt on the part of Ontario members to change the party's western character.

Another concern, primarily expressed by Stephen Harper, was that fragile new constituency associations might easily be taken over by other organizations on the right, such as the Confederation of Regions Party (CoR), Campaign Life, the National Firearms Association, and the Association for the Protection of English in Canada (APEC), all of which were already well entrenched in Ontario.[52] In principle, the solution, or at least part of the solution, to this problem was to draw a clear line around party policy on the right to exclude extremists. Thus the Reform Party's policy committee — in effect, Manning and Harper — prepared several resolutions for Saskatoon to delimit some of the party's more controversial policies. In addressing the assembly, Harper emphasized: "Do not back down on the Party's insistence that issues like language and immigration be addressed. Just the same, do not allow the Party to be shot in the foot on these issues by radical elements, as has happened far too often to new parties."[53] A motion was passed to condemn legislated unilingualism,[54] thus distancing Reform from APEC's and CoR's position that English should be Canada's only official language. Immigration policy was also revised to remove any reference to ethnicity, to ensure that it would be purely economic in character.[55] In the field of multiculturalism, the phrase "national culture" was also removed to counter the misconception that the Reform Party favoured forcible assimilation of immigrants.[56] These measures did not suffice to ward off all problems in Ontario (there was the much publicized case of the Heritage Front in Toronto, and less well-known difficulties with CoR and APEC members in several ridings), but they were in the right direction.

In view of the obvious care with which the party approached expansion, it is surprising that one of the most important issues was never discussed — the effect of the first-past-the-post electoral system on a new party's chances. As mentioned previously, a new party must be regionally concentrated to have any chance of breaking in under a system of plurality voting. As The Party of Western Canada, Reform had achieved this concentration in the West, more particularly in Alberta and parts of British Columbia. There was obviously new support to be gained in parts of Ontario, but would the quest for those voters jeopardize the party's hard-won standing in western Canada?

This question was all the more critical because of the frankly regional strategy that the party had initially pursued. In the election of 1988, Manning had related everything to the interests of the West. He had thereafter moved onto a national level with his Quebec policy, but it was still a huge gamble to give up the local advantage of being a regional party. How quickly could western voters readjust their thinking? Having just become comfortable with the idea of Reform as The Party of the West, could they transfer their support to Reform as a national party?

The fact that the underlying strategy of national expansion was never fully clarified made matters still more difficult. On the one side was Manning's hinterland theory that the Reform Party might represent the interests of thinly populated resource-producing areas across Canada. This showed up in early suggestions that the party might limit its expansion to northwestern Ontario, or "ignore southern Ontario and Quebec completely, but actively explore the development of a party organization in Atlantic Canada."[57] On the other side was Harper's critique of the hinterland theory and his counterproposal that the Reform Party acknowledge itself as a conservative party and attempt to replace the Progressive Conservatives as the main vehicle of the moderate right in federal politics. Within this strategic perspective, the main short-term purpose of expanding into Ontario was to confront the Conservatives in their historic heartland, split their vote, and destroy them as a party, with the hope of replacing them in the future as The Party of the Right. In fact, this aspect of the strategy worked superbly in the 1993 election.

The strategic debate was never resolved, nor indeed was it ever made known outside a small circle of party insiders. Thus the party opted to go national without developing an internal consensus about the type of voters it would target. For a purely western party, Manning's talk about the obsolescence of left and right made some sense because he offered an alternative — advocacy of western regional interests — that did actually cut across ideological lines. In practice, the party was always perceived as right of centre, but it could still draw support from other westerners on regional grounds. Going national changed all of this. If the party was no longer western, and if Manning insisted that it was not a new conservative party, what was it? The Reform Party went national with a case of unresolved identity.

Manning, however, made a major effort to position the party with his nationally televised address to the assembly, entitled "The Road to New Canada." The speech continued what he had begun at Edmonton when he first positioned Reform as The Party of English Canada. It opened with a long reference to the Lincoln-Douglas debates, thus evoking connotations of secession and civil war. It went on to characterize "Old Canada" as "a house divided" by adherence to the doctrine of "equal partnership between two founding races, languages and cultures, the English and French."[58] In a quick review of Canadian history drawn from an undelivered speech written by Stephen Harper for Deborah Grey, Manning tried to show that "the equal partnership model leads to a constitutional cul de sac." In his own words:[59]

1. It has been attempts to more tightly integrate the institutions, languages, and cultures of the French and the English by political and constitutional means which have been the greatest cause of political disunity in the Northern half of the North American continent over the past two hundred years.

2. In each instance where these efforts have produced a political crisis, that crisis has been resolved, not by pursuing a more intimate relationship between the two but by the establishment of a more separate relationship within a broader political framework....[60]

Now, said Manning, the time had come to define a "New Canada" as well as a "New Quebec":

First of all, let me say charitably but clearly that I do not look to Quebec or Quebec politicians to define New Canada. New Canada cannot simply be a reaction to Quebec's demands and aspirations. New Canada must be open and big enough to include a New Quebec, but it must be more than viable without Quebec.[61]

To define New Canada without Quebec was a powerful piece of symbolism, even if Manning insisted that the New Quebec would be welcome in the New Canada — albeit on Canadian terms, not on its own. He then called for a separate process of constitutional conventions — one in Quebec, and a set of regional conventions elsewhere — that would lead to a "National Constitutional Convention."[62] It is not clear whether this body was supposed to include Quebec, but in any case there would have to be a "Great Constitutional Negotiation" to "see if the vision of the New Quebec can be reconciled with the vision of a New Canada within a broader constitutional framework."[63]

At this point, according to Manning, electoral politics entered the scenario:

In other words, I am saying that the Great Canadian Constitutional Negotiation — the real thing, not a charade — cannot proceed in earnest until a Quebec provincial election and a federal general election have been held.

The principal issue in that Quebec provincial election will be "Who really speaks for the New Quebec, and who should be entrusted to negotiate on its behalf with the representatives of New Canada?"

The principal issue in the next federal general election will be "Who really speaks for New Canada, and who should be entrusted to negotiate on its behalf with the representatives of the New Quebec?"

Any political party Leader who cavalierly seeks to occupy that position for purely partisan or personal reasons is a fool, for he or she will face a task even more difficult and dangerous than that which faced Macdonald in 1867.

But it is our task as Reformers, and my task as your Leader, to so position and conduct ourselves in the months ahead that we will not be found wanting or deficient should Canadians ask us to shoulder a portion of that awesome responsibility.[64]

Observers have pointed out that there was an internal contradiction in these words. While rejecting the two founding nations theory, Manning was calling for negotiations between Quebec and the rest of Canada to define a new constitutional order. Jeffrey Simpson later wrote:

By his own words and prescriptions, Manning acknowledged that there are two major groups or peoples or political entities or races or nations, one in Quebec, one lying elsewhere. Reform has not organized, recruited candidates, raised money or attempted to influence opinion in Quebec, because a party that tries to represent Canadians everywhere — to appeal simultaneously inside and outside Quebec — cannot adequately represent only Canada outside Quebec. Two nations, in other words.[65]

As Simpson noted, Manning tried to launch the Reform Party into the national political fray as the only party that could really speak for the New Canada (i.e., Canada outside Quebec) without being compromised by also trying to represent Quebec. Hence the logic of his decision, which was not compelled by the assembly's resolutions or the party referendum, not to run any candidates in Quebec in the next election — it was to avoid a conflict of interest in the impending showdown.

This was a particularly refined example of Manning's tendency towards calculated ambiguity. At one level, the phrase New Canada sounded like an all-inclusive vision of the country. But at another level, the New Canada referred only to Canada outside Quebec. It thus worked on two levels to position Reform confrontationally as The Party of English Canada while simultaneously offering reassurance that Canada could emerge from this hour of peril.

The manoeuvre proved successful and led to the party's explosive growth during the rest of 1991. But it was also a tricky bit of political surfing. Manning recurred to aquatic metaphors in his speech, saying, "There is a tide in the affairs of men, and it is not governed by the whims of Robert Bourassa or Brian Mulroney."[66] The reference was apt, for being The Party of English Canada depended on a high level of anxiety about the failure of constitutional talks, that is, on a tide over which Manning had little control. If the tide went out before the government chose to call an election, what was the use of being positioned as the party of the New [English] Canada? And if the constitutional issue was lost or abandoned, what would give identity to the Reform Party? As we will see in subsequent chapters, these are exactly the contingencies that the party had to face. For a time in late 1992 and early 1993, it seemed that it might become the "Manning Party" without any clear orientation other than the thoughts of the leader; but in the end Manning reverted to conservatism and successfully positioned Reform as The Party of the Right in the 1993 election. However, the uncertainty about what the party really stands for will never fully disappear as long as populism continues to dominate the leader's thinking.

5

Going National

At an early morning meeting in May 1991, strategy for the next federal election was discussed. Summarizing many previous discussions, Reform Party chairman Cliff Fryers articulated the so-called two-election strategy. Much of the thinking went back to Stephen Harper's original memo on expansion, but it was now stripped of its ideological and social elements and presented purely as an electoral strategy. According to Fryers, the Reform Party would win a large number of seats in the next election; he seemed to have in mind about 50 to 80. The party had to win seats in all western provinces and Ontario, so it would not fall into the old Social Credit trap of becoming an Alberta-only party. It also had to finish no worse than third, thereby displacing one of the existing parties in English Canada. The resulting minority Parliament would last only a year or two, after which there would be another election in which Reform would come to power.[1]

The two-election strategy provided the working premises for the Reform Party's national expansion up to and including the 1993 election. It was reaffirmed in all essential details by Manning and Fryers at a pre-election planning meeting held in July 1993. Fryers told the assembled group, "We are trying to put Preston in 24 Sussex Drive after the second election." Manning said, "I'm not interested in winning a few seats in Parliament and spending the next 40 years trying to build on that."[2]

As initially carried out after the announcement of national expansion, the two-election strategy had a number of implications, which included some sharp discontinuities with previous practice:

• The party was supposed to become a full-scale contender at the national level, acquiring all the political technology and tools the other parties had at their disposal (polling, advertising, public relations, computer network, private jet for the leader's campaign, and so forth).[3]
• The party had to raise a large sum of money to fight two national elections in short order.
• The party had to shed its western image to become truly national, for its ambitious objectives could not be achieved solely with victories in the West.

In effect, by pursuing national expansion under the guidance of the two-election strategy, Manning was gambling that he could catch the wave during the 1990s.

Prior to this time, the party had been run with a minimum of staff. In addition to Manning himself, there had been a series of financial officers to deal with fundraising, accounting, and the party's computerized membership list, and a series of press secretaries to deal with the media. Manning hired a personal assistant when money became available, and of course there had to be a receptionist and secretaries, as well as clerks for data-entry and shipping. But overall it was a very lean organization because members of executive council and other volunteers did most of the political work.

As early as the summer of 1990, a plan had been devised to expand this tiny staff into something much larger.[4] In addition to a campaign manager for the election, there was to be a full-time paid executive director of the party who would preside over four departments, each headed by a director. The departments were:

• Finance and Administration, for fundraising, accounting, membership, and the party's business dealings in general;
• Constituency Development and Election Readiness, for liaison with the riding associations and candidates around the country;
• Policy, Strategy, and Communications, to deal with policy development, polling, public relations, and advertising;
• Special Projects, to take such matters as might be assigned, particularly elections for Senate seats, the eastern expansion and the planning for assemblies.

This plan proved too grandiose for the party's needs and financial resources and was never fully implemented, although right up to the election it remained theoretically in place with many empty boxes on the organization chart. But it was not just a case of thinking too big; the party's organizational difficulties illuminate the paradoxes of populism. Caught between the mythical supremacy of the grassroots and the practical reality of the leader's close control of all important matters, the organization languished.

Manning's reluctance to delegate authority and his concern with detail presented a serious problem. Throughout this period, he wrote almost all of his own speeches, often drafted press releases, and carefully edited the ones he did not write. He also composed nearly all of the party's direct-mail fundraising letters (dubbed "sustainer letters") as well as much of the material for *The Reformer*, the party's newspaper; and what he did not write, he usually edited, rewrote, and proofread. Inevitably, the necessity of clearing everything through the leader led to long delays in getting things done and valuable time was lost when the leader decided to reverse an initiative taken by someone else.

Ultimately, the problem was Manning's difficulty in entrusting important business to other people. Because he had trouble doing this, key positions in the organization chart were never filled. Despite the fact that the national office staff clearly lacked experience in running campaigns, the party never did really hire a campaign manager for the 1993 election. Cliff Fryers acted as chairman of the campaign management committee, while Rick Anderson, nominally the campaign director, was hired only for the writ period, travelled with Manning on the leader's tour, and was more of a tour director and spin doctor than an overall campaign manager. The position of executive director of the party remained unfilled until January 1992, when Gordon Shaw was prevailed upon to leave his comfortable Vancouver retirement and return to Calgary. One of Manning's closest confidants, Shaw had been vice-chairman of the executive council under Diane Ablonczy's chairmanship and was the volunteer director of Special Projects, a position he continued to hold even after becoming executive director.

A Calgary headhunting firm conducted searches for a campaign manager and executive director, but this proved an inappropriate and ultimately fruitless approach. Manning was simply unwilling to hire anyone not already part of the small circle of people in whom he reposed trust. His instinct was sound in a sense, given the special position of the leader in a populist party, but it impeded the building of a competent organization. In practice, it meant that throughout 1991 and early 1992, until Shaw could establish some control, the people who were hired lacked direction. Trying to create a new and much larger organization without someone in charge on a day-to-day basis was a recipe for failure. The constitution made Cliff Fryers, as chairman of the party, chief operating officer; but he ran a full-time law practice and could not function effectively as CO, while Manning himself was either on the road or preoccupied with writing *The New Canada*.

This book, incidentally, arose from Manning's personal desires and not from any strategic plan or group decision. Although it did eventually bring the party some useful publicity, the writing of it entailed a heavy cost because it consumed Manning's attention for almost six months at the precise time when the party was trying to build a larger organization. Some of the later breakdowns might have been averted if Manning had not been distracted during these months.

Trouble hit first in Finance and Administration, whose director, Hal Kupchak, had been hired in June 1991. Although the first to bear the title of director, Kupchak was only the latest in a series of chief financial officers; the portfolio had always been troublesome. From the start, Kupchak found himself in a delicate position. Since there was no executive director in place, he reported for many purposes to a committee of executive council; yet two members of that committee, Dick Harris and Don Leier (who was also the vice-chairman of executive council), took paid positions, theoretically under Kupchak, to run fundraising operations. The difficulty of supervising men who were his own superiors contributed to a breakdown in relations, and Kupchak was fired in January 1992 and not replaced until May.

Unfortunately, this was a particularly crucial period for the party's finances. The Save Canada campaign, a fundraising drive, had yielded much less than expected, and the party should have immediately begun to downsize its operations. But the financial systems were still shaky because the party had never had a formal line-item budget. Indeed, the absence of a formal budget was symptomatic of a lack of planning at a more fundamental level. Although the party avoided going into debt, spending decisions often reflected the enthusiasms of the moment rather than long-term strategic priorities. Kupchak had started to introduce a more formalized budget process but was fired before he could fully establish it. The party thus drifted through the first half of 1992 without a proper budget, at a time when it should have been making efforts to economize.

The problems in Policy, Strategy, and Communications proved just as serious but took longer to come to a head. After commencing work, I took a few people who were already working for the party, hired several more, and eventually put together a group of 10 to carry out the many functions suggested by the department's name. These tasks included answering telephone queries and correspondence, making a daily clippings package, preparing press releases and dealing with the media, doing research, drafting speeches, putting out party publications, supporting the party's policy-development processes, contracting polls and advertising, and much more. As an academic political scientist, I had no practical experience in most of these activities; I had to learn as I went along, and I made many costly mistakes.

The job proved educational and exhilarating, but also increasingly frustrating as time passed. My most basic frustration was that I wasn't really in charge. With no executive director in place, I reported to three "bosses": Cliff Fryers, who only came into the office for a couple of hours a week; Manning, who was gone or unavailable most of the time; and a committee of executive council. Also, each of these three bosses frequently dealt directly with staff who nominally reported to me. It was "matrix management" with a vengeance, and I spent much of my energy just trying to find out what was happening.

Manning, in particular, managed around rather than through me as director. Anything he was really interested in, he directed himself: media relations through Ron Wood, party publications through Diane Ablonczy and later Laurie Watson, platform development through Stephen Harper. I found the director's position to be redundant because Manning was his own director, for all practical purposes. After eight months, I resigned as director of Policy, Strategy, and Communications and took the more modest title of director of research. After one more year, I resigned altogether from the party's employment.

The broad reach of Policy, Strategy, and Communications presented another problem. Supposedly, these functions were unified so that policy would always drive communications. That was a laudable goal, but in practice the opposite came closer to the truth. Manning's deepest interest was and still is in communications. During his years as a management consultant, his work had often been in the field of corporate communications. As leader of the Reform Party, he has spent endless hours refining the wording of speeches, press releases, and advertisements. With limited success, he repeatedly tried to impose his 12-point COMMUNICATE 500 checklist upon all staff. He devotes great effort to devising slogans and communications "hooks," such as the notion of the so-called Debt Hole in the Zero in Three budget-balancing package of 1993. (Typically, graphic representations of the debt show it escalating exponentially year by year, heading upwards and to the right. Manning reversed the chart to show it sinking downwards, so he could speak of it as a hole and link it with a favourite saying: "If you're in a hole, the first thing to do is stop digging.") To the extent that Manning functioned as the real director of Policy, Strategy, and Communications, he naturally conveyed his concern with communications to staff, leaving little time for serious policy development.

Any policy development that did take place during my tenure was usually impelled by the needs of the moment. Manning would decide that he ought to make a speech on a certain subject, or that he had to have an answer to a question that someone had asked, or that it was time to satisfy a demand from within the party to enlarge upon a point in the Blue Book. Staff would then scramble to pull some ideas together. The driving force was always communications.

Of the three full-fledged departments with a complement of paid staff, Constituency Development and Election Readiness worked out the best, largely because that department's main function — keeping in contact with constituency associations — continued an activity that was already under way. Hence, Manning was willing to let the director, Virgil Anderson, and his staff do their work. After national expansion began, the number of recognized constituency associations grew to over 200. Of course, there were problems: constituency squabbles, arguments about procedures at constituency nominating meetings, the unwelcome attempt by ex-Tory John Gamble to get himself nominated in Don Valley West,[5] the resignation of a few nominated candidates over policy disagreements, and the embarrassment caused during the 1993 election campaign by one candidate's racist remarks. But these were trifles in comparison to what might have gone wrong.

All in all, the organizational record was a chequered one. Policy, Strategy, and Communications never fulfilled expectations, partly because of Manning's leadership style, partly because of my academic orientation and inexperience in practical politics. Finance and Administration went through an administrative meltdown but was finally rehabilitated and now runs smoothly. Constituency Development and Election Readiness did relatively well.

Although the various departments suffered many reverses, there is evidence to show that the party can learn from experience and eventually build a functioning organization. Manning, Fryers, and Rick Anderson finally assembled a group that got the job done in the 1993 election campaign. However, the composition of that group points to the challenge that lies ahead. It consisted of senior people who operated with absolute loyalty to Manning and junior people who were mainly following orders. There were few if any of the middle-ranking persons that one would find in other parties — pollsters, advertisers, researchers, policy experts, speechwriters — with independent professional credentials and experience. Manning and his circle have not yet solved the problem of how to integrate professional expertise into a populist movement, but they will have to do so if Reform is going to be effective as a national party with a substantial voice in the House of Commons.

Political parties that have money to spend make use of consultants with special skills, especially in polling and advertising. At the time of national expansion, the Reform Party already had a loose relationship with the Vancouver ad agency of Scali McCabe Sloves, but Manning and Fryers saw this as inadequate and wanted to establish closer ties with a Calgary firm, Hayhurst Associates. Manning had known Alan Wiggan, the head of this firm, for some years and had long hoped to get him working for the Reform Party; but Wiggan had been reluctant because Hayhurst had important advertising contracts from the provincial governments of Alberta and British Columbia. Wiggan was also a close friend of Fryers; he had done advertising for Fryers' law firm, and the two shared a ski cabin in winter and had neighbouring cottages as well. In the spring of 1991, after the problem of provincial contracts was overcome, Fryers worked out an agreement with Wiggan in strict secrecy and presented it to the executive council for ratification as a fait accompli.

The motives for bringing in Wiggan and his company at this time were understandable enough. The party was starting to plan for an election and expected to put on a national advertising campaign. If political advertising is going to be effective, whoever is responsible for it should sit on the campaign committee before the actual campaign begins in order to become imbued with the party's ideology and strategy. And there was not a lot of choice. Calgary is not a major location for advertising companies; and of those present in the city, many already had connections with other political parties.

But even if Hayhurst seemed worth trying, several factors conspired to ruin the relationship, which lasted only about a year. The major problem was cost. Hayhurst wanted to follow the normal procedure for handling corporate accounts, which was to send over one or two account executives for all meetings. These people and often Wiggan himself would then serve as intermediaries between the party's requests for service and the creative people in the agency. Good reasons exist for proceeding this way in the corporate world, but it is too expensive for a fledgling political party. Even though Hayhurst billed at a discount, the invoices were huge by Reform Party standards because so many Hayhurst employees were involved. The difficulty was compounded by Reform's loose organization, which meant that many different people from the party's side were meeting or telephoning Hayhurst staff, who had their meters running all the time.

Another factor that contributed to the demise of the relationship was that no one at Hayhurst had any experience doing political advertising, so the party was spending money for Hayhurst to learn on the job. With the failure of the Save Canada fundraising campaign, it was obvious by the spring of 1992 that Reform could not afford to keep the relationship going; and Gordon Shaw, who as executive director was most aware of the cost, managed to terminate it.

Considerable discussion ensued about how to replace Hayhurst. One option would have been to do what the Liberals and Conservatives do, namely, to bring together a few politically supportive advertising executives as volunteers to do the creative work, but no progress ever seemed to occur on that front. It was impeded by objections from Wiggan and Rick Anderson; but in any case bringing in newcomers at that point would have overstretched Manning's capacity to trust others. As a result, the party had to fight the referendum campaign of 1992 without professional advertising advice. The resort to simple "talking head" ads during that campaign was motivated not only by the shortage of funds but also by the absence of any-one able to create anything better (it also allowed Manning to exercise control over content and format).

As soon as the party began trying to plan the election campaign in the summer of 1991, those involved felt the lack of their knowledge and experience. This led to the hiring of a second consultant, the American pollster Frank Luntz, whom Virgil Anderson had met at a campaign management seminar in Washington, D.C. Although still very young, Luntz had been involved in campaign work since his early teens. He had a Ph.D. in political science from Oxford and was the author of *Candidates, Consultants, and Campaigns*, a study of the effect of computers, polling, television, and other modern technologies on politics.[6] After getting his Ph.D. and going out on his own as an independent consultant, he had worked briefly for Richard Wirthlin when the latter was Ronald Reagan's White House pollster. Although often described in the Canadian press as Reagan's pollster, Luntz only did one small project for the White House in the short time he was with Wirthlin.

For several reasons, he was well suited to Reform's needs. He was not only a pollster but was knowledgeable about all aspects of political organization and technology. Having studied in Great Britain and worked on a campaign in Israel for the Likud, he was acquainted with multiparty races. Of course, it was a concern that he was an American, and other parties would undoubtedly criticize Reform for hiring a foreign consultant; but the NDP had used an American pollster in 1988 without creating a campaign issue,[7] and the federal Conservatives had been using an American direct-mail consultant for years.

After a get-acquainted meeting in July, Luntz was retained as a consultant. His first project was to conduct a national baseline poll, which he fielded through Canadian Facts at the end of August for a cost of $85,000. His presentation of the data in September caused a good deal of optimism because he measured Reform's national support at 19% outside

Quebec. He also found that Manning was popular, although not well known outside the West, and that the party's major policy positions had broad public support. A set of 12 Reform positions drawn almost verbatim from the Blue Book all received a high level of endorsement ("strongly agree" or "strongly approve" from at least 43% of respondents, and most were well over 50%).[8] Broadly speaking, his findings reinforced the theory of the two-election strategy in which the populist Reform party was poised to catch a wave of public dissatisfaction and ride it to prominence, maybe even to power.

Curiously, however, this poll marked the peak of the wave as far as Luntz's own influence on the party went. In his work in American elections, he was used to being close to the candidate and consulted on all sorts of issues, but Manning would not grant him that kind of access. Although he pleaded for the opportunity, Luntz never really got a chance to spend any time alone with Manning. Instead, a planning committee was set up, on which Luntz was one of six members. Known as TEAC (for Technical Election Advisory Committee) and chaired by me, this body met several times in the fall of 1992 and produced massive amounts of paper, but not to much effect. Manning kept his distance from TEAC, joining it occasionally but not committing himself to any conclusions.

As far as Luntz was concerned, the main thing that happened in TEAC was that he was outmanoeuvred by Wiggan and Rick Anderson (about whom more will be said below). In view of Luntz's findings, and thinking that the money would be available, it seemed logical for TEAC to recommend a campaign of paid advertising in the pre-writ period to heighten the public's awareness of Reform. Wiggan recommended using billboards; but Luntz said billboards were a waste of money for political advertising, and if we could not afford television, we would be better off not to spend money on a campaign. When Anderson sided with Wiggan, the committee opted for billboards, though the campaign was subsequently cancelled altogether because of lack of funds.

From that point on, Luntz was never a major factor in decision making at the national level, though he continued to play a role in candidate-training seminars. In February 1992, Manning vetoed any further polling on grounds that it was too expensive and that a populist party could not use the results anyway. In retrospect, that was his way of saying that he was not prepared to use Luntz as a major adviser, so there was no point in spending a lot of money to let him poll. From then on, Luntz attended occasional meetings and sometimes sat in on teleconference calls, but his best efforts went elsewhere. First he was hired as Pat Buchanan's pollster in his primary challenge to President Bush, then he became Ross Perot's pollster; and these commitments made him mostly unavailable to the Reform Party.

Consequently, after September 1991, the party was "flying blind," trying to navigate without polling data. Manning was ignoring the conventional wisdom of contemporary politics, as expressed in John Laschinger's Ten Commandments for campaign managers: "Always choose a pollster who gives advice. . . . Use the numbers to drive the strategy. . . . Always poll, even when broke. . . ."[9] Of course, polling is expensive, and money became a serious issue with the failure of the Save Canada campaign, but it was not the real issue. The deeper problem was how to use polling in a populist party where the leader is the interpreter of "the common sense of the common people." Again, this problem remains to be solved.

The third consultant to get involved in the Reform Party was Rick Anderson, then manager of the Ottawa office of the giant consulting firm Hill and Knowlton. Anderson at one time had been deeply involved in the Liberal Party; since 1974, he had worked on more than a dozen Liberal federal, provincial, and leadership campaigns. He had been manager of Donald Johnston's leadership campaign in 1984,[10] and served as a briefer for John Turner in the federal election later that year. His father-in-law, Blair Williams, had been national director of the Liberal Party from 1973 to 1975.[11] Anderson had broken with the federal Liberals, but was still an active member of the Ontario provincial Liberals.

Apart from Liberal politics, Anderson had also worked since 1980 for David McNaughton in the consulting business, where he developed many connections with important Conservatives. His first achievement was to help McNaughton and Alan Gregg get the *Decima Quarterly Report* on a sound business footing.[12] Decima, of course, was subsequently acquired by Hill and Knowlton. One of Rick Anderson's brothers, Bruce, also worked for Decima until he left to set up Anderson Strategic Research, the polling arm of Earnscliffe Associates, a consulting group that includes prominent Conservatives Bill Fox, Harry Near, and Nancy Jamieson (Bruce Anderson's wife). Anderson Strategic Research emerged as a polling company that, after Decima, got a major chunk of business from the Conservatives and the federal government.[13] Another Anderson brother also worked in Ottawa doing observation and liaison for the NDP government of Ontario.

Rick Anderson and Blair Williams organized a dinner for Manning in Ottawa in September 1990 so he could meet some political insiders, mostly Liberals.[14] Anderson subsequently joined the Reform Party and attended the Saskatoon Assembly as an observer from Ontario. Manning kept him in mind and had him invited to the session in July at which it was decided to retain

Frank Luntz. Anderson brought along Jamie Deacey, another consultant with a Liberal background. Deacey was the president of Association House, a consulting group that included Michael Marzolini, who subsequently took over from Martin Goldfarb as pollster for the federal Liberals. Anderson and Deacey made a presentation on what they could offer the Reform Party, but those who heard the presentation preferred to retain Luntz.

Anderson, however, kept in touch, and in September Cliff Fryers announced that he would be put on the team as Canadian political strategist. He subsequently sat on TEAC, worked on candidate training, and did some other things for the party — all without pay except for travel expenses. After adroitly neutralizing Luntz in the early months by forming a tactical alliance with Fryers' friend Wiggan, he became a major source of advice to Manning, as much through private telephone conversations as through formal group meetings. In the end, he was the only one of the external consultants to last and to become a major player within the party, in spite of the episode, described in the next chapter, in which he took the Yes side in the referendum campaign.

There is no question that Anderson was helpful to the party. He had a fund of practical political knowledge and experience in polling, advertising, public relations, and organizing a leader's tour that was largely lacking in the national office and executive council. He also had many useful personal connections to politicians, consultants, and journalists. Nonetheless, his becoming a close adviser to Manning occasioned difficulties. For one thing, it looked bad. Manning was supposed to be a populist leader involved in a crusade against the traditional parties, whereas Anderson was completely at home in the world of the Ottawa political establishment.

Moreover, Anderson's political views differed from those of most Reformers, as shown by his decision to support the Yes side in the referendum. Perhaps because he had grown up in Montreal, keeping Quebec happy has a priority for him that it does not have for most Reformers.[15] As early as April 1992, he advised Manning not to oppose any constitutional deal that might be forthcoming because, he said, "the country is bone-tired of the constitutional process."[16] Anderson also has little objection to official bilingualism in its present form, and he advised Manning to dissociate himself from the criticism of bilingualism that Alberta premier Don Getty made in January 1992.[17] Most importantly, Anderson rejected the strategy of The Party of the Right. In his view,

Canadian voters are ideological only in the broadest sense; they eschew ideological purity and prefer practicality on virtually all specific issues. That's what the Tories and NDP have found out election after election, except where they muddied the ideological waters by presenting themselves as more mainstream. That the Tories now lack a sense of direction or purpose is certainly an argument for them to be replaced, but not an argument to replace them with an ideologically-pure party. Principled, yes. Honest, yes. Committed to a more open process, yes. Determined to live within our means, yes. Ideologically pure and consistent, forget it. Most voters don't think that way, and most issues don't present themselves this way.[18]

Anderson thus reinforced the non-ideological side of Manning's populism, his belief that left, right, and centre are obsolete categories and that "the common sense of the common people" is the ultimate test of policy.

This fundamental agreement between Manning and Anderson explains how Anderson came to be Manning's closest adviser and was ultimately appointed campaign director for the 1993 election. "Rick Anderson," Manning once said, "represents the kind of person that we must eventually reconcile ourselves with if we are going to win Ontario." In other words, Anderson fit into Manning's non-ideological strategy of sweeping to power in a short period of time on a broad wave of discontent rather than invading from the margin by espousing a consistently conservative ideology.

In spite of not having a formal budget process, the Reform Party was quite frugal in its early years. Volunteers performed most functions, and things were done as cheaply as possible. At the time of the national expansion, the party had a substantial nest egg of about half a million dollars in the bank.

Reform's financial base was its direct-mail program of "sustainer letters" to members. In this program, the Reform Party was as advanced as any party in Canada, primarily because from the very start it had maintained a single computerized membership file at the national office and did not have to negotiate with anyone for access to mailing lists. But this base, although adequate for the party's routine needs, was thought to be too narrow to sustain the expense of a national campaign because it depended on repeat donations from a relatively small number of people. The party had experimented a couple of times with direct-mail "prospecting" to build up a donor list outside the membership, but without success. Corporate giving was virtually non-existent, except for small companies owned by Reform supporters.

The party's leadership thought at this time that the two-election strategy would require much more money than could be wrung out of direct mail, even if Reform membership grew, as hoped, to 150,000–200,000 (in fact, it peaked at 133,000 during the referendum and was only about 100,000–110,000 during the 1993 election campaign). With the help of Compton's International, an Australian fundraising firm, an imaginative plan was devised for a grassroots fundraising campaign called Save Canada. In every constituency association, a team of volunteers would be recruited and each volunteer would personally visit 10 other party members. The volunteers would disclose the amounts they were pledging and ask their targets to make a contribution comparable in the light of their own financial circumstances.

The concept seemed ideal for the Reform Party: it was new and fresh, it involved lots of volunteers, it built on acquaintanceships within the party, and it did not depend on getting large contributions from corporations or wealthy donors. And in fact the campaign did raise $2.3 million — not an insignificant sum. But it failed to live up to the expectations of the planners, who had hoped to raise $12 million, to be split more or less equally between the national office and the constituency associations. If it had achieved that goal, Save Canada would virtually have bankrolled a full-scale national election campaign. It was estimated that, depending upon how many Reform candidates were nominated, the national party would be allowed under the Canada Elections Act to spend about $6 million on its campaign. With their half of the cash, the constituencies would also have been well fixed for their local campaigns, which would be subject to a limit of about $60,000 depending on the size of the riding.

When the campaign was launched on November 6, 1991, the party, with confidence born of hope and inexperience, publicly announced a target figure of $12 million,[19] even though skeptics had pointed out that there was no evidence to show that this amount could be raised. There was even an expensive billboard campaign in major cities to advertise Save Canada to the public. But it became obvious within a very few weeks that results would be far below the target figure. Attempts were made to spur the troops on to greater efforts, but in the end only $2.3 million came in, spread out between 1991 and 1992. Of that, the national office got to keep only about $500,000 because it had to split the proceeds with constituencies and had also committed itself to pay all the costs of the campaign, including a fee of about $500,000 to Compton's — an exorbitant fee in terms of results but one that had seemed reasonable in terms of expectations.

Why did Save Canada not do as well as anticipated? Most obviously, the expectations, not being based on practical experience, were inflated.

The campaign actually proved a modest success, and constituted a failure only in relation to the unrealistic expectations. But there was also an administrative lesson to be learned. Save Canada had been conceived by a small circle of people in the executive council and then suddenly sprung on the membership of the party. When the leadership assiduously fosters a cult of populism, it cannot realistically expect the mass membership of the party to respond like soldiers to commands. After the Save Canada fiasco, executive council made a point of proceeding more carefully in trying to get constituencies to line up behind national office initiatives.

The failure of Save Canada represented a setback for the two-election strategy and its full-scale national campaign. Unless it changed direction, the party was now on the road to insolvency because, in anticipation of the success of Save Canada, it had been making expensive commitments throughout 1991 — hiring new staff, signing contracts with consultants, getting accustomed to doing everything on a grander scale. The proceeds of the sustainer letters, which had kept the party going for five years, were no longer adequate.

In retrospect, there should have been an immediate, sharp downsizing at the beginning of 1992, together with a re-evaluation of what could be expected for the campaign. A few steps were, in fact, taken, such as cancelling the polling program; but for the most part serious cuts and rethinking were put off until late summer. This was partly because of a lack of control at the top. There was no campaign manager, and the director of Finance was fired in January. Gordon Shaw came on as executive director in early 1992, but his time was taken up with a major change in the party's computer system.

Another reason for putting off the necessary adjustments was the belief that corporate fundraising might fill the void. The party had run a small corporate campaign in 1991 and had raised $328,000, which, after deducting expenses of $97,000, left a net yield of $231,000. Now it proposed to spend $300,000 on corporate fundraising in 1992 in the hope of generating $2.5 million in contributions.[20] In the event, the $300,000 was spent, but it generated only about $200,000 in contributions, for a net loss of $100,000.

At the kickoff of the referendum campaign, Manning cited the party's opposition to the Charlottetown Accord as the reason for corporate reluctance to give to the Reform Party,[21] but this was a fanciful rationalization. The simple fact is that the party was just not able to get the donations. Corporate fundraising requires the efforts of people who have business connections, and Reform lacked such people at this time. In Toronto, the central location for corporate donations, the party's efforts in 1991–1992 were headed by David Andrus, who got into one quarrel after another and was eventually expelled for his role in trying to nominate John Gamble in Don Valley West. But even more fundamentally, corporate giving to political parties is a hardheaded business decision, calculated to gain access to politicians in office. Until the Reform Party proves it can elect MPs and exercise influence in the House of Commons, it is not likely to get much from the corporate world, no matter how attractive its program might be in theoretical terms to the business community.

The net result of the failure of Save Canada, the failure of corporate giving, and the postponement of necessary cuts was that the party used up what it had gotten from Save Canada plus most of its accumulated reserves. When the referendum campaign was announced, the party was incapable of funding an expensive campaign out of existing resources and had to resort to exacting a voluntary levy upon the constituency associations ($311,000 was committed, not all of which was paid). The party reported referendum campaign expenditures of about $350,000, but over half that amount consisted of salaries of party employees and other expenditures that would have been incurred even if there had not been a referendum. In cash flow terms, the national office actually made a profit on the referendum (subtracting expenses from the amount raised from the sale of pamphlets, contributions earmarked for the referendum, and the special constituency assessment).

The Reform Party undertook national expansion with a strategic concept derived from Manning's understanding of a populist party. It required the party to build a large national organization very quickly in order to catch the anticipated wave. But the organizational effort proved more a failure than a success. The party could not raise the necessary funds, and the unsuccessful effort left it in worse shape financially than before it started. Relationships with consultants did not work out, and the party never acquired sophisticated polling and advertising capacity. Finally, the research and communications staff at national office dissolved in acrimony after the referendum campaign, leaving Manning surrounded by a combination of junior staff and senior loyalists.

There are various explanations for why things went wrong. One has to do with the leader's personality: Manning's rather solitary nature and his reluctance to restrain his own autonomy by creating a collegial team made it impossible to bring the necessary expertise into the organization. At the end of 1993, the people closest to Manning were still the same as in 1990, except that Rick Anderson had moved inside the circle and Stephen Harper had moved outside it. This inability to bring highly skilled people into the party and employ them constructively helps explain the party's weaknesses in fundraising, advertising, and public relations. For some things it tried to do, it never did "have the horses" or could not keep them in harness.

Moreover, it may be questioned whether a populist party as Manning conceives it can acquire and use all the sophisticated tools of contemporary politics, such as polling, advertising, public relations, and fundraising. Effective use of the "black arts," as Laschinger calls them, requires the creation of intermediate structures between the leader and the grassroots, structures that are bound to conflict with Manning's role as interpreter of "the common sense of the common people."

On the other hand, Reform has now achieved two major successes — the victory in the referendum campaign and the election of 52 MPs in the 1993 election — without use of the black arts. There has been almost no polling, little corporate giving, only small-scale and unsophisticated advertising, and nothing but simple attempts at media management. With the benefit of hindsight, it now seems that the attempt to build a full-scale apparatus comparable to that of the existing parties was misguided, and it is probably a good thing that it failed. At least for the time being, the party has managed to succeed without the money and technology that were previously considered essential in Canadian politics.

The Reform Party will eventually have to acquire Laschinger's black arts, but it will have to find a populist way of doing so. For example, it needs polling, but the effort should probably start with a solid research program based on the opinions of party members, and work up from there. And it will want to advertise in future elections, but should probably cultivate the whimsical, folksy, humorous approach that worked well on a small scale during the 1993 election. Similarly, it will always need fundraising, but it might be better to voluntarily forego corporate support and work for a change in the law to prohibit political donations by corporations and labour unions.

Figure 5-1 shows Gallup Poll support figures month by month for the Reform Party from April 1991, when the Saskatoon Assembly endorsed national expansion, through August 1992, after which the public's attention became focused on the Charlottetown Accord and the referendum. The basic pattern is easy to describe. Reform started strong, with 16% national support of committed voters in April 1991 at the time of the Saskatoon Assembly and the expansion announcement. Since the party was not seeking support in Quebec at that time, 16% national support translated into 21% in the rest of Canada, a respectable figure and enough to win a significant number of seats if it held up during an election. With 20% of the popular vote, the NDP

Figure 5-1
Reform Support, April 1991–August 1992

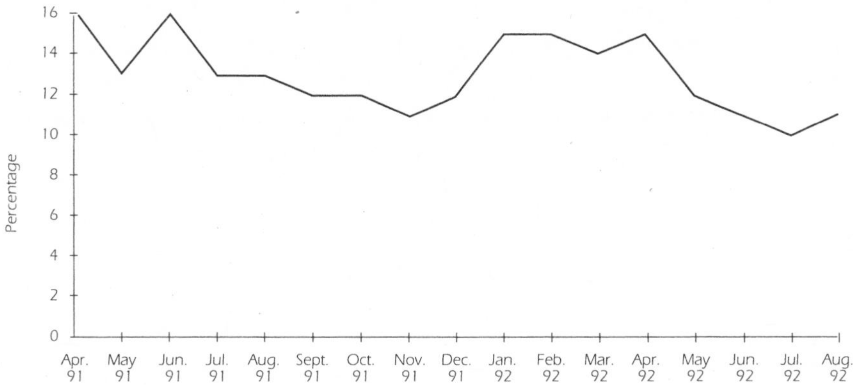

SOURCE: Gallup Monthly Poll

won 43 seats in 1988, all outside of Quebec. But Reform support started to erode almost immediately, sliding to 11% by November 1991. The trend then reversed itself, with Reform staying around 15% from January through April 1992. After that the erosion resumed, so that Reform was down to 10% in July and 11% in August 1992.

These may seem like marginal changes, but they were important to a party in Reform's position because of the effect of Canada's first-past-the-post electoral system. With 16% of the national vote, given that its support was concentrated in certain parts of western Canada and Ontario, it could hope to elect 40 MPs representing several provinces. At 10%, it would struggle to elect 12 MPs, the minimum for an officially recognized caucus in the House of Commons, and they would all probably be from Alberta.

In the early months of expansion, the party got a relatively easy ride in the media. There were lots of puff stories at first, commenting on the mere fact of national expansion, on the size of Reform's membership, its ability to turn out crowds and raise money, and Manning's rapport with audiences. In the fall of 1991, Stephen Harper appeared several times as a commentator on a political panel after the Sunday night CBC television news — another sign that the party was arriving in national politics.

But by that time, the party was also in danger of becoming old news. After covering the novelty of the expansion, the media had to have something else to report, and Manning wasn't giving them much. He was preoccupied during the summer and early fall with writing *The New Canada*, which kept him out of the public eye. Characteristically, he wrote almost all of it himself, although he did integrate some small bits drafted by others.

Moreover, even when he did appear in public, he said little that was news-worthy because he essentially gave the same speech over and over. This was fine for the audience in the room but did not satisfy the need of the media for something new to report, so coverage of the party declined.

The rebound in Reform's support coincided with a period of intense media attention in the winter of 1992. One reason for the attention was that some long-term projects came to fruition. Manning's book appeared and the pub-lisher sponsored a coast-to-coast tour to promote it. Global did a TV special on Manning and a long article on Reform women appeared in *Chatelaine*.[22] Also, there were some hotly contested nomination fights that produced news-worthy nomination meetings, like the race in Lethbridge, ultimately won by Ray Speaker, that generated new membership sales of 4,000.[23]

Partly due to my prodding, Manning temporarily revamped his media strategy for speaking tours. Particularly during a major tour of Ontario in January, and to a lesser extent on some other tours, he paid closer attention to the needs of the media. He spoke on a different subject each day and put out press releases summarizing the new material. It was the tried and true "Gainesburger a day" approach but on a fairly high intellectual level, offer-ing policy ideas, not just photo opportunities or attacks on opponents. For example, during one week in Ontario and Quebec, he spoke about Reform's potential appeal to Liberals, advanced education vouchers, pro-portional taxation, and Reform's theory of territorial bilingualism. Each topic generated newspaper headlines, lead stories in broadcasts, and attacks from opponents that prolonged the publicity.[24]

Manning has continued to use this approach to the media from time to time, but he has difficulties with it. His personal conscientiousness, coupled with his determination to control the Reform message, compel him to write all his own speeches. He can sometimes use drafts from other people, but not without investing a large amount of time in rewriting. George Koch, a reporter for *Alberta Report*, was hired as a speechwriter in the spring of 1992, but Manning rarely used him and gave up altogether after about three months. It may be admirable for a leader to write all his own speeches, but it severely limits what he can do. In particular, it makes it extremely difficult for him to deliver a series of speeches on different sub-jects, simply because of the necessary preparation time. Also, as a serious rhetorician, Manning is sensitive to audiences and occasions, which often leads him to continue working on speeches right up to the minute they are delivered. This is wonderful for the audiences, but reporters become con-fused when they find that the speech doesn't entirely match the press release, which in turn leads to garbled stories in the media.

In this period there was also a large amount of negative publicity, generated by Reform's own mistakes as well as by attacks from other parties. Interestingly, the bad press did not seem to depress Reform's popularity; in fact, the party's standing in the polls did not drop off until May 1992, when the attacks, as well as positive coverage, tailed off. For a new party in Reform's position, trying for the first time to gain nationwide recognition, there may be no such thing as bad press; being ignored is probably worse than being attacked. However, it is also obvious that negative publicity can lead to loss of support in the long run. In Reform's case, what seems to have happened is that the negative coverage cut off the prospects for future growth before it cut deeply into existing support. People who might have been willing to look at Reform were deterred by bad publicity.

Hard evidence for this interpretation is lacking, but it is consistent with the fact that Manning's net personal approval rating dropped in the year after national expansion (see Figure 5-2). To be more precise, the percentage endorsing his performance remained more or less constant in the range of 30% to 35%; but the percentage of disapproval increased while the percentage of "don't know" responses declined. Since Manning was synonymous with the party, a decline in his popularity was likely to limit its growth potential and ultimately lead to actual decline.

Given the importance of bad publicity, it is essential for any party to learn how to deal with it. With this in mind, let us look briefly at half a dozen episodes to see how well the party performed. Did it do the best for itself in difficult circumstances? How much of the media damage it suffered was self-inflicted? And how much of this self-inflicted damage is related to the nature of a Manning-style populist party?

Figure 5-2
Preston Manning's Approval Rating July 1991–July 1992

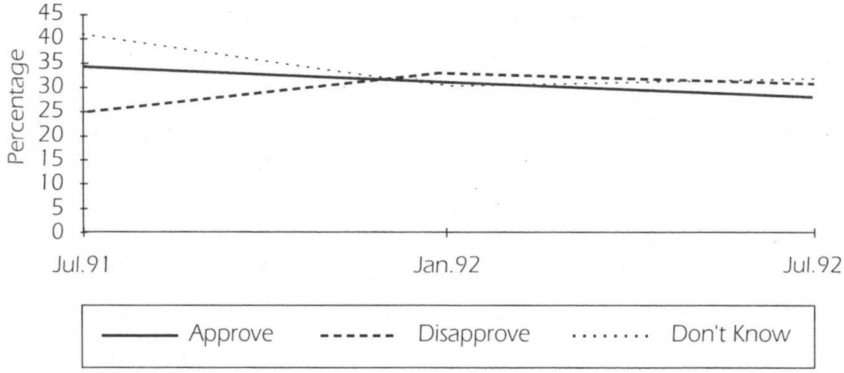

SOURCE: Angus Reid Poll

Three of the six episodes involved membership problems. In December 1991 a long-running dispute between the party's leadership and several of the most active members in Winnipeg started to get into the press. It eventually resulted in the expulsion of four members and dozens of unwelcome stories, reported mostly in Manitoba but echoed around the country.[25] Then, between Christmas and New Year's, reporters discovered that Gordon LeGrand had been elected to the executive of the Ontario constituency association of Leeds-Grenville.[26] LeGrand was the man who had been filmed stepping on the Quebec provincial flag in a 1989 demonstration about provincial bilingualism in Ontario; the resulting footage was shown over and over in Quebec during the Meech Lake debate and became a symbol there of English Canada's supposed hostility towards Quebec. Although Manning had been warned that LeGrand had joined the party and was becoming active in the Leeds-Grenville riding association, he did not order any preventive action to be taken. After media exposure, however, he had LeGrand expelled from the party as soon as executive council could meet.[27]

The most damaging publicity occurred on February 28, 1992, when front-page headlines in the Sun chain of newspapers broke the story that four members of the neo-Nazi Heritage Front, including the leader Wolfgang Droege, had joined the Reform Party. Not only was Droege a member, he and some friends had helped provide crowd control at a couple of events during Manning's trips through Toronto (Droege and his friends are bailiffs and thus have some expertise in providing security services). It was only through chance that the *Toronto Sun* reporter did not succeed in getting a photograph of Manning standing next to Droege or, even worse, shaking hands [28] The Heritage Front members were expelled as quickly as possible as executive council members communicated through a conference call and fax ballot rather than waiting for a scheduled meeting.[29] However, the headlines still reinforced the impression that the Reform Party was a magnet for extremists and would not clean house until forced to do so by exposure in the media.

In these three instances of bad publicity, the damage arose not from incompetence in handling the media but from the organizational structure of the party itself. Each episode illustrated some of the intrinsic difficulties of a Manning-style populist party. On the one hand, Reform is supposed to be a mass party. Membership sales are encouraged at all times, not just during nominating meetings. Anyone can join the party without checks of any kind. Thus a Gordon LeGrand or Wolfgang Droege can be signed up without setting off alarm bells. At a higher level, too, people whose past record radiates danger signals have sometimes been recruited into the party and

given responsibility. For example, Herb Schultz, one of the Manitoba dissidents, is the brother-in-law of Ed Schreyer and had been expelled from the
NDP before he became a Reformer. However, Manning thought Schultz
could be useful and encouraged his participation instead of exercising cau-
tion. He also personally recruited and encouraged others who eventually
became troublesome and were expelled: Ron Gamble in British Columbia,
George Van Den Bosch in Manitoba, David Andrus in Ontario.

A related problem is that the rhetoric of populism gives rise to a cult of
local autonomy. Constituency associations are encouraged to have large
executive committees — over two dozen in some cases — and to think of
themselves as the voice of the members in their riding. But this spirit of
grassroots autonomy can collide with the reality of Manning's unique role
as interpreter of the Reform message; and when it does, dissident members
tend to become outraged, as happened in Manitoba. At that point, the
national executive council has virtually no tools to use to control local constituency associations except the expulsion of dissidents from the party.

The ultra-centralization of Reform's organizational structure creates another
problem. The national office and executive deal directly with all riding associations; no provincial or regional organizations, or even informal potentates,
exist. No one is out in the field charged with the task of ensuring that people
like Gordon LeGrand and Wolfgang Droege are not enlisted as members and
given positions of responsibility. Hence the tendency to be caught by surprise.

Finally, even when an organization has been created, such as the Reform
national office, it can be hamstrung by reliance on loyalists rather than professional staff. The Heritage Front episode provides a pertinent illustration.
On June 19, 1991, the *Toronto Star* reported a statement by Wolfgang Droege
that the Reform Party had "given [the Heritage Front] some hope."[30] The paper
did not report that he had joined the party, but it should have been cause for
concern that Droege was speaking favourably of Reform. Not long afterwards, Al Muxworthy, a Toronto Reformer who had had a meeting with the
Canadian Jewish Congress, wrote to the national office to sound a warning
about Droege. However, no one acted upon that letter and I could not find it
in the files when I learned of its existence six months later.[31] Closer to the
event, a member of executive council who was doing fundraising work in
Ontario in early 1992 was warned by the Canadian Jewish Congress that
Droege and other extremists might have joined the party. He started an inves-
tigation of membership rolls when he returned to Calgary, but it went forward
slowly and without involving the people with the necessary research skills. If
the search had been done more quickly, the party might have been able to
clean house before the Sun chain published its damning story.

The other three episodes of bad publicity involved incompetence in handling the media. The first began on November 18, 1991, when Sheila Copps compared Manning to the American racist David Duke, who had just been defeated in the race for governor of Louisiana. "The policies of Preston Manning, which appeal to people's latent fears in a recessionary period," she said, "are the same kinds of policies that permit a David Duke to come forward in a state like Louisiana."[32] The obvious response to Copps's attack, as Rick Anderson correctly pointed out at the time, would have been to refer the media to Reformers who belong to racial minorities. While most Reformers are white, there are non-white activists in the party. Manning's own brother-in-law, an active Reformer later elected to executive council, is a Métis. The husband of another member of executive council is from Nigeria. The numbers may not be large, but probably every major ethnic and racial group is represented somewhere in the party. In fact, after a couple of weeks, journalists started finding a few of these people and writing about them,[33] but they did not get much help from the national office or the leader. Manning could not be reached when the story broke and never did reply except to deny that he was a racist, which was not very imaginative or effective.

The party did not directly lose support as a result of Copps's attack; she is not a major cue-giver for those drawn to the Reform Party, and her statements were generally criticized by media commentators and even politicians from other parties as outrageously unfair. Ironically, political opponents came to the defence of the Reform Party even as the leader remained silent. The NDP's Howard McCurdy, the only black MP in the House of Commons, called Copps's remarks "gross" and said she needed a lesson in American history.[34] Even the prime minister intervened: "David Duke is a racist and a member of the Ku Klux Klan and an anti-semite, and she said that Preston Manning was David Duke, the equivalent of David Duke. He is no such thing! He is just a political opponent."[35] But that does not mean her manoeuvre backfired. It sent a strong negative signal to Liberal supporters who might otherwise have taken a closer look at Reform, and it thus helped erect barriers to expansion, particularly in Ontario. At the very least, by not responding quickly and vigorously, Manning missed an opportunity to display the party's multiculturalism policy in an attractive light.

A second problem arose from my attempts to implement a TEAC decision to create a program of opposition research, that is, the systematic tracking of other parties' policies, activities, and candidates. From the standpoint of pluralistic politics this seems like common sense: know what your competitors are up to. But it clashes with the mythology of populism, which depicts Reform as a regenerative movement building the New Canada. Manning had been present when opposition research was discussed and approved it at least tacitly, but subsequent events showed he was not committed to it.

In December I sent a memo to all constituency associations outlining a suggested program of research to be undertaken at the local level in preparation for the next election. It included a suggestion to maintain clipping files on the other parties and their candidates at the local level. Unfortunately, I stupidly included the following sentence: "Search to see if they [opposition candidates] have violated legality, morality or propriety in their public lives." When I wrote it, I was thinking of the many seamy episodes of the Mulroney years — MPs and senators faced with criminal charges, conflict-of-interest scandals à la Sinclair Stevens, resignations from cabinet, the phenomenal growth of the lobbying industry. However, I failed to consider how the sentence would look if a reporter with a penchant for "gotcha" journalism pulled it out of context and turned it into a headline such as "Reform to Probe Morality of MPs."[36] The headlines started popping up around the country in January and continued into February. Even though I am a Canadian citizen and have lived in Canada for more than 25 years, the stories and editorials often brought in the fact that I grew up and was educated in the United States, thus making my error symbolize the alleged American character of the party.[37]

Caught in my first "gotcha" experience, I compounded the mischief by trying to explain the memo's context and intended meaning, which is worse than useless because it just generates more stories. I should have made a quick apology along these lines: "I made a mistake. There was no sinister intent, but it was a dumb sentence to write. I'm sorry for it, and I have sent out a revised memo to all constituencies. End of story." That might have worked, although in the leader-centred Reform Party it is often only Manning who can spike a bad story. But he seemed unconcerned about the whole thing and let the story rattle around the country for weeks. Then he finally sent his own memo to constituencies saying that we had no use for opposition research except to defend ourselves against opposition attacks, but he never did anything to kill the story in the media.

The final episode of bad publicity may have hurt the party the most, precisely because it was so ridiculous. The party's February sustainer letter contained an insert describing a gift to the Reform Party made by an Edmonton woman we will call Anne. With the help of Gordon Wusyk, an executive councillor who is in the financial services industry, Anne had purchased a life insurance policy and transferred it to the Reform Party. The party would

pay the premiums while she would make an annual donation in the same
amount, thus obtaining the standard income tax credit. It was similar to a
procedure that is widely used in philanthropy, except that the beneficiary of
the policy was a political party, not a registered charity. The purpose of
sending the notice along with the sustainer letter was simply to make party
members aware of the option, not to encourage them to undertake a campaign of selling life insurance policies.

Unfortunately for the party, however, the matter got into the media
through expelled dissidents in British Columbia and Manitoba, who put a
bizarre interpretation on it. "What they're really saying is, 'When you die —
and we hope it's soon — we will get money.' What about the old boy whose
brain may be a little addled who has a small insurance policy to leave to his
wife?" said Roger Rocan to the Victoria *Times-Colonist*.[38] The article also
featured a photograph of NDP MP Dave Barret, who was quoted as asking,
"Are they going to bump off some of their members?" In Manitoba,
expelled Reformer Lloyd Kirkham told the *Winnipeg Free Press*, "In many
cases, older people are being asked to sign over their life insurance to the
party, without any considerations as to what their family circumstances
are."[39] Highly misleading and damaging headlines ricocheted around the
country, such as "Reform's Life Insurance Scheme to Raise Money Shocks
Party Renegade," and "Reform Seeks Loyalty from Beyond the Grave." The
CBC comedy show "Double Exposure" included a skit about Preston visiting a nursing home and standing on the oxygen tube after selling an insurance policy to a senior citizen.

This theatre of the absurd continued as minister of Revenue Otto Jelinek
and his junior minister John McDermid denounced the plan as "totally illegal within the tax system" and "highly unethical." Sheila Copps, ever ready
for a smear, said, "This scheme smells like what we have is a Preston
Swaggart." Rod Murphy of the NDP blustered that it was a "slick, sophisticated, sleazy, step-by-step guide on how to abuse the tax system." Only a
careful reader would have noted that these denunciations were just personal
opinions and that Revenue Canada had not yet begun its consideration of
the plan's legality.[40] In fact, the plan was perfectly legal, as an embarrassed
Jelinek had to admit two weeks later.[41]

Once again, Reform was confronted with a problem of damage control. As
usual, the choice came down to either apologizing for having made a mistake
or defending what had been done. The second option might have worked in
this case because the party had done nothing illegal or immoral and was
being victimized by unscrupulous attacks and slipshod reporting. But
Manning did not really want to defend the idea. He had not participated in

developing it, had not been consulted about sending it out with the sustainer letter, and actually seemed to agree with the spirit, if not the letter, of the criticisms. He did at one point authorize a combative press release in the name of Deborah Grey,[42] but it had no effect because he would not defend the plan personally. Given his unwillingness to stand and fight on the issue, it would have been better to have repudiated the insurance-giving plan as soon as possible and put a stop to the headlines that were making the party look ridiculous. But he did not do that, either, and the party ended up in the worst possible position, like a prizefighter out on his feet and trapped in the corner, taking blow after blow without defending himself.

These three episodes all highlight certain problems of the Reform Party in dealing with the media that persist to the present day. Manning was functioning, in effect, as his own director of communications; no one else had the authority to state positions or issue news releases. But he did not stay in close contact with staff. He would be gone for days at a time on speaking tours without using the telephone to keep in touch. Ron Wood, his press secretary, eventually purchased a cellular phone, but Manning seldom used it. Even when Manning was in Calgary, he would usually be unavailable to staff. Thus, because of his tendency to ignore criticism unless personally directed at him, damaging situations were allowed to develop and drift for days and even weeks.

But more was involved than the technical problem of getting the right people in place and letting them do their jobs. In Manning's conception of the populist party, the leader's direct relationship with members and public audiences is crucial. Although he is an introverted person, he is a master rhetorician who thrives on the performance aspect of speaking. He navigates his course through the waters of policy largely on the basis of what he hears from his audiences. His standard response to the worries of staff members that we were being savaged in the media was always to say in effect, "Don't take the media so seriously. People weren't talking about that last week when I was in Peace River [or Swan River, Battle River, Grand River]."

Manning's problems with damage control relate to some other technical difficulties he has with the media. At various times, he has been reluctant to give reporters the "Gainesburger a day" they need to file their stories, to stick with the concise press releases they require, or to throw out the pithy one-liners that would enliven their reports. All these difficulties stem from the same root cause: Manning visualizes the rhetorical situation as speaking to the audience in the room, not to the much larger audience one reaches through the media.

None of this is to say that Manning is not skilled at using the media; of course he is. Yet all political leaders experience media problems, and

Manning's problems are of a specific kind, deriving both from his personality and his populist brand of politics. But modern politics is media politics. A populist party that cannot obtain technical mastery of the media will have grave difficulty in achieving its political objectives.

6

The Referendum Campaign

The referendum held on October 26, 1992, to determine the fate of the Charlottetown Accord was a double triumph for the Reform Party. Not only did the referendum result block the adoption of a constitutional package that most of the party's membership intensely disliked, but also the very fact that the referendum was held established an important precedent for

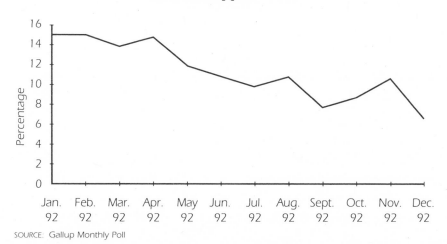

Figure 6-1
Reform Support 1992

SOURCE: Gallup Monthly Poll

Figure 6-2
Preston Manning's Approval Rating July–November 1992

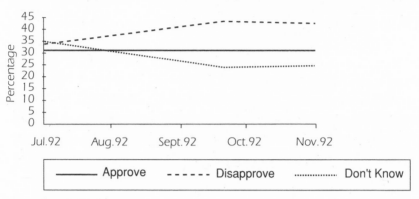

SOURCE: Angus Reid Poll

the future. Most observers of Canadian politics think it unlikely that major packages of constitutional amendments will ever again be adopted without referendum approval, which in itself was a Reform demand. Yet the conduct of the party's referendum campaign revealed certain strategic, organizational, and financial weaknesses, which contributed to the party's continued slide in the polls in the second half of 1992. Figure 6-1 shows the Reform Party's share of committed voters in the Gallup Poll throughout 1992. The erosion that was already under way was temporarily reversed as the party went back up to 11% in November in the immediate aftermath of the referendum campaign. The effect, however, was short lived; the party went down to 7% in December, the lowest it had been since March 1991.

Alarmingly, the drop was most severe in Alberta and British Columbia, precisely the provinces where Reform had the deepest roots and the most exposure during the referendum campaign.

Paralleling the party's slide was the continuing decline in Preston Manning's net popular approval rating (see Figure 6-2).

As in the previous 12 months, the percentage of people who approved of Manning remained unchanged, while the number of people who disapproved of him continued to grow. By a curious coincidence, exactly 31% of respondents said they "generally approved" of Manning's performance in the July, October, and November Angus Reid surveys. But the percentage of those who "generally disapproved" jumped sharply from 34% in July to 44% in the October peak of the referendum campaign and remained at 43% in November. The November balance was negative for Manning (43% "approve" vs. 45% "disapprove") even in the Reform stronghold of Alberta.

How could it happen that, even while the Reform Party was playing a crucial role on the winning side, its political standing and that of its leader actually declined? To answer this riddle requires a close look at the referendum campaign.

It was announced on Saturday, August 22, 1992, that the first ministers and native leaders had agreed in principle on what would become known as the Charlottetown Accord. Preston Manning convened a meeting of national-office political staff — Stephen Harper, Ron Wood, Laurie Watson, George Koch, and me — for Monday morning to consider the party's response. Although we had only newspaper accounts to go on, we had to meet immediately because Manning was leaving that day for a week's vacation with his family.

Manning opened the meeting by saying, "At times like this, we have to remember why we're in politics." No one asked what this meant. Did it mean that we should not oppose the accord because it was good for the country? Or that opposing the accord, which seemed popular at the moment, might jeopardize Reform's long-term chances of winning an election and coming to power? Manning then made it obvious that he had little inclination to lead a fight on the No side against the newly announced agreement. Two considerations seemed uppermost in his mind: a feeling that some parts of the agreement were not all that bad, and a perception that the accord would pass easily because of widespread constitutional fatigue among the general public. He spoke at some length about how Reform could use the restructured Senate to its advantage. Having campaigned so long for Senate reform, he said, the party should be able to elect large numbers of senators and then show the public how an elected Senate could represent the interests of Canada's outlying regions.

What happened that morning capped a trend in Manning's thinking on the Constitution that had been growing for almost a year. He had said surprisingly little in public about the Constitution during 1992. At least since April of that year, Rick Anderson had been advising him not to fight a constitutional agreement but rather "to move the agenda along quickly to the rest of the 'New Canada' agenda of parliamentary, fiscal and economic reform."[1] Manning had made economic issues the theme of most of his speeches during his extensive public tours in May and June. At this time he also introduced the subject of criminal justice reforms, including amendments to the Young Offenders Act, a referendum on capital punishment, and deportation of non-citizens convicted of serious offences. In early June he told a reporter that he was going to use his Ontario tour to introduce positions on social policy and criminal justice to fill the vacuum that would be left by a constitutional settlement.[2]

By the end of the month, Manning was proposing a moratorium on constitutional talks until after federal and Quebec elections could be held.[3] "Most Canadians," he said, "want their politicians to tackle Canada's pressing economic and social problems instead of fixating on ramming through an unworkable constitutional deal which the public does not accept."[4] As usual, he justified his position by referring to the mood of the people who attended his speeches, claiming that they were asking questions about economic competitiveness, violent crime, and the accountability of politicians, not about the Constitution.[5] In one sense, Manning's new stance was consistent with Reform's constitutional position; the party had always denounced constitutional revision through executive federalism and had called for a constituent assembly. But in another sense, Manning's statements marked a major change because he was now suggesting that the public did not really care much about constitutional reform. This represented a potentially momentous departure from his previous position that constitutional change was essential to the New Canada.

Reform's constitutional position became even more contorted after Joe Clark and the premiers of all provinces other than Quebec reached the so-called Pearson Accord (named after the building in Ottawa in which it was negotiated) on July 7. As was often the case that summer, Manning was away from Calgary and unavailable to the media; so, after consulting with Rick Anderson, Stephen Harper issued a statement partially endorsing the agreement: "Although there is not quite a Triple-E Senate — elected, effective, and equal — the premiers have gone much of the distance towards such an institution." However, Harper expressed reservations about other aspects of the package and called upon the prime minister to submit any deal to a binding national referendum.[6] Manning subsequently refined this position into something like a personal campaign against the prime minister. Without actually endorsing the agreement as such, he called upon Mulroney to hold a first ministers' conference to try to get Quebec's support for the Pearson Accord. "As imperfect as this agreement is, it offers a chance for constitutional peace which should be pursued."[7] As the days went by, he became a virtual defender of the Pearson Accord, accusing Mulroney of wanting "to have this latest constitutional round fail so he can run on a new package."[8] When he was in Ottawa in mid-August, he told a columnist: "If there ever was an elected Senate, we would have a very good chance of ending up with a majority of seats in it. If we ever got a foothold like that, then we could do something to demonstrate what we're talking about — a new style of representation, a new attention to regional fairness."[9]

Manning was playing a double game in this period: on the one hand trying to blame any final constitutional breakdown on Mulroney, on the other preparing himself and the Reform Party to live with a new Constitution should it be passed. This may have made short-term tactical sense, but it was far removed from a forthright defence of the Triple-E Senate and opposition to special status for Quebec. Thus the stage was set for a collision between Manning and the party.

The press later reported that Manning really wanted to be on the Yes side in the referendum debate,[10] but that was not the impression he gave at the August 24 meeting. He did not actually favour the Charlottetown Accord, but neither was he interested in leading a struggle against it. At that stage, he wanted the party to remain neutral, to run an information campaign and comment critically on some features of the deal, but not to oppose it as such. A telltale sign in this direction was the way he phrased the alternatives in the September membership mailout questionnaire:

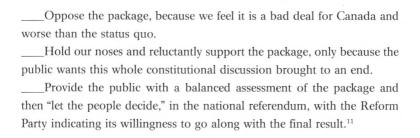

_____Oppose the package, because we feel it is a bad deal for Canada and worse than the status quo.

_____Hold our noses and reluctantly support the package, only because the public wants this whole constitutional discussion brought to an end.

_____Provide the public with a balanced assessment of the package and then "let the people decide," in the national referendum, with the Reform Party indicating its willingness to go along with the final result.[11]

As anyone who has ever worked with him knows, it is Manning's practice to formulate his preferred course of action as a moderate compromise between two extremes. The third alternative in the list was clearly the one he personally preferred.

Three reasons may help explain the position he took that day. One is the fact that in the preceding months he had been drawing closer to Rick Anderson, who did end up on the Yes side. Another is his general dislike of conflict. Third is his populist tendency to interpret public opinion directly without analyzing it through an objective process. However, the fact that his own experience would lead him so far away from the real feelings of the party, and of Canadian voters, shows the unreliability of this version of populism.

Manning's unexpected proposal produced obvious tension in the meeting. Not fully understanding what was going on, I was taken with the effrontery of doing the unexpected and started to play out loud with the idea. Watson and Koch were visibly upset at what they saw as a betrayal of Reform. Harper was calmer but equally opposed, and made it clear that he would oppose the accord no matter what happened. In the end, Manning agreed that we would take steps to consult members of the Reform Party and postpone any decision until he returned from holidays.

After the meeting broke up, I spoke with the other participants individually and quickly became convinced that being on the No side was the only realistic course of action for us to take. There might be legitimate debate about the adequacy of the new Senate, but in other crucial respects the agreement was opposed to what the Reform Party stood for. Specifically, we objected to the murky wording of the so-called social charter, the fact that 25% of House of Commons seats were forever guaranteed to Quebec, and the sweeping and open-ended provisions for aboriginal self-government. Even if the fight was hopeless (which was the prevailing view at that time), we had to oppose the accord. If we did not, it would be the end of Reform as a party with a distinctive agenda, and maybe the end of the party altogether.

While Manning went on holiday, we worked to prepare the way for an entry on the No side. Watson set up a telephone hotline that produced an avalanche of calls advising us to go No (93% of 1,300 calls in the first 10 days).[12] She and I also rewrote the September membership fundraising mailout, which had been almost ready to go to the printer, so that it dealt with the constitutional agreement and the expected referendum; if we had not done this, there might have been little money to fight the referendum. Koch undertook a media survey to look for signs of opposition to the accord and also analyzed the dozens of letters received from our candidates and constituency organizations (only one among the first 70 to reply recommended support for the accord).[13] In Manning's absence, Harper took over the main responsibility of dealing with the media. Although he did not stray from the official position that we were in the process of consulting our members, he took pains to describe the defects of the agreement.[14] I drafted a memo on the reasons for going No and included some ideas for getting the campaign started. I stressed that, even though public opinion seemed to be on the Yes side at this stage, the government had set itself the difficult task of winning a referendum in every province. The Yes side had to win 10 times, while we only had to win once in order to block or at least seriously impede the deal. Thus the fight was not as hopeless as it seemed.[15]

After Manning's return to Calgary a week later, talk of adopting a neutral position ceased; the momentum towards No had become unstoppable. The overwhelming majority of the party wanted to fight the agreement; 69% of respondents to the September mailout supported No,

while only 2% supported Yes and 29% favoured Manning's original preference of a "balanced assessment," even though the questions had been
set up to encourage the neutrality option.[16] The next step, therefore, was
to develop a strategy — that is, to articulate our reasons for opposing the
accord and to decide how we would communicate them. Stephen Harper
and I reviewed the text independently over the Labour Day weekend, and
we worked out the party's detailed position on September 8 at a meeting
with Manning.

Manning, Harper, and I all agreed in a broad way about what was wrong
with the accord from a Reform point of view; the problem lay in settling
upon an emphasis and arrangement that would be most likely to influence
undecided voters. Manning contributed one firm position based on his perception of constitutional fatigue: there had to be a five-year moratorium on
future constitutional talks. It was clear that this was settled in his mind.
Even while we met, he experimented with campaign slogans, trying to link
up "No more," "Know more," and "moratorium." This led to what one
reporter aptly called Manning's campaign "mantra," "No Means No More."[17]
Beyond the call for a moratorium, we decided to put our critique of the
accord in the following order:

1. The accord was "not a true agreement but only a framework for future
negotiations." Adopting it would bring "more years of negotiations." We
headlined this as the accord's greatest flaw in the party's major campaign
publication.[18]

2. It was fiscally irresponsible. It did little to reduce interprovincial trade
barriers and nothing to reduce the deficit, while the social charter and the
provisions for opting out and aboriginal self-government might mean
increasing demands on the federal treasury.

3. The Senate was "less than 2-E" and hence too weak to protect the interests of Canada's outlying regions.

4. The extension of the unanimity amending formula, plus the double-
majority rule in the Senate and various guarantees for aboriginals, would
produce an inflexible constitution.

5. Because the deal did not provide the control over language legislation
within Quebec that had always been the key demand for that province, it
could not possibly bring constitutional peace.

6. Underlying the accord was an unacceptable collectivist vision of ethnicity that gave special status to francophones and aboriginals.[19]

We deliberately constructed this list in almost the opposite order of priority that one might have predicted, assuming that this strategy would influence larger numbers of Canadians than a purely Reform-oriented critique would. Voters who did not share Reform's views on the Senate or on the "distinct society" might well be open to the argument that the accord was a phantom deal that did not really settle anything. Also, at this stage we were still concerned about being painted as the "enemies of Canada," as the prime minister had put it.[20] Giving low priority to issues of language and ethnicity seemed like the way to avoid such attacks. Thus we agreed that in the early weeks of the campaign when Manning was to entrench our critique in the public mind he would emphasize the accord's incompleteness above all other considerations.

In some ways, this strategy worked very well during the campaign. Although the party never made much yardage with predictions of fiscal irresponsibility, the charge that the accord was just an agenda for future negotiations became a common criticism among all the No forces by the end of the campaign. It certainly contributed to the widespread view that voting Yes was risky and uncertain compared to the status quo.

Initially, we were quite pessimistic about our chances of winning; we would have been glad to defeat the accord in one or two western provinces. At the meeting of September 8, I speculated that support for the Yes side might cascade away as voters realized that few people actually liked the contents of the accord. Because most of those who favoured it did so only because they thought it was widely acceptable and would put an end to the interminable wrangling over the Constitution, a trickle of defections could easily turn into a torrent. But this was just a hope, not a prediction. I was not aware at the time that research on Californian referendums had shown that ballot propositions that were both complex and controversial — two characteristics that certainly applied to the Charlottetown Accord — typically begin with high but superficial support and then lose it during the campaign. For the No side in such situations, "the initial strategy is to raise doubts about the need, implementation, or impact of the measure. This may result in persons shifting from 'yes' to 'no,' or it may mean that voters shift from support to indecision and then later respond to the appeal — 'When in doubt VOTE NO.'"[21] The logic of the situation led Reform to rediscover a No strategy that had often proven successful elsewhere.

However, there was another side to the strategy that created difficulties. In postponing the obvious and expected Reform critique of the accord, Manning became an easy target for a damaging type of criticism. Editorialists and columnists agreed that it was legitimate to be on the No side, but they accused Manning of insincerity. One columnist wrote: "Preston Manning showed more nerve than I'd expected. He also showed the cuteness and oblique tactics which have made him the number one sly-boots in Canadian politics. . . . Preston Manning is, after all, if you didn't already believe it, just another politician."[22] "Reform takes a stand on both sides of the fence," brayed the editorialists of the *Calgary Herald*, always ready to condemn Manning no matter what he did.[23] The *Globe and Mail*'s Hugh Winsor made the most perceptive criticisms:

> But in playing to the fatigue, and calling for a moratorium on future nego-tiations for at least five years, he [Manning] is turning his back on one of the major themes he has been talking about since his party was formed — the need for constitutional reform and the need for an elected Senate to ride herd on the government in the Commons. . . .
>
> By trying to be on all sides of the issue, while skating over the senti-ments of many of his members and still claiming to be a populist, Mr. Manning risks losing his principal asset — the perception that he is a straight shooter and not just a politician like the rest of them.[24]

In fact, as part of his ever-fluid populism, Manning was ready to back away from the Reform Party's constitutional agenda and move on to other issues. He would have preferred not to be in the referendum fight at all but found himself constrained by the desires of the party he led. Harper and I helped articulate an intellectual rationale he could use to oppose the accord, which he then used to jettison the party's constitutional agenda. He never moved to the second stage of dealing seriously with the substance of the accord. Instead, he politicized the referendum by raising partisan ques-tions about political leadership, which made him look like an opportunist and thus contributed to the party's decline.

Manning made several remarks that left him open to charges of oppor-tunism. For example, he told an Ontario audience that they should delay deciding how to vote until they saw how opinion was heading in other provinces. If they could see a negative trend in provinces such as Quebec and British Columbia, they should then vote No for the sake of national unity.[25] But what happens to concern for principle in this scenario? This incident caused a minor buzz in southern Ontario for several days and must have boosted the perception that Manning was becoming a politician like any other. Then, after the referendum was over, he made a major effort to demand that the government of Alberta hold an advisory Senate election on the Stan Waters model to fill a vacancy.[26] Although this did not technically conflict with his call for a five-year moratorium on constitutional discussions, since the election would be advisory only, ordinary viewers of the news might well have missed the nuance and assumed that he was trying to reopen the constitutional file, an accusation levelled of course by the prime minister.[27]

But most damaging of all were the two articles run by the *Globe and Mail* which revealed that Manning had not initially wanted to be on the No side. Unfortunately, this story broke during the Winnipeg Assembly, just before the referendum vote.[28] This revelation gave the prime minister another excuse to excoriate Manning: "He's passing himself off as a politician different than all the rest of us grubby politicians. We're supposed to be in a lower league. He's supposed to be in a league of a higher calling. He changed his mind secretly on this deal on the advice of a pollster. This is a strange kind of principle."[29]

Although Mulroney would find it hard to believe, no polling had been involved in Manning's decision. Moreover, no one was predicting a No victory at the time the decision had been made; only with the benefit of hindsight did it look like a cunning move to be on the winning side. Nonetheless, the whole episode generated an unfavourable round of stories and commentary at the time when Manning should have been able to bask in the glow of the No side's anticipated victory. The impression created by the negative headlines must have contributed to Reform's inability to capitalize politically on the referendum outcome.

Prior to the referendum campaign, the main decision-making body had been the campaign management committee. In fact, it was more of a discussion group than a decision-making body; Cliff Fryers had announced at the first meeting of CMC that important decisions were to be reserved for Manning, Gordon Shaw, and himself, which in practice meant that Manning's personal judgment would prevail on political issues. However, at least CMC existed and held more or less regular meetings.

But now Manning decided that CMC was too large and cumbersome to run the referendum campaign. In the first week of September, he created a smaller steering committee, consisting of himself, Fryers as chairman, and Shaw, plus Virgil Anderson as campaign manager, Rick Anderson as strategic adviser, and the young Ian Todd as secretary to the committee. (Todd had recently been brought in from British Columbia.) This removed Laurie Watson and me; both of us had had numerous disagreements with Manning and Fryers.

Ostensibly Manning had created the steering committee for reasons of efficiency, but the real reason obviously had more to do with his perceptions of loyalty and political orientation. By excluding Watson and me and not inviting Stephen Harper to participate, Manning was marginalizing the people who had really wanted to fight the referendum campaign and had helped develop the strategy for doing so. Now, the only strategist on the committee was Rick Anderson, who was in fact a Yes supporter. This change reflected Manning's desire to move away from the party's constitutional agenda. It is also noteworthy that with the exception of Manning himself the committee did not contain anyone accustomed to fighting the party's political battles by speaking to the public, giving interviews to the media, drawing up statements and ads, and so forth.

Not surprisingly, problems arose almost immediately. Manning had the inspired idea of printing up the Charlottetown Accord with all the unclear passages marked with handwritten Xs and Os in bright green ink. The No side in Quebec later did something similar but even more sophisticated with great effect: they inserted handwritten comments in the margin of the accord's text. On a Thursday Manning told Laurie Watson to have the new pamphlet ready for him to take to Ontario the following Monday. She assembled some people who worked through the weekend to get the job done, but Manning then decided he would postpone distributing the pamphlets until after the official campaign launch on September 18. In the rush to meet Manning's initial deadline, no one was assigned to review the content of the pamphlet. Consequently, it was printed without an adequate explanation of what the Xs and Os meant. In the end Manning decided to pulp the first run of 50,000 and print an entire new run with a better explanation. Due to administrative errors, two weeks of valuable time were lost in distributing the pamphlet at the point in the campaign when it would have had the most effect because the Yes side had been so slow in getting out its own version of the accord.

Another blunder occurred when Cliff Fryers revealed to the press that the Reform Party had virtually no cash reserves to fight the referendum campaign. This generated a front-page story entitled "Money Running Low for Reform Party; Reform Party Faces Cash Crunch,"[30] which unfortunately ran the day the campaign was launched. There was no reason to reveal our financial problems to the press, but Fryers had not consulted anyone before doing the interview.

At first I did not protest being left out of the steering committee because I had been assured that I would still be consulted. But when it became obvious that I was excluded not just from the committee but from any significant role in the campaign, I gave Manning a written ultimatum: put me on the steering committee or I would quit my job as director of research. For the sake of appearances, Manning then included me and I participated in committee meetings from late September until the end of the campaign. But I soon learned what I should have known in advance: the steering committee was no more a decision-making body than CMC had been. Manning hardly ever attended sessions of the steering committee because he was on tour. He would discuss matters privately with Anderson, Fryers, or Shaw and then make a decision.

For all practical purposes, Manning became the referendum campaign. After using Stephen Harper to draft the positioning speech of September 10 and George Koch to write the launching speech of September 18, he became his own speechwriter. He also wrote pamphlets, advertising copy, even some press releases. And, with Rick Anderson's assistance, he served as his own strategist. (Frank Luntz was preoccupied with American politics, Stephen Harper was infrequently consulted, and my interventions in the steering committee were generally ignored.) And of course he did all these things at odd hours in hotel rooms because he was on tour throughout the campaign, and had to give several speeches and interviews every day, as well as appearing on talk shows. With so much riding on one man, it is remarkable, and a tribute to Manning's attention to detail, that things went as well as they did. Nonetheless, his insistence on doing everything himself was the Achilles heel of the Reform Party's campaign.

The worst fiasco connected with the steering committee was the Rick Anderson affair. Manning had come to rely on Anderson's advice more and more throughout 1992, and Anderson's appointment as sole strategist on the steering committee confirmed his ascendancy. In fact, Manning and Fryers hoped to entice him to fill the chief-of-staff role that no one had been able to fill before. However, one major stumbling block existed: Anderson didn't want to be on the No side in the referendum. No later than September 8, he had told Manning that he intended to vote Yes.[31] Nevertheless, Manning put him on the steering committee as strategic adviser.[32] He wanted to keep Anderson in the loop because of his desire to make him his chief aide if the money could be found. Also, and perhaps even more importantly, keeping Anderson involved sent a signal to the political class in Ottawa that Reform was not totally opposed to their values, that in spite of opposing the Charlottetown Accord a rapprochement might be possible at some future time.

Anderson's understanding is that he never sat on the steering committee but continued to volunteer his time for the party in other respects, particularly in candidate training. In that capacity, he attended Manning's meeting with candidates on September 10, at which it was conclusively decided to take the No position; and he came to Calgary later in September for a candidate-training session, at which he was asked for advice about referendum matters, specifically the "Mulroney deal" ads. He did give advice on some matters, but felt uncomfortable about doing so and in general tried to stay out of the referendum.[33] But regardless of how Anderson viewed the arrangement, Manning and Fryers saw him as a committee member. A memo dated September 15 and sent to all candidates and constituencies identified Anderson as such.[34] Cliff Fryers stated the same fact to the party's executive council when it met on September 18, adding that Anderson was responsible for gathering strategic advice from people such as Frank Luntz, Stephen Harper, and me and conveying it to the steering committee.

On October 1, Anderson flew to Calgary via Edmonton for a confidential dinner meeting with about a dozen businessmen who supported the Reform Party. The purpose was to introduce them to Anderson as a possible chief of staff for Manning in the hope of securing extra contributions to pay his salary. They were not told that Anderson was a Yes supporter; there would have been no dinner if they had known. Afterwards, Anderson went for a drink with the *Globe and Mail*'s Alberta reporter, Miro Cernetig, whom Anderson had bumped into on the way down to Calgary. In the course of the evening, he told Cernetig that he planned to vote Yes, but Cernetig decided not to do a story about it.[35] On October 7, a CBC reporter from Calgary called Anderson in Ottawa to ask about his position on the referendum. Anderson confirmed that he was on the Yes side but declined to be filmed. The result was a story that evening on CBC television news that used file footage of Anderson and announced his position.[36]

Why did Anderson decide to let the news out after keeping quiet for so long? The answer may lie in the fact that the October 1992 edition of the *Financial Post Magazine* identified him as a major player on the No side. He was quoted as saying, "The referendum is only a way station until the next general election." The story concluded: "The fledgling Western party is a babe in the political woods when it comes to strategy and communications. Anderson, meanwhile, has Hill & Knowlton's polling expertise — they own Decima Research — at his fingertips. Watch for Anderson to be making a few more trips to Calgary before October 26."[37] Anderson could hardly let this stand uncorrected; the implication that he was using Decima polling results to help the Reform Party would have damaged Hill and Knowlton's reputation among clients.

The news hit the Reform Party's staff and activists like a mortar round, for all of us thought that Anderson was on our side as an active member of the steering committee (although some staff members had previously heard rumours from journalists that Anderson really supported the Yes side).

Tempers flared as Manning, Fryers, and Shaw clung to Anderson. The few who knew the truth about Manning's early wavering on the referendum saw the Anderson affair as further evidence that Manning's populism combined with Anderson's advice was leading him to depart from the Reform agenda. This was the last straw for Stephen Harper. Although he decided to continue with his candidacy in Calgary West and not to raise a public challenge against Manning, he withdrew from national office activities. The whole affair, combined with the other events of the campaign, had a similar effect upon me. On October 14, I asked my department head at the university to arrange a return to full-time teaching effective January 1993.

As a result the party's roster of strategic advisers was temporarily wiped out. Alan Wiggan was long gone, Frank Luntz was marginalized, Rick Anderson had rendered himself suspect in the eyes of party members, Stephen Harper didn't want to be involved, and I was returning to the university. Important operational staff became casualties, too, as communications manager Laurie Watson and speechwriter George Koch were fired the day after the referendum.

This departure of personnel from the national office was a costly loss for the party. Harper, Watson, Koch, and I, together with junior staff, had done much of the work of communicating with the public; we had prepared position papers and media releases, written speeches and correspondence, set up the leader's press conferences and given background interviews to reporters. Our sudden departure certainly contributed to the party's difficulty in getting media coverage in the post-referendum period.

At the official launch of the Reform Party's referendum campaign on September 18, Manning challenged the prime minister as well as the leaders of the Liberals and the NDP to a televised public debate.[38] Although Mulroney and Chrétien did not reply, Audrey McLaughlin accepted the challenge almost immediately. This took courage on her part, for most observers predicted that she would not do well in an abstract argument about the Constitution. But she was obviously eager to heighten her role in the campaign, since official plans left her overshadowed by the leaders of the larger parties as well as by the non-political citizens' committees.

Her eagerness to debate was reflected by the fact that her staff set no conditions when they accepted Manning's challenge. Stephen Harper and I wanted to propose conditions that we thought would help Manning's performance: an Alberta or British Columbia venue, a relatively long time for answering questions from the floor as opposed to reading prepared speeches, and questions from journalists or constitutional experts rather than just the audience. However, we were not in the decision making at this stage; when I tried to offer our advice, I was told that Rick Anderson had the arrangements well in hand. Harper and I were brought in for consultation at a later point; but by this time the big decisions had already been taken and it was too late to make any but minor adjustments.

In the end, the arrangements were more or less neutral for Reform. The debate was in Ontario rather than the West; but at least it was at Guelph, in rural Ontario, rather than in a hostile inner-city setting. Although the university venue favoured the NDP somewhat, the ticket arrangements allowed a fair number of Reform supporters to get into the hall. Questions would come from the floor rather than from journalists or academic experts, but the fact that the questions would be addressed alternately to one party then the other minimized the risk that seasoned NDP activists would seize control of the floor. French questions were to be translated to avoid highlighting Manning's inability to speak French. Overall, the arrangements worked out, but the steering committee was unable to approach the debate strategically. There was little attempt to identify strategic goals for the debate and work towards them systematically.

This absence of a strategy manifested itself most strikingly in Manning's inadequate preparation for the October 5 debate. He squeezed the engagement into his already crowded schedule without setting aside time for rehearsal, briefing, and consultation with advisers. His preparation for the event consisted in spending a few hours alone in his hotel room the afternoon of the debate and calling Stephen Harper to read him his prepared closing statement. Afterwards, there was no review of his performance, either.

Manning's performance during the debate reflected the general difficulty he has had in adapting his style to the demands of national prominence. For the most part, he spoke effectively to the audience in the room but not very calculatingly to the television cameras. An exception came at the closing, when he left the national audience with the powerful message, "If you vote Yes you are following the politicians, if you vote No you are leading them."[39] This was the best line of the night, perhaps the best line of the entire referendum campaign. Observers present at the debate in Guelph tended to think that both McLaughlin and Manning had done well but that the latter had won "on points."[40] But those analyzing the televised presentation tended to be more impressed with McLaughlin. According to William Gold she was, "forceful, articulate, passionate, focussed, crystal clear and unintimidated." Manning, in contrast, "demonstrated that his formidable intellectual and communications skills are better suited to his own style of one-man, one-audience dominance. He doesn't shine in cut and thrust." Gold concluded that "someone reading a transcript might award the evening to Manning on points," but in the all-important context of television, "McLaughlin clearly won, and not just on points."[41]

Rick Salutin came to a similar conclusion, though with a different evaluation:

> On news reports that night, McLaughlin won because she clearly gave better clip: short bursts of emotion-charged rhetoric. But for those in the hall or watching live on TV, including some NDP supporters, Manning often seemed more impressive: low-key and self-effacing, really listening to questions and apparently trying to answer them, providing helpful details from comparable places like Australia. He lost the last news because it's hard to highlight that kind of discourse. It was odd. There was the iconoclastic left-wing woman from the North more or less personifying conventional politics. And the right-wing Manning, looking like Central Casting's idea of an undertaker, as he had on his referendum ads, yet coming across as essence of the new desire for democracy. It was an interesting night on Newsworld.[42]

There is no simple answer to the question of what Manning should do differently to improve his image on television. He certainly should not abandon his low-key, laconic style in pursuit of bombastic "good clip"; but anyone who leads a national party must think strategically about reaching, not just the people in the room, but the larger audience that will view the debate live on television, and the much larger audience that will learn about it through news reports. This issue should have been raised and thoroughly discussed before the debate, and a strategy should have been adopted and later analyzed for effectiveness.

Although other parties did not know about the failure of Reform's internal decision-making process, they could see the weakness of Manning's performance in the debate. Not surprisingly, several politicians and other public figures challenged Manning to a debate during the final weeks of the campaign. There were offers from Tom D'Aquino, president of the Business Council on National Issues; Kim Campbell, the minister of Justice; and, at the last minute, Joe Clark himself. However, Manning turned them all down, sticking to his established policy that he would only debate other party leaders (although he did debate Conservative MP Bobbie Sparrow in his own riding of Calgary Southwest). It was the right decision. The No side was doing well and had nothing to gain by exposing Manning to another debate.

Manning's performance in the debate did not harm the referendum campaign, but as a missed opportunity it contributed to the relatively low standing with which he and the Reform Party emerged from the campaign. In subsequent months, NDP workers even managed to get the press to repeat the false assertion that McLaughlin had "wiped the floor" with Manning.[43] It is an unfair but inescapable fact of political life that if you lose momentum during a campaign you will be hurt by negative comments that could easily be brushed aside under other circumstances.

Towards the end of the Reform Party's referendum campaign, nothing generated more controversy than Manning's repeated use of the slogans "Mulroney's deal" and "the Mulroney deal." The way in which these phrases emerged illustrates a good deal about Reform's management process at the time.

In early September, Laurie Watson, the party's communications manager, was asked by the steering committee to develop some print advertisements. Although the national party had almost no money to spend on advertising, some constituency associations could afford to run ads in local newspapers. These ads would also serve as a basis for designing the radio and television ads for which the party would be guaranteed free time under the terms of the Referendum Act.

Watson brought in some mock-ups produced by a small Calgary communications company, but Manning did not like them and countered by faxing in prototypes that he designed himself while on a speaking tour. The steering committee, in consultation with Rick Anderson and Frank Luntz, who both came to Calgary in late September for a candidate-training seminar, then wrestled with various concepts until a consensus was reached. It is not clear who first thought of the phrase the "Mulroney deal," but in the end it was supported by everyone in that circle: Manning, the steering committee, and the consultants. It seemed rather ironic that Anderson supported it, for he had written to Manning on April 8 that a constitutional agreement "will not be seen as Mulroney's deal."[44] Stephen Harper, Laurie Watson, and I were opposed to the concept, but we had no part in the decision-making process.

Those who favoured the concept did so for straightforward and self-evident political reasons: Brian Mulroney was extremely unpopular, so tying the Charlottetown Accord to him personally seeming like a winning tactic. They were probably right, at least from a short-term perspective. An Angus Reid poll taken on October 15, 1992, showed that Mulroney was unique among national leaders in that his influence on voters in the referendum was perverse, that is, they chose to do the reverse of what he recommended (B.C. Premier Mike Harcourt had a similar effect in his own province). Thirty-four percent of respondents said that Mulroney's performance in the campaign made them want to vote No, whereas only 16% said it made them want to vote Yes.[45] The Reform Party did not have the money to measure the effect of its ads, but it seems plausible that the impact, if any, was in the intended direction.

Opponents of the phrase "Mulroney's deal" acknowledged that it might well be effective but were worried about long-term implications. First of all, referring to the Charlottetown Accord in this way misrepresented the process that produced it. To be sure, Mulroney came up with the strategy of attracting support from Quebec nationalists by promising to change the Constitution; but he had remained aloof from the negotiating process until the very end. The accord was ultimately a collective production, which indeed accounted for many of its peculiarities. Attributing it exclusively to Mulroney was certain to involve a debate about the fairness of the charge.

The situation differed fundamentally from the 1988 general election, in which both the Liberals and the NDP spoke of the Free Trade Agreement as the "Mulroney deal." An NDP strategist wrote at the time: "First, the less we use the words free trade the better. We should instead focus our attack on the Mulroney deal or on the Mulroney/Reagan deal."[46] Now, whether one supported or opposed the FTA, it had clearly resulted from federal government policy, and hence it did not seem unreasonable to name it after the prime minister responsible for the policy. But because the provinces and aboriginal organizations were involved in negotiating the Charlottetown Accord, it represented a collective effort and could not be named after one individual. (Incidentally, it is curious that observers of the referendum campaign never mentioned that the phrase had also been used in 1988. But Manning has carefully read Graham Fraser's book *Playing for Keeps*, which describes the use of the phrase the "Mulroney deal" in 1988; he often refers to the book in public, and indeed at one point wanted to purchase a copy of it for every member of the Reform Party's executive council and senior staff.)

A second problem with associating the accord with Mulroney only stemmed from Manning's promise that his campaign would operate at the level of issues, not personalities. In announcing his position on September 10, he said: "We will campaign on principle and specifics, and avoid the simple bashing of opponents and the manipulation of symbols."[47] And again on September 18 at the campaign launch: "I also want to emphasize that we in the Reform Party are not interested in personal attacks on individuals or in bashing any group or region in Canada. Our campaign is firmly based on principles, substantive disagreement with specific elements of the deal."[48] To start talking about the "Mulroney deal" so soon after making these statements was hypocritical and invited trouble.

It would have been better to have called the accord the "politicians' deal" and not have targeted Mulroney specifically. The phrase, like all campaign slogans, would have been debatable, but it would not have been unfair. (Who had negotiated the accord if not Canada's politicians?) It would have fit the direct-democracy philosophy of the Reform Party, and it would have captured the dissatisfaction with politicians that prevailed at the time.

As soon as it had been approved by his advisers, Manning tried out the new slogan in a speech in Vancouver on September 21: "It may be Mulroney's deal, but it's your choice."[49] The slogan created a headline but drew no particular response from the other side. On October 2, ad mats for seven newspaper advertisements went out to the constituencies. Each bore the heading "Mulroney's deal is no deal at all," or something similar.[50] For mass distribution, there was also a pamphlet that amalgamated the text of the various newspaper ads; it used the phrases "Mulroney deal" and "Mulroney's deal" 14 times.[51] Finally, in Reform's TV ads Manning uttered the same lines in front of the camera. He was nothing if not consistent!

The TV ads were unveiled at a press conference on October 7 and began to run on free time the next day. They received curiously respectful treatment at first. In the topsy-turvy world of the referendum campaign, it was an asset that they looked as if they had been shot in a basement by someone's brother-in-law armed with a camcorder (the party spent only $28,300 on radio and TV production).[52] Professors of marketing murmured on CBC that the ads looked refreshingly different. No criticism came until October 14, when the roof started to fall in.

Joe Clark was first off the mark with a well-aimed shot. He accused Manning of wanting to make Canadians vote No without even reading the text of the accord. "His [Manning's] popularity is as an anti-politician and here he is acting in a very political way."[53] This was a jab that hurt, for Manning had invested much political capital in promoting the idea that Reform offered a "new breed" of politician. Sheila Copps and Audrey McLaughlin quickly chimed in, setting off a chorus of editorialists and columnists across the country. "Manning is surely a politician now," one columnist wrote. "By constantly referring to the Charlottetown accord as 'Mulroney's deal,' Manning has changed his act from prophet to politician. He has now shown himself every bit as capable of fogging the issues and having it both ways as any bona fide elected official."[54] The denunciations were predictable, coming as they did from political opponents and columnists who had never approved of anything Manning did; but they still had a damaging effect, particularly because they appeared at about the same time as the *Globe*'s story that Manning had originally wanted to be on the

Yes side. Together they highlighted the opportunistic side of Manning's populism and undercut his credibility as the leader of a reform movement.

Unfortunately the party was unable to mount an effective defence. The steering committee realized that it had made a mistake and substituted slightly different versions of the TV ads in the final week, but it was too late to undo the damage. Having already decided to return to the university, I refused to defend the "Mulroney deal" and even joined in the public criticism.[55] Stephen Harper did not openly criticize the slogan but also refused to defend it. Laurie Watson tried to suggest that the idea wasn't really Manning's but had come from "external influences."[56] Gordon Shaw said that in hindsight it was probably a "tactical error."[57] Manning's own response was inconsistent. Sometimes he defended the phrase vigorously. "The prime minister's fingerprints are all over this thing," he said. "People see this as a deal for the sake of a deal — that it's not a principled agreement. And that is part of the prime minister's style."[58] At other times he resorted to the pseudo-populist argument that "we think it is justified" to use the phrase because pollsters have found ordinary people using it.[59] Then he referred the question to the grassroots of the party in the November mailout and received a measure of vindication when 78% of the respondents indicated that they approved of the words "Mulroney deal." However, despite this approval, he later admitted that the slogan had been a mistake.[60] But by then it didn't matter what he said; the damage had been done.

The referendum was unquestionably a victory for the Reform Party. The very fact that it was held can be traced in large measure to the party's activities. Reform had called for a referendum on Meech Lake and had made constitutional referendums a major plank in the Blue Book. It is no accident that in 1991 and 1992 British Columbia and Alberta passed legislation requiring provincial referendums on constitutional change; these were the two provinces where Reform support was the strongest. And it was the actions taken by British Columbia and Alberta that forced the prime minister to hold a referendum he had never wanted. It might have been acceptable for Quebec to hold its own referendum on an offer from the rest of the country while the other provinces proceeded with ratification in their legislatures, but it was scarcely tenable for some provinces in the rest of Canada to hold referendums while the people in other provinces would not get a chance to vote.

Reform's intervention in the campaign also made a difference. An Angus Reid poll taken in Alberta in late August showed 58% of respondents intended to vote Yes. A subsequent poll taken on September 11, the day after Manning's announcement that Reform would run a No campaign, showed that Yes support in the province had fallen to 46%.[61] Manning's announcement may not have been responsible for the entire drop, but it must have accounted for some of it. A very large Angus Reid poll taken in mid-October asked respondents whether the performance of certain individuals had made them more likely to vote Yes, more likely to vote No, or had had no impact. Table 6-1 summarizes the results for seven national political leaders:

Table 6-1
Impact of Leader's Opinion during the Referendum

Leader	Balance of YES over NO	No impact
Brian Mulroney	−18	47
Preston Manning	−15	53
Audrey McLaughlin	2	68
Jean Chrétien	4	63
Pierre Trudeau	−27	44
Ovide Mercredi	10	57
Joe Clark	16	55

SOURCE: Canada West Foundation, "Public Opinion and the Charlottetown Accord," January 1993. N = 3577.

These data suggest that Pierre Trudeau's opposition was the single most important factor on the No side. This is confirmed by the tracking poll conducted by UBC political scientist Richard Johnston and associates, who found a sharp fall in Yes support and a rise in No support outside Quebec immediately after Trudeau's "Egg Roll" speech of October 1.[62] But if Trudeau was the star, Manning's role was still significant. His impact on the No side was similar to Joe Clark's on the Yes side, and both seemed to far outweigh Jean Chrétien and Audrey McLaughlin as factors in the campaign.

In at least two ways, the referendum results expressed a political configuration that the Reform Party should have been able to build upon. First, as shown in Figure 6-3, the tendency to vote No was strongly and inversely related to the warmth of one's feeling about politicians.[63]

Respondents in this survey were asked to rank their feeling about politicians in general on a thermometer in which 100 was very warm, 0 was very cold, and 50 was neutral. Of those who scored themselves between 0 and 20, that is, they felt very negatively towards politicians, 77% reported that they had voted No; whereas of those who scored themselves between 61 and 80, that is, they felt fairly positively towards politicians, only 45% voted No. This could have been grist for the mill for Reform's rhetoric

Figure 6-3
Voting Yes and No on the Accord, According to Feelings about Politicians—Rest of Canada

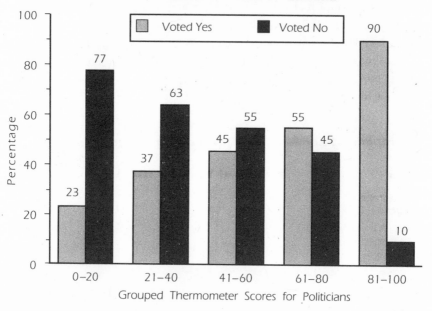

SOURCE: 1992 Canadian Referendum Survey

about a new populist party challenging the so-called traditional or old-line parties, except that Manning's conduct during the referendum campaign had eaten away at this advantage. His initial reluctance to be on the No side, his avoidance of discussing fundamental principles during the campaign, and his "Mulroney-deal" ads all made him look just as much a politician as any of the old-line leaders.

Interestingly, the voting pattern in the referendum also instantiated Manning's original populist hinterland vision of Reform as a "truly national party with its roots in the resource-producing regions."[64] All four western provinces were united in voting No, showing that there can sometimes be a transcendent western interest. Also, there was a very obvious split in Ontario between metropolitan Toronto and Ottawa, which went strongly Yes, and most of the rest of the province, which went just as strongly No. This validated Manning's theory that rural Ontario was just as alienated from the centres of power as western Canada. This urban-rural split also occurred in the West. In British Columbia and Alberta, the only constituencies to give more than 40% to the Yes side were in Victoria, Vancouver, Calgary, and Edmonton. Indeed, Yes won in Manning's own riding of Calgary Southwest and came close in three other Calgary ridings. In Saskatchewan, Yes won in Regina Wascana; and while it did not win anywhere in Manitoba, it was strongest in two Winnipeg ridings.

Beyond this urban-rural split there was also a class cleavage that could perhaps be identified with Manning's notion of populism as well as with Harper's idea of a split between the urban "knowledge class," on one side, and the urban working class and rural population, on the other side. Within large urban areas in the West and Ontario, upper-income ridings supported the Yes side more strongly than blue-collar ridings. This pattern was clearest in Calgary, where Yes won in Calgary Southwest and polled over 48% in West, Centre, and North — all mainly middle-class areas. It was also visible in Vancouver, Edmonton, Regina, and Winnipeg, where Yes did its best in the affluent ridings. It could even be seen in Ontario, although it was obscured somewhat there because the large visible minority population in Toronto and francophone population in Ottawa supported the deal. But the pattern was crystal-clear in blue-collar Windsor's two ridings, where 64% of the constituents voted No. The deal was also defeated in Hamilton East and Hamilton Mountain (Sheila Copps's riding), both working-class ridings.

The analysis cannot be pushed too far, because outside Ontario and the West other factors were clearly driving the vote. Ethnic factors were particularly important: anglophones in Quebec, Acadians in New Brunswick, and natives in the Northwest Territories all went strongly Yes, while francophones in Quebec went strongly No, but not for the same reasons as No voters outside Quebec. And Newfoundland's and Prince Edward Island's fiscal dependency on the government, as well as the popularity of the premiers in those provinces, presumably contributed to the strong Yes vote there.

Nonetheless, the pattern of results in the West and Ontario suggested that Manning's hinterland and populist vision was based on something real, that at least on certain issues and under certain conditions, it might be turned into support for his "new national party."[65] This should have been profoundly encouraging.

Unfortunately for the Reform Party, however, it was difficult to capitalize on these results in the short run. Partly to blame were the failures of funding, strategy, organization, and leadership displayed during the campaign, as well as Manning's seeming insincerity. The party's opponents and the media were merciless in calling attention to these weaknesses, but essentially the damage had been self-inflicted.

In the longer run, however, the party rebounded and Manning proved able to learn from his mistakes. In comparison with the referendum, Reform's 1993 election campaign was much better organized and conducted, without public displays of disunity; Manning advanced the party's core agenda in a straightforward way that did not leave him open to charges of opportunism; he did not repeat the mistake of taking the leaders' debate too lightly; and Reform's paid advertisements stayed away from self-defeating attacks on the leaders of other parties. In perspective, then, the referendum campaign proved to be an invaluable learning experience for Manning, and he deserves credit for drawing lessons from it. No political leader can expect to lead without making mistakes, but a successful leader will learn from experience and avoid similar mistakes in the future.

Moreover, as we will see in Chapter 8, Reform's pattern of success in the 1993 election bore some similarity to the pattern of No votes in the referendum. For the 220 constituencies outside Quebec, the correlation between the 1992 No vote and the 1993 Reform vote was a moderately strong .61 (1.0 would indicate a perfect association and 0 would indicate no connection).[66] Reform did well in western Canada, especially Alberta and British Columbia, and in rural Ontario — all areas where the No vote was strong. The biggest difference was that in the election Reform was not able to dominate the blue-collar, low-income voters who had nearly all voted No in the referendum in cities such as Vancouver, Edmonton, Windsor, and Hamilton. When the election came, these voters stayed with the NDP or the Liberals.

In retrospect, then, the referendum can be seen as an event that partially paved the way for Reform's success. Especially in the West and rural Ontario, it helped shake many voters loose from the Conservative Party and thus helped Reform to replace the Conservatives. It also helped shake many voters loose from the NDP, but most of those voters chose the Liberals rather than Reform. Yet that might not always be the case. In a future election, Reform might succeed in re-creating something like the referendum No coalition in English Canada, that is, rural voters combining with large numbers of middle-class and working-class urban voters. The most obvious scenario in which that would occur would be in a campaign that highlighted identity issues, such as the threat of Quebec's separation, which would pull English voters together. In other words, if events develop in a certain way, the referendum No coalition may turn out to be the prototype of The Party of English Canada.

7

Intermission

Reform did not gain any support from its not-very-well-managed referendum campaign. The party quickly slipped into single-digit figures in public opinion polls and stayed there for 10 months, until the beginning of the 1993 election campaign. Likewise, membership was declining; from a peak of 133,000 reached during the referendum campaign, the numbers fell to about 100,000. Finances were also a continuing problem; enough money came in to pay the bills but not to build up a war chest for the coming election.

All of this worried Reformers at the time; however, in retrospect, it may all have been for the best. The party's standing was so low on the eve of the election that the other parties took it far too lightly. The Conservatives, in particular, made the mistake of assuming they no longer had a serious rival on the right and thus veered to the centre in the campaign, causing their traditional voters in the West and rural Ontario to desert in droves to Reform. Manning did not exactly feign weakness in order to trap the Conservatives into making fatal errors, but this turned out to be the effect of his patient waiting for the right moment to fire his best shots.

Figure 7-1 shows Reform Party support among committed voters as measured by the Gallup Poll for the months between the referendum and the beginning of the 1993 election campaign. Support was up to 11% in November 1992, probably as a result of the party's exposure during the referendum campaign, but then dropped off precipitously to 7% in December. Although it fluctuated in the following months, it never went above 10%

Figure 7-1
Reform Support between the Referendum and the Election

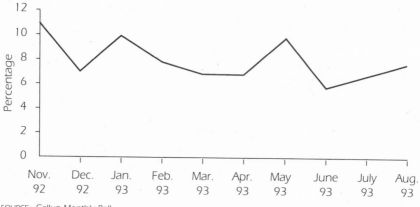

SOURCE: Gallup Monthly Poll

and usually stood at 6% to 8% — a level at which Reform no longer looked like a serious contender.

The national downward trend was paralleled by a similar decline in Reform's Alberta base. At its height in 1991, Reform support in the province had been over 40%. Now a number of polls showed it slipping into the 20% to 30% range and even falling below 20% by June 1993.[1] This again was an alarming sign of weakness; for, if the Reform Party was going to elect a viable caucus, it had to do well in Alberta. Remember that the party had polled 15% in Alberta in 1988 without electing a single member. Now it again appeared to be in the danger zone of political irrelevance, where the first-past-the-post electoral system would nullify the effect of its remaining support.

Of course, part of this decline was related to external factors that the party could not control. For example, the Conservatives enjoyed a surge in popularity when they replaced Brian Mulroney as leader. Nonetheless, it is also true that Reform abetted its own decline in the polls by virtually falling off the political stage after the referendum. Except for brief interludes, it became almost invisible in the media, thus creating a vicious circle. Lack of media presence drove down polling numbers, creating a sense of the party's irrelevance among both reporters and the general public. Journalists thus ceased to cover the party except for occasional articles on the theme of "What ever happened to Reform?" which contributed further to the decline in support.

Because of his call for a constitutional moratorium, it was now impossible for Manning, even if he had wanted to, to talk convincingly about the need for a Triple-E Senate or the danger of giving in to exaggerated demands from Quebec. When he tried to resurrect the idea of Senate elections in

Alberta, it only antagonized the new Conservative premier, Ralph Klein, who resumed the formal alliance with the federal Conservatives that Don Getty had broken off.[2]

Another possibility would have been to work on the theme of elitism. Before the referendum many political observers had speculated that it would be a watershed in Canadian political history, marking the rejection of elites by the public. The Reform Party, with its rhetoric of populism, direct democracy, and "the common sense of the common people," should have been able to take advantage of an anti-elitist current in public opinion. But this was never a realistic option for Manning because of the peculiarities of his populism, namely, his emphasis on universal reconciliation and his inability to posit opponents. The very night of October 26, even amid the party's victory celebration, he drafted this message of reconciliation to be published as an ad in the *Globe and Mail*:

> Thank you, Canadians, for participating so enthusiastically in the national constitutional referendum. If you voted YES, not because you were told to, but because you honestly believed that this would help unite the country, thank you for your faith and generosity. If you voted NO, not for narrow or selfish reasons, but because you honestly believed the Charlottetown accord was a bad deal for Canada, thank you for expressing the courage of your convictions. NOW LET'S MOVE FORWARD TOGETHER.[3]

These words could just as well have been written by someone on the Yes side as on the No side. It is interesting that Manning addressed the Yes supporters first — surely significant in view of his invariable practice of organizing his thoughts in prioritized lists. As if to reinforce the point, Manning said in his first major public address after the referendum, delivered in Ottawa on November 9: "The Reform Party is not anti-elite. We are not interested in pitting one group of Canadians . . . against another."[4]

The party now faced a dilemma about which positioning strategy to use. National expansion had reduced the efficacy of The Party of Western Canada, the referendum result had temporarily put The Party of English Canada out of play, and Manning's ethereal brand of populism made it difficult for him to use the referendum as a springboard for The Party of the People. In the event, he recurred to The Party of the Right, as he generally does when he senses himself in difficulty.

The first bullet that Manning fired in the new campaign was a plan to downsize the federal cabinet to 24 ministers, which he proposed in November in his Ottawa speech. The plan could stand alone on its own merits, but it was also a step towards the key conservative goal of reducing federal expenditure. Manning had actually asked that the proposal be developed in the summer, but publicizing it had been delayed because of the referendum. Getting the number of cabinet ministers down to 24 was easy; one only had to eliminate the junior and associate ministers, plus a few positions that Reform opposed in principle, such as minister of Multiculturalism.

While Manning's instinct was sound in returning his attention to federal spending, there was a secondary strategic problem. He thought that the Conservatives were going to downsize the cabinet in any event, so he wanted to get out in front and claim credit for originating the idea. At the time it seemed like a cunning ploy, but events showed that it was not cunning enough. If you demand that the governing party do something that you are sure they are going to do anyway, how do you react when they do it? You risk appearing irrelevant precisely because they have done what you demanded.

Moreover, a new party trying to carve out a niche for itself cannot succeed simply by attaching itself to widely popular ideas. An idea that is generally popular is bound to be picked up quickly by at least one of the established parties, leaving the small party without a pony to ride. The logic of the situation demands that the new contender espouse controversial policies that attract intense support from a poorly represented segment of the electorate. On election day, there must be a cadre of voters that have positive reasons to cast their votes for a new and untried party. Having run interference for the established parties will not provide a good enough reason.

In the event, the Conservatives responded predictably; Kim Campbell reduced the cabinet to 25 as soon as she became prime minister. Manning attempted to up the ante by calling for a cabinet of 16 just before she made her announcement, but this looked rather silly. "Call it Preston Manning's incredible shrinking cabinet," said the Southam papers in the lead sentence of their story.[5] When Campbell downsized the cabinet in June 1993, the public gave Reform no credit for having originated the idea.

Unfortunately, the party also got little credit when Manning first made the suggestion in November 1992 because he mishandled the announcement. In the course of answering a question, he allowed himself to ruminate in public on civil service staff cuts, a topic on which he was not briefed:

> "But if you're talking about trying to take $30 billion out of $150 billion in (annual) spending, you're talking about a 15 to 20 per cent reduction that could ultimately translate into staff requirements of that type."
>
> Manning said he was aware there are more than 525,000 Canadians getting paid directly or indirectly by the federal government.[6]

It was a bad mistake. Since most of the federal budget consists of transfer payments, a cut in total spending simply does not translate into a proportional cut in federal employment. Frightening headlines about Manning firing 100,000 civil servants started to ricochet around the country; and his cabinet-cutting proposal, which should have been almost universally popular, was hardly covered at all.

Reform's other main initiative in the pre-writ period, the Zero in Three plan to balance the budget, was better handled, received more extensive and more favourable attention in the media, and was almost surely responsible for the brief surge in the spring poll results (13% in the April Angus Reid, 10% in the May Gallup).[7] Again, this was Manning's idea and it pre-dated the referendum. It began when he started getting questions from nominated candidates about how a Reform government would erase the federal deficit in three years, as stated in the Blue Book and election platform: "A Reform government will balance the revenues and expenditures of the Government of Canada by the end of its third fiscal year of office or it will call an election."[8] As a first step, Manning asked me to prepare a one-page cash-flow chart showing in aggregate terms how this could be done. After I put together some hypothetical numbers demonstrating the magnitude of cuts required in different areas of federal spending, even allowing for reasonable revenue growth, Manning decided to develop the chart into a more detailed set of proposals. Given that politicians are notoriously averse to discussing spending cuts before an election, he made a courageous decision; and in the end it turned out to be key to Reform's success in the 1993 election.

The developmental work started after the referendum and carried on into February 1993. Manning handled it the way a leader should: he established goals and insisted they be reached, but allowed other team members to do their work. Dimitri Pantazopoulos, a young Reform staff member with a degree in finance, combed the main estimates for specific spending programs incompatible with Reform policies. Stephen Harper, who has a master's degree in economics, developed a set of assumptions about inflation, interest rates, entitlement payments, and federal revenue growth dependent upon general economic growth and unemployment rates. Harper was also assisted by an Ottawa group of Reform sympathizers, most of whom were employed in the federal public service and had considerable knowledge of federal spending. With the aid of data from the Fraser Institute, I developed some proposals for restraint in the big-ticket items of transfers to persons and transfers to provinces. After our group of four had completed its work, Manning tested the plan before a couple of audiences, including nominated Reform candidates.

Some junior staff members and executive councillors developed a way for communicating the plan to the public. The big risk in bringing out such a complex set of proposals is that it will be dumped on the table, so to speak, receive one round of stories in the media, and then be forgotten as reporters move on to something more digestible. To counter that possible reaction, Manning was advised to give four separate speeches on the Zero in Three plan over a period of four weeks, each time emphasizing a different aspect of it.[9] All Reform candidates were invited to participate in this Speaking with One Voice initiative by holding local news conferences to coincide with Manning's speeches. The national press, of course, focused on Manning; but the local press release helped to get attention in local media, especially weekly newspapers, which tend to be more receptive to Reform than the big dailies.

Most of the Zero in Three plan consisted of "black box," or global, cuts in large areas of spending without saying precisely where the cuts would be — for example, a "15% cut in budgets of institutions at the top of government."[10] Others amounted to putting numbers on long-standing Reform policies, such as a saving of $50 million to be made by eliminating the bilingualism bonus in the federal civil service.[11] Although such statements were useful in giving a sense of Reform's priorities and approach to deficit reduction, they did not constitute new policy.

But there were also some new measures in the Zero in Three package, of which the most important was the proposal to switch from individual income to family income in calculating the taxback on old age security. This built on the Blue Book idea of developing "a family or household-oriented comprehensive social security system administered through the income-tax system."[12] At that time, the OAS taxback kicked in at $53,215 of *individual* income at a rate of 15%, and all benefit from OAS disappeared at $83,170. At the end of 1992, the average *family* income in Canada was $53,854; and, according to Fraser Institute calculations, about 25% of the roughly $20 billion expended on OAS was going to seniors whose family income was above the Canadian average.[13] Basing the taxback on family income promised to return about $2 billion to the federal treasury while carrying out the position expressed in the Blue Book: "The Reform Party supports greater focusing of social policy benefits. We prefer to target benefits on those who need the help, and to do so in a rational and compassionate manner."[14]

Admittedly, Zero in Three contained some weaknesses, some of which were obvious at the time, others of which were pointed out by critics during the election campaign. To mention only the four biggest problems:

• Too many of the proposed cuts remained at the "black box" level, especially cuts in federal subsidies to agriculture, small business, Crown corporations, and "special interests." Reform's opponents might have done damage by demanding details, but in the event they virtually ignored these topics, preferring to concentrate on the plan's impact on social programs.

• We did not use an econometric model to estimate the temporary recessionary effects that will result from a reduction in federal spending. In the long run, it is true, a reduction in the debt burden will help the private sector; but in the short run there will be negative effects caused by sudden changes in expectations. That is, discharged civil servants, as well as people whose transfer payments are cut, will find their purchasing power reduced, leading to some economic contraction and a decline in federal tax revenues. Because we did not try to estimate these effects, it may have been true that the arithmetic did not add up, that the plan would not in fact have gotten rid of the deficit in three fiscal years.

However, the strength of this criticism should not be overestimated. Econometric models are not true in the sense of physical laws; they are empirical descriptions of the economy as it has functioned in the past. Major changes in government policy are bound to have a major change in the parameters in the model's equations. Thus, existing models might accurately foretell some short-term effects of balancing the budget but would soon lose their predictive validity.

• There were problems with the Fraser Institute's figures on OAS. Their analysis showed that one quarter of OAS payments goes to "economic households" with incomes above the national median, but it is not clear how that applies to families in the normal sense. Many seniors live with their adult children, but would such arrangements be considered families for tax purposes? Manning exacerbated this difficulty by raising the OAS taxback target from $2 billion to $3.5 billion after it became clear that the federal deficit would be larger than predicted when work had begun on Zero in Three. It was undoubtedly true, as critics later alleged, that it is impossible to save $3.5 billion simply by cancelling OAS for those seniors whose family income was above $54,000.

• We eventually settled on an annual savings target of $4 billion from unemployment insurance. While $4 billion could be cut from this program and Canada would be better off for it, a technical problem exists that was never addressed. Because UI is funded mainly through payroll taxes levied on workers and their employers, the achievement of substantial savings by making the program less generous would either mean that payroll taxes would be reduced, which would not help the deficit situation, or that the revenue from UI premiums would have to be used for other purposes. However, this objection should not be overstated. Any excess revenue from premiums could be treated as repaying the cumulative deficit in the UI account (about $6 billion at the time of writing).

Being aware of these and other problems, I was in fact rather dubious about the whole Zero in Three idea. I feared that Manning was turning complex problems of public policy into a simple exercise in arithmetic, and I would have preferred him to make a series of statements on specific issues rather than advance an overall set of numbers. In retrospect, however, it is clear that he exercised good judgment, as he usually does with regard to issues of communications. Producing an overall set of numbers, even simplistic ones, was essential from a communications perspective because it allowed Manning to claim that he had a plan. It gave the Reform Party credibility on this issue, because the plan, even if imperfect, was at least marginally better than what any other party offered. Also, by focusing attention on the overall objective, it deflected criticism of the individual policies contained in the package.

Moreover, as an academic I was too worried about the specifics of policy. Whatever problems there were in the OAS and UI proposals, they certainly pointed in the right direction. No one will ever balance the federal budget without curbing the generosity of OAS and UI, and the most politically acceptable way to do so is to start at the upper-income end. In the larger scheme of things, it didn't matter whether the projected OAS savings of $3.5 billion were precisely correct. Similarly, UI is a well-known work disincentive and leads to overallocation of labour to seasonal and temporary occupations; until it is returned to something like its original purpose, it will always be a drag on the Canadian economy. The important thing at election time is to point to the need for reform, not to have a plan that is unassailable from all angles.

Zero in Three was too complex to get much attention in the electronic media, but it did generate extensive coverage in newspapers. There were the usual attacks,[15] but at least columnists were writing about Reform, which is what the party needed most at the time. Indeed, the *Calgary Herald*'s ombudsman publicly reproved that paper for not devoting enough space to Zero in Three, thus prompting some additional coverage.[16] There were also some favourable columns in usually hostile papers such as the *Toronto Star* and Vancouver *Province*,[17] but the biggest boost was undoubtedly a *Globe and Mail* editorial endorsing the package:

> The Reform Party has been unveiling a detailed, considered, entirely cred-
> ible plan to shrink the deficit to zero over three years. . . . the Reform mix
> of cuts in spending and tightened tax breaks is so sensible most of us
> wouldn't feel a thing. Certainly it would not require any sacrifice of those
> truly in need. As an exercise in the "new politics," which is to say telling the
> truth, it sets the standard.[18]

The fact that all of this occurred during the Conservative leadership race shows that a small party can, indeed, deliver its message in the media if it has something to say and goes about it intelligently. However, Manning did not sustain the momentum past May, and the party once again disappeared from sight in the media, thus leading to lower polling numbers and resuming the downward spiral. This downward trend can partly be attributed to the media's insatiable requirement for "news"; they cannot report and discuss the same topic forever, no matter how important it may be. Another problem arose from the promises of the leading Conservative leadership contenders, Jean Charest and Kim Campbell, to balance the budget in four or five years respectively. This made Reform look like "Tories in a hurry" and transformed Zero in Three from a unique proposal into a matter of degree.

To carry the struggle further, Manning would have had to be ready with speeches on particular policies implied by Zero in Three, which would stress their novelty and challenge the other parties to match these specific policies with something other than vague promises. It would have been a high-risk strategy because specific policies are always open to criticism, to say nothing of appropriation; but given Reform's precarious position in the polls, it might have been worth running the risk. However, it was probably not a realistic alternative. Years of delay in fleshing out the Blue Book meant that Manning did not have much additional material about the policies included in Zero in Three, and his insistence on writing all his own speeches makes it almost impossible for him to make quick use of lengthy documents prepared by others, such as Stephen Harper's consultative group in Ottawa.

In retrospect, it may have been a good thing that Manning dropped Zero in Three at that time, even though it caused Reform to slip back in the polls. If he had continued to push it hard, it might have grown stale by the time the election was called. Also, continued exposure might have drawn attention to the plan's weaknesses, which largely escaped notice at the time; and it might have encouraged the Conservatives to come out with a more realistic deficit-reduction package of their own.

Whatever the merits of that argument, it is also true that Manning's populist instincts were leading him elsewhere. In May, he began preparing to go off in a different direction with his less confrontational speech, "The Reformer's Guide to the New Economy." As mentioned in Chapter 1, he wrote this speech to counter what he called the "slash and burn" tone of Zero in Three.[19] Manning was driven in this direction by his deep-seated desire to be positive, and to give people hope. The problem with the speech was that the initiatives it advocated could have been recommended by any party. There was nothing distinctively Reform-oriented about them. Of course, Manning never fully accepted the strategy of invading from the right, so according to his own philosophy he was being consistent in returning to broad generalities.

As discussed in the previous chapter, Manning was already thinking during the referendum campaign of appointing Rick Anderson his top political aide. That plan was delayed when Anderson came out on the Yes side and thus made himself suspect in Reform Party circles. He stayed away from the Winnipeg Assembly and in general lay low while Manning decided what to do. Ultimately, Manning opted for a course of gradual rehabilitation.

Anderson was invited to meet in Calgary with a group of executive council members, senior officers, and other insiders on the morning of January 15, 1993. With his distaste for confrontation, Manning stayed away and left Cliff Fryers with the difficult job of chairing the session. Anderson claimed at this session that he had informed Manning of his Yes views at the outset of the referendum and had never served as a member of the steering committee. When I asked Fryers why he had informed the party that Anderson was on the committee, he became embarrassed and said, "I have no explanation for that." But since no one else was interested in probing deeper, Anderson's account went unchallenged, and he was immediately reinstated as an adviser, sitting in on a strategy meeting that lasted for the rest of the day.

In the following months, Manning would occasionally send up trial balloons in his tape-recorded "Fireside Chats" about the need to get Anderson more involved in the campaign, perhaps as coordinator of the leader's tour.[20] The appointment in May of Allan McGirr as director of communications at the national office indicated which way the wind was blowing. McGirr, a long-time Liberal activist from Hamilton, was also an old associate of Anderson's; both of them had worked as assistants for the Liberal cabinet minister Judd Buchanan during the 1970s, and Anderson had introduced McGirr to Manning.[21]

By July 9, it was obvious that Anderson would become campaign director, the highest position under Manning and Fryers. At a strategy meeting I attended that day, an organizational chart was passed out that showed the campaign director's position was vacant.[22] Since Anderson's name did not appear in any other box, and since anyone else who might conceivably have played a responsible role had been assigned to another job, it was clear that the position had been reserved for him. Subsquent conversations I had with junior staff confirmed this.

I decided then that it was time to make my opposition to the appointment known. I called Ken Whyte, western columnist for the *Globe and Mail*, to compliment him on a recent *Saturday Night* profile of Manning,[23] and mentioned that Anderson would soon be campaign director. He already knew this and decided to do a column about it, in which he portrayed Anderson as a "consummate Ottawa insider" and a "surprise choice" to manage the campaign — surprising for all the obvious reasons: Anderson was an Ottawa lobbyist, a Yes supporter in the referendum, and, in ideological terms, a centrist. Whyte wrote:

> It's becoming clear that the Reform Party has no future as a moderate, national party. Without its old regional flavour, its old conservatism, its old readiness to oppose Quebec's domination of the Canadian political agenda and its old bogey of a fat and corrupt Ottawa establishment (which, incidentally, once included lobbyists), the Reform Party is left pushing fiscal responsibility, law-and-order and parliamentary reform, just like everyone else. Why should westerners vote for it? And outside the West, why choose Tory clones over the real thing?[24]

Although Whyte did not attribute any quotations to me, I wanted to be on the record in the future. So I faxed Manning a letter saying that I strongly disapproved of the Anderson appointment and would not refrain from criticism in the media.[25] He responded by doing what he had to do if he was going to appoint Anderson: he fired me from my position as policy adviser. Typically, he avoided commenting on the bone of contention — whether Anderson should be campaign director —, and framed the problem as one of relationships: "Because I no longer enjoy your confidence, and because you cease to enjoy the confidence of an increasing number of our key people, I believe the time has come to end the relationship between the Reform Party and yourself as Policy Consultant."[26]

Stephen Harper was as opposed as I was to the Anderson appointment, but because of his position as a Reform candidate he did not want to get involved in an open dispute. He contented himself, therefore, with oblique comments to the media that were clear enough to insiders but did not convey to the public an impression of a rift.[27] He did, however, resign from the Reform Party's national campaign organization. Manning was thus deprived of the services of a gifted strategist.[28]

Another loss for the party was a weakening in support from the previously reliable *Alberta Report*. Ted and Link Byfield were seriously upset by the news of Anderson's appointment. Ted proceeded to write blistering columns in the Sun newspapers and the *Financial Post* that far exceeded any criticisms I had made.[29] There was also a sudden change in the tone of the coverage given to Reform by the *Report*. While not openly hostile, it became cooler and more analytical than before, and the Anderson appointment received extensive coverage. Meanwhile, I continued to speak freely to reporters drawn to me by the scent of controversy, and I enlarged upon my fears that the Manning-Anderson team would veer towards the centre, both in terms of geography and ideology. Specifically, I feared that the Reform campaign would place undue emphasis upon Ontario at the expense of Alberta and British Columbia, and that it would draw upon the technocratic platitudes of Manning's New Economy speech while downplaying the Reform Party's earlier agenda. With the increased interest caused by the kickoff of the election, some of these stories made front-page headlines,[30] so that Cliff Fryers felt compelled to send out an internal memo in an attempt to discredit me: "Re: Negative comments about Reform Party by Dr. Tom Flanagan. The reason Tom is a 'former' advisor is because we came to the view that his judgement is lacking. He is proving that again."[31]

Perhaps partly because of the negative reactions of Whyte, the Byfields, and myself, Manning did not in the end run a centrist campaign. After the initial phase, he veered sharply to the right and, with considerable help from Kim Campbell, managed to position Reform as the only genuine conservative alternative. This was exactly the sort of campaign the critics had wanted, but does this mean that our fears were unfounded? Maybe, but probably not. Even apart from the Anderson appointment, a good deal of objective evidence in the summer of 1993 indicated that Manning was preparing to run a centrist campaign:

• In May he stopped talking about Zero in Three and drafted the New Economy speech.

• He directed that a brochure based on the speech be prepared for use in the campaign. (The broadsheet that staff eventually produced was rewritten so many times that most of the New Economy material disappeared.)[32]

• In his July and August "Fireside Chats" to candidates, he emphasized that during the campaign he would talk less about how the budget could be balanced and more about the positive benefits of deficit reduction. It would be the time to present the New Economy as the "light at the end of the tunnel."[33] (He actually tried to do this during the campaign, but his New Economy speech created little interest and he dropped it.)

• In July he put considerable effort into drafting an "Open Letter to the Electors of Quebec" in an endeavour "to lay to rest the charge that the 'Reform Party's Canada does not include Quebec.'"[34] The letter touched upon the Reform Party's history and some of its policies on language and federalism, but it remained silent about Reform's history of opposing Quebec's demands for special status and recognition as a distinct society. Instead, it tried to strike an inclusive note: "Those who tell you that Reform's vision of a new Canada does not include Quebec are particularly misguided and malicious."[35] With his penchant for historical references, Manning even evoked the memory of Baldwin and Lafontaine:

> I am reminded that in the days prior to Confederation, it was Reformers from Lower Canada (Canada East) under Louis Lafontaine, who eventually joined together with Reformers from Upper Canada (Canada West) to end colonial rule, to bring about representative and responsible government, and to lay the foundations for the new Canada of Confederation.
>
> Perhaps history will repeat itself, as history sometimes does, and you will be able to assist me in identifying who are the contemporary equivalents of Lafontaine and his supporters in your province.[36]

• He also drafted an "Open Letter to the Members of Local 222, Canadian Auto Workers," and an "Open Letter to Federal Public Servants."[37] The first letter condemned Bob Rae's Social Contract as a "one-year crash program," mentioned that Deborah Grey had voted against NAFTA, denied that Reform had a right-wing agenda, and emphasized that the "Reform Party supports the rights of workers to organize democratically, to bargain collectively, and to strike peacefully." (He did not mention Reform's opposition to public service strikes!)[38] In fact, the letter abounded in centrist and leftist phraseology that almost amounted to conservative-bashing, for example, "We are a party that believes in free trade, but not at any cost." The second letter offered federal civil servants a "cooperative approach to federal public sector/public service reform" and reassured them about "opportunity counselling and re-training, priority staffing, attrition (5% per year), early retirement, and an extension of portability of benefits." Although neither open letter departed explicitly from the Reform agenda, both certainly suppressed essential elements of it, and both reflected a rosy view of Reform policy without any hard edges. As Bob Dylan sang in "Blowing in the Wind," you didn't have to be a weatherman to see where the wind was blowing.

However, airing concerns in the media may have amounted to a sort of self-denying prophecy. From calls and letters I received, as well as from journalistic reports, I know that the fears expressed by Ken Whyte, Ted Byfield, and myself about Manning's centrism had some currency with Reformers, and that party activists began asking questions of Manning and other members of the election team. As a populist politician, Manning is guided above all by the reactions he elicits from the people he is trying to reach. Thus, the fact that we had voiced concerns about centrism may have contributed to a mood within the party that helped to keep him focused on the already established Reform agenda. Just as in the case of the Charlottetown Accord, in which Manning eventually joined party members on the No side, in the 1993 campaign he moved away from his personal preference for technocratic centrism and towards the conservative ideology espoused by most Reformers.

By the summer of 1993, candidate recruitment was well in hand. Anyone with a reasonable chance of getting elected had already been nominated, so the party could proceed to finalize its campaign preparations. The campaign strategy was laid down by Manning at a meeting in Calgary on July 9 to 10 attended by about 30 people. The key premise was that this election was the first stage in the two-election strategy. That is, in this election the Reform Party would break into the system, and in the next it would win enough seats to form a government. Manning explicitly said that he wasn't interested in getting a toehold and then working for 40 years to enlarge the caucus. Even more dramatically, Cliff Fryers said he doubted that the party could fight three or more elections. To an outsider, these might seem like rhetorical flourishes calculated to excite the troops to greater efforts; but in fact they faithfully represented Manning's conception of a populist party that comes to power by catching the wave.

The key to success in this election, according to Manning, would be polarization. Reform had to make itself appear to be a systemic alternative to all the old parties. The party would accomplish this by concentrating on two major themes (economic reform and democratic reform), with help from two other themes — criminal justice reform in urban ridings and agricultural reform in rural ridings. Manning also speculated, correctly as it turned out, that questions of strategic voting and minority government might loom large in the latter half of the campaign.

This limitation of themes made the content of the campaign fairly definite. Task forces appointed earlier in the year had recently submitted reports on direct democracy, criminal justice, and agriculture, so the party's proposals in these areas would be reasonably clear. The main area of ambiguity lay in economic reform. On the one hand, the Zero in Three package would allow Manning to go to the right if he wished; but there was also his New Economy speech, which could take him towards the centre if that was where he decided to go. The biggest strategic issue of the campaign was never discussed, so Manning was left free to do whatever he wished.

The communications strategy for the campaign was supposed to unfold in three phases. The first, which would last about a week after the writ was dropped, would be called "Let the People Speak." Rather than expound Reform policies directly, Manning and the other candidates were to turn over the microphone to the audience. This populist approach was supposed to highlight the contrast between Reform and all the other parties. It also had two unstated advantages. It would give Manning a chance to tour the whole country before committing himself to specific positions; and it would allow "the people" to talk about controversial subjects such as immigration, multiculturalism, and bilingualism, even though they were not official campaign themes.

The second phase, which would take up most of the campaign, would be called "Now You Have a Choice," or something similar. It would be devoted to presenting Reform's positions on the major themes and the supporting ones mentioned previously. For some reason, opponents never picked up on the contradiction implicit in the fact that party positions had already been set and literature had already been printed in preparation for this phase, even though it was supposed to follow and depend on "Let the People Speak."

The theme of the third and final phase of the campaign, to last about a week, would be "Make Your Vote Count"; the point would be to explain how a vote for Reform would not be "wasted," as critics of new parties always claim, but would have an impact on the political system — by helping to elect the official Opposition, or a caucus holding the balance of power (or both), and by sending a message to traditional elites. In the event, this phase became redundant, because by the end of the campaign, it was the NDP and PCs who had slipped so badly that they could be accused of having split an anti-Liberal vote.

Although the three-stage plan seemed clear and definite, it is worth noting how much discretion was left to Manning to execute it. Instead of committing himself to one campaign slogan, he had three slogans, and therefore three approaches, to work with. Within the framework of the campaign plan, he was free to emphasize the populism of "Let the People Speak," the policy orientation of "Now You Have a Choice," or the strategic calculations of "Make Your Vote Count." And under policy, he could go to the right with Zero in Three or to the centre with the New Economy. Although this amount of latitude might not be desirable for most parties, it was probably unavoidable for the Reform Party in this campaign, given Manning's unique position as personal expositor of "the common sense of the common people."

The campaign organization was also designed in a way that would not constrain Manning or place him in conflictual situations. The senior personnel on the campaign management committee were the same people that had been in the referendum campaign of the preceding year: Preston Manning was the leader; Cliff Fryers, the campaign chairman; Rick Anderson, campaign director; Gordon Shaw, executive director of the Reform Party; Virgil Anderson, assistant campaign director; and Ian Todd, campaign assistant. Other campaign staff were either junior people, who were not in a position to contradict Manning and the CMC, or executive councillors and other loyal activists brought to Calgary as volunteers. There was also a National Election Resource Network of approximately 50 persons scattered around the country. Comments from this group were to be collected and funneled to CMC by Delcy Walker, a friend of Sandra Manning's.

Originally, Manning wanted Stephen Harper and me to be policy advisers; but I was fired for criticizing Rick Anderson's appointment, and Harper declined to serve. He had not wanted to be involved anyway, but the final straw for him was a written pledge sent out by Cliff Fryers to be signed by everyone in the campaign organization, which required them to refrain from publicly criticizing CMC decisions. The pledge was heavy-handed at best, and especially inappropriate for a nominated candidate, who has independent responsibilities to the constituency association and voters of his riding.

Financial plans were made to run the campaign on a shoestring. An estimate made in July indicated that the national office would have at most $150,000 on hand when the writ was dropped. A direct-mail appeal would go out to all members as soon as the campaign began, but the returns would come in gradually over a period of several weeks, so it would not be possible to pre-pay expensive media services. The campaign, therefore, would have to be low-tech with no polling and little advertising. The main emphasis would have to fall on the leader's tour and local candidates' posting of signs and distribution of literature.

To supplement the meagre funds available, Rick and Virgil Anderson undertook a cross-country tour to present the party's tentative advertising plans to nominated candidates. The purpose of the tour was to persuade candidates to contribute local money to pay for "cooperative advertising."[39] The national office would have the ads produced and carry out the media buy with money put up by candidates, who were assured that the money raised in their area would be spent in their area. However, the Andersons could not make any commitments about the content of the ads, which caused some candidates to worry that the referendum advertising fiasco would be repeated. Some constituencies joined the arrangement while others stayed out. About $400,000 — a minuscule sum by contemporary advertising standards — was raised in the four western provinces, and there was a local TV buy in all the major regional markets of the West. However, not enough money could be raised in Ontario to fund a useful media campaign in that province. The ads were developed in-house by young staff members Jennifer Grover and Bob Van Wegen, who worked with a few candidates. Manning stayed out of the process, in contrast to the referendum campaign, when he had virtually written the ads himself.

In relative terms, more effort went into planning the literature campaign. In addition to the already existing Zero in Three pamphlet and the Blue Sheet, which contained the Blue Book and the election platform approved at Winnipeg, the national office prepared a piece of literature for each phase of the campaign, as well as special items on agriculture and criminal justice. It was an old-fashioned approach, but one the party could afford, and it proved effective. "The raw troops of populism," as Manning calls the politically inexperienced people who have joined the Reform Party, could distribute literature but would have had problems with more sophisticated campaigning techniques such as personalized direct mail.

The leader's tour was also carefully planned, although as always with the Reform Party, detailed preparations were left to local people. The advantage of this approach is that it allows much to be done with a few paid staff; the disadvantage is that it is relatively inflexible. Once local people have arranged a major event for the leader, it is almost impossible to cancel it even if other factors make it advisable to go somewhere else that day. But this did not prove a major handicap for the Reform Party because no great efforts could be made to target particular ridings. Reform's best chances were obviously in Alberta and British Columbia, so those provinces would get the most time; but the leader of a western party also had to be seen in

Saskatchewan and Manitoba. In addition, he had to be seen in Ontario, which was of further importance because of the opportunities it offered for national media exposure; and he also had to make token appearances in the Atlantic provinces. Within the various provinces, the choice of specific constituencies to visit was based on rough estimates of winnability combined with constraints of proximity to airports and satellite uplinks. There was no great need to preserve flexibility in the tour because there would be no constituency-level polling data during the campaign to pinpoint winnable ridings for special attention.

Finally, arrangements were made to allow Manning to participate fully in at least the English-language leaders' debate.[40] Rick Anderson and Cliff Fryers handled these arrangements, which involved a fair bit of negotiating, and were assisted by various junior staff members. Whether consciously or not, they had learned from the McLaughlin debate of a year ago that one had to approach such debates with strategic objectives in mind. In the end, Reform got a satisfactory outcome: full participation for Manning in the English debate, plus cameo appearances with translation at the beginning and end of the French debate. The latter was much better for Reform than full participation, for Manning could have been damaged by persistent questioning from French journalists about his nebulous "new federalism."

Overall, this campaign was well planned, given the party's limited financial resources. Its low-tech and old-fashioned nature suited a Manning-led populist party, as did the fact that it gave the leader almost complete autonomy to determine the content of the message. Regardless of whether such autonomy is desirable in an abstract sense, it was the only way Manning could function at that time; and any strategy that attempted to constrain him, or force him to argue heatedly with advisers about what he wanted to say, would have been bound to fail.

8

Riding the Waves: The 1993 Election

In the 1993 election Reform increased its complement of MPs from one to an astonishing 52, and elected members in five provinces. The party's remarkable success was due more than anything else to the waves caused by the sinking of the New Democratic and Progressive Conservative parties. Of course, Reform's own actions in the campaign contributed to its rise, but it would not have been nearly as successful without the remarkable collapse of the NDP and PCs.

First, the NDP. That party turned in its best performance ever in 1988 — 20% of the popular vote and 43 MPs. It topped the Gallup Poll for four months starting October 1990 and at its peak registered the support of 41% of decided voters in January 1991. It then started to decline gradually but steadily, reaching single-digit levels by July 1993 (8%) and never recovering. Thus, in polling only 7% of the popular vote and electing only nine MPs on October 25, 1993, the NDP vacated a large chunk of political turf. Few disenchanted NDP supporters switched their votes to Reform; but by lowering the NDP's vote total, they allowed Reform to win seats previously held by the NDP, particularly in British Columbia.

The decline of the NDP cannot reasonably be attributed to the rise of the Reform Party; it was caused by weak leadership, spillover from the unpopular policies of provincial NDP governments, and the mismatch between NDP ideology and the current need for fiscal restraint and government retrenchment. But whatever the causes, the decline of the NDP made waves that helped propel Reform towards its goal.

It was a matter not just of realigning voters but also of redirecting media attention. The NDP had sunk so low by the start of the election (8% in the first Angus Reid poll) that it was trailing the Reform Party (10% in the same poll).[1] Even though Reform was not doing very well at that point, it was now the third party in English Canada, and the media had to give it some attention; whereas, if the NDP had been in its traditional range of 15% to 20%, Reform would have looked like a fringe party by comparison and would have attracted much less coverage.

The relationship between Reform and the PCs was more complex than that between Reform and the NDP. The fact that Reform had taken a large share of the Conservatives' western base was a major long-term cause of the latter's decline. Nonetheless, the selection of Kim Campbell as leader and the stretch of easy publicity she enjoyed over the summer of 1993 had gone a long way towards restoring the Conservatives' standing in the polls. They were in a virtual dead heat with the Liberals when the writ was dropped (34% to 33% in Environics, 36% to 37% in the first Angus Reid), and far ahead of Reform.[2] However, as is now widely recognized, the 1993 Conservative election campaign was the most incompetent in Canadian history. A long string of mistakes drove the party's support down to 16% on election day. However, this collapse need not have benefitted Reform; the alienated Tory voters could have gone en masse to the Liberals. That Reform did benefit substantially is due to the precise nature of one of Campbell's major mistakes — the way in which she vacated the right of the political spectrum, leaving Reform as the best option for small-c conservative voters. This stirred up the biggest wave to carry Reform to Ottawa.

Early in the campaign, Campbell tried to occupy the right by making the deficit her main theme. "It always came back to the deficit," two reporters wrote. She "was on a crusade, it seemed, a woman possessed."[3] But she came under increasing pressure for refusing to discuss the details of how she would fulfill her leadership campaign pledge of balancing the budget in five years. Her undocumented position on this issue looked vague in comparison to Reform's Zero in Three paper or even the Liberals' Red Book. This pressure led to a series of contradictory statements that demolished her credibility on fiscal responsibility, which was the main issue for conservative-minded voters in the election. In the end, she seemed to demonstrate what many disenchanted Conservatives had long thought, that the Conservative party no longer espoused a conservative philosophy.

On September 20 Campbell said that, contrary to earlier statements, she would release some details of her deficit-cutting plans.[4] But only three days later, while confirming that her government intended to "completely rethink our system of social security," she refused to discuss the substance of the issue: "You can't have a debate on such a key issue as the modernization of social programs in 47 days. . . . [The election campaign] is the worst possible time to have that discussion . . . because it takes more than 47 days to settle anything that is that serious."[5] The next day, however, she partially backtracked by promising to set out "the principles that I believe must guide any useful debate on how we as a country must modernize our social programs."[6]

On September 27, in a speech to high-school students in Surrey, British Columbia (surely a strange audience for the occasion), Campbell put some deficit-reduction numbers on the table;[7] but it quickly became evident that they did not add up. In particular, she revealed in a visit with the editorial board of the *Globe and Mail* that she was confused about the difference between a decrease in the annual budget and a cumulative saving over five years.[8] Then, during the English-language leaders' debate, she was unable or unwilling to answer Lucien Bouchard's pointed question about how large the current year's deficit was estimated to be: "A simple figure. What is the real deficit?"[9]

Immediately after the debate, the Tories launched a series of attack ads against the Reform Party, using the image of a magician sawing a woman in half to satirize Manning's Zero in Three deficit-reduction program.[10] At the same time, Campbell began to attack Manning as "a right-wing ideologue who has completely lost sight of . . . the values that we have to preserve [in] our social programs and to create a caring society."[11] Emphasizing her new role as defender of the welfare state, she told Peter Gzowski that she "would throw [herself] across railway tracks to save the health care system."[12] Although she continued to criticize the Liberals for fiscal irresponsibility, her position lacked conviction because she was simultaneously posing as the defender of social programs against Reform. She thus marched away from the traditional ground that the Conservatives had always occupied in the West and rural Ontario.

To put it another way, the Conservatives showed they were not willing to lose a single election to preserve their philosophy and core vote. Rather than fight Reform over the traditional ground of conservatism, they tried to occupy new ground in the centre, in the desperate hope that this might return them to power. But in the end they lost everything. Their move to the centre not only failed to pay off, it alienated their core voters, who defected en masse to Reform.

Figure 8-1
The Voters Speak

A look at how major political parties have fared in 1993 public opinion polls

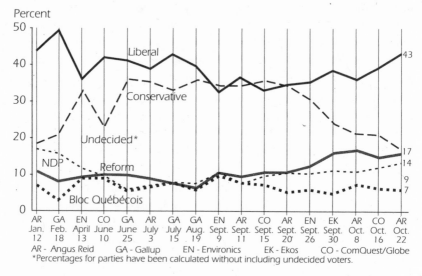

SOURCE: Canadian Press and the Globe and Mail

The data show that the period when Campbell was vacating the right was precisely the time when Reform support shot upwards. Figure 8-1 is a compilation of several major national polls taken during 1993.[13]

It shows that Reform support was static at 10% to 11% until about September 20, then rose quickly to 17% to 18% by the end of September and stayed at that level through election day. Correspondingly, Conservative support stayed at about 35% until September 20, then fell precipitously to the low 20% range by early October. It also dropped sharply again in the last week, due to Campbell's repudiation of the Tory ads that drew attention to Chrétien's facial palsy as well as to her public criticism of Brian Mulroney and other leading Conservatives.[14]

The timing of these developments is crucial. Although Campbell made mistakes from the very beginning, most notably her comment on the first day of the campaign that unemployment could be expected to stay high for years,[15] these early mistakes neither benefitted Reform nor particularly hurt the Tories. Reform did not move ahead until Campbell began to vacate the right. Similarly, the Conservative mistakes at the end of the campaign, which had no ideological bearing, moved voters to the Liberals and the Bloc Québécois, not to Reform. While the implosion of the Conservatives raised several waves that pushed voters in different directions, the wave that carried Reform forward was clearly caused by the vacuum on the right that resulted from Campbell's mid-campaign decisions.

However, it would be misleading to attribute Reform's progress during the campaign solely to the mistakes of the Conservatives. Those mistakes were necessary for Reform's success but not sufficient. Reform could profit from them because, at the crucial time, Manning's statements had the effect of positioning the party on the right. Whether intentionally or not, he invaded from the right with perfect timing.

As planned, Manning began the campaign with a "Let the People Speak" phase. "In this election," he said on the opening day, "don't let anyone else tell you what the agenda is. This time, *you tell* the oldline politicians what is important and what is not. *You tell* the oldline politicians what is good for us and what isn't. *You tell* the oldline politicians what they can do with their political correctness!"[16] He then pursued this theme for about a week in an initial tour of Canada's major cities. Although he did not say much about policy during this phase, and the party did not move ahead in the polls, it may have been a useful exercise, allowing him to reconnoitre the landscape, so to speak, while he crisscrossed the country. It also allowed Reform supporters to express conservative sentiments without the leader having to endorse them explicitly.

Meanwhile, Ted Byfield and I kept up our campaign to steer Manning to the right. On September 14, we were both quoted in the Vancouver *Sun*. I asked, "When is the last time Preston spoke out about bilingualism, about multiculturalism, taxes, immigration?" Byfield commented: "If they [Reform] go back to where they started from — a small-c party prepared to question the assumptions of small-l liberal Canada — they will probably do well. If they say that they are not like that at all — they'll lose and they should."[17] Two days later, the *Calgary Herald* ran a provocative question on the front page: "When was the last time the word Western crossed Preston's lips?" In response, Manning acknowledged that the party was concerned about his apparent reluctance to talk about Reform's policies; "there is the feeling on the part of some of our people that maybe we have backed off."[18] Shortly thereafter, he veered sharply to the right. In a speech in his own riding on September 18, he touched on bilingualism, multiculturalism, and immigration, as well as fiscal responsibility and the Triple-E Senate.[19] More importantly — probably the turning point in the Reform campaign — he re-released the Zero in Three plan in a speech on September 20 in

Peterborough, Ontario. Setting up an empty chair for Kim Campbell, Manning quipped: "We have done all the homework on this and all she has to do is to take notes."[20] The *Globe and Mail* again endorsed the plan, as it had done in the spring, giving Reform's campaign a major boost:

> Reform is the one party to date to trust Canadians with the truth. This might not be so bold as it appears: the public is way ahead of the major parties on this issue. Indeed, if there is one candidate in this election who is truly offering "hope," that much-advertised elixir, it is Mr. Manning: hope that the economy might one day break out of the death spiral of high debt and higher taxes, as much as the hope that Canadian politics might climb out of the slough of cynicism and deception in which it has been wallowing for so long. The other parties might do well, as Mr. Manning advises, to "take notes."[21]

The Zero in Three package, released at just the time that Campbell was giving up the ground of deficit reduction, was bound to position Reform firmly on the right. The other parties attacked it so vigorously that it took on a life of its own and set the tone for the rest of Reform's campaign. In being forced to defend various aspects of Zero in Three, particularly the controversial cuts to old age security and unemployment insurance, Manning had to appear as a conservative critic of social programs.

Interestingly, just as he had said he would,[22] he made efforts to go beyond the "slash and burn" tone of Zero in Three.[23] Only a few days after his Peterborough speech, he started talking about hope and "the light at the end of the tunnel."[24] But the media were not interested; they wanted to report the controversy over Zero in Three. Manning made one last try, delivering his New Economy speech to students at Trinity Western University in Langley, B.C., on October 8, but again the media were not interested.[25] Having effectively put the party on the right, Manning could no longer position it elsewhere.

In any case, it would almost certainly be wrong to think of Manning intentionally positioning the party anywhere in particular on an ideological spectrum. Since he holds that left, right, and centre are irrelevant categories, he does not strive for ideological consistency. Hence the variety of positions on various issues that he adopted during the campaign. Some of these positions were definitely on the right, even quite far to the right, as when he recommended the partial privatization of health care,[26] demanded that the annual flow of immigrants be cut in half,[27] and called for violent offenders to be put on "lifetime parole."[28] At other times he sounded rather middle-of-the-road, as when he talked about hope, "the light at the end of the tunnel," and the generic positions of the New Economy speech. And when he mused about Canada's unilateral withdrawal from NATO,[29] a position long advocated by the NDP, he seemed to flirt with the left. However, while Manning was his usual eclectic self during the campaign, the overall impression his statements created situated the party on the right; and that positioning, coupled with Campbell's evacuation of the same territory, allowed Reform to dominate the right in much of the West and rural Ontario, which became the key to winning seats. In that sense, Manning invaded from the right, even if it was not his intention.

Of course, this strategy by itself never had the potential to win the party enough seats to form a government. Throughout the campaign, concern about the deficit remained the top priority of only a minority of voters. For example, in a ComQuest poll carried out October 11 to 14, 57% of respondents said that "the government should invest money in job programs and training programs, even if it means increasing the deficit," while 31% said that "the government should concentrate on reducing the deficit, even if it means more unemployment."[30] Around the same time, Environics found that 41% of respondents named unemployment as the most important issue, while 22% named the deficit the most important issue.[31] In emphasizing the deficit, Reform was appealing only to a minority of voters, but a minority concentrated geographically in Alberta and British Columbia,[32] and demographically in small towns and middle- to upper-income suburban residential areas. The concentration was sufficient to allow a party to win seats if it could come to "own" the deficit issue, as Reform eventually did. Thus the strategy worked well for breaking into the system, although a broader base of support will be necessary if Reform is ever to fulfill Manning's dream of forming a government.

As he had promised during the summer, Manning put much emphasis on the idea of minority government in the final phase of the campaign. He repeatedly called upon voters to deny the Liberals a majority, thereby letting Reform hold the balance of power and become the "fiscal conscience" of Parliament.[33] He also suggested that voters should make Reform the official Opposition by giving them more seats than the Bloc Québécois: "It is absolutely imperative that the balance of power in any minority Parliament be held by federalists rather than separatists. This is the way Reform can 'beat the BQ' even though we are not yet present in Quebec."[34]

Even though Manning pushed these themes hard in the final days, they do not seem to have attracted any further support; as Figure 8-1 shows, Reform's share of the vote remained at the level achieved in the middle of the campaign. This reinforces the view that dominating the right was the key to Reform's success in the 1993 election.

However, we must not lose sight of the nuances involved in the general idea of dominating the right; a number of issue clusters are involved in the broad concept of conservatism. Using methods that are too technical to discuss in this book, the Canadian National Election Study team measured the ideological differences between Reform and Conservative voters outside Quebec.[35] By far the biggest differences were in attitudes pertaining to the welfare state and "out groups" (the latter included attitudes towards the French language and Quebec, affirmative action for racial minorities, and admission of more immigrants). It is interesting that Reformers and Conservatives were strongly differentiated on these issues even though they did not figure prominently in the campaign, and Manning spoke little about them except for his suggestion of cutting immigration levels in half. The pattern of Reform support was obviously influenced not just by the campaign but by the general profile that the party had acquired over its history.

The welfare-state cluster included attitudes towards cutting programs such as health care, pensions, and unemployment insurance for the sake of deficit reduction. Reform voters were much more willing than Conservative voters to accept cuts in these areas. However, on questions about deficit spending that did not specify cuts to welfare programs, Reformers and Conservatives offered very similar responses. This makes sense in relation to the positions of the two party leaders. Both called for balanced budgets, but Campbell seemed to imply that social programs could be protected from cuts, whereas Manning was frank about the need to cut OAS and UI.

If Reform's positioning was necessary for success, it was not the sole factor. It was also essential to execute the campaign competently, to avoid making mistakes that might have turned away voters who were sympathetic on ideological grounds. Hence, it is worth looking at some of the practical things that Manning and Reform did right during the campaign.

First, the leaders' debate. There is no evidence that Manning's marginal presence in the French debate made any difference to the campaign; but in the English debate he turned in a performance which, if not brilliant, was sufficient under the circumstances. Clearly the most relaxed of the five leaders, he deliberately acted in an informal way, calling the other participants by their first names. He also asked questions of the others and sometimes tried to mediate in arguments, rather than simply taking positions and denouncing other opinions. Some viewers may have found this approach odd; others may have recognized it as Manning's attempt to get away from overt conflict. Media pundits were not impressed. The *Globe and Mail* wrote that "Mr. Manning did not have a good debate,"[36] and *Sun* columnist Bob Fife gave him a B-, higher only than the C he gave Kim Campbell.[37] But of course the real test was the impact on public opinion; and the data suggest that, while Chrétien won the debates (but not in an overwhelming way), Manning did well enough to preserve the momentum of the Reform campaign. A week after the event, Environics collected the following responses in its tracking poll:

Table 8-1
Perceived Winner of Leaders' Debates

	French	English
None/all the same/no opinion	44	38
Jean Chrétien	29	24
Kim Campbell	6	16
Preston Manning	—	12
Lucien Bouchard	18	2
Audrey McLaughlin	1	7

SOURCE: Environics tracking poll, October 11, 1993.

These results were quite satisfactory for Manning. First of all, about 40% of respondents perceived no clear winner in either debate. Manning did better in the English debate than either Bouchard or McLaughlin, both of whom had had extensive parliamentary experience, thus showing that he "belonged" in the forum. According to the data, he did not do as well as Campbell, but the two leaders were in entirely different situations. The Conservatives were in free fall; to rebound, Campbell needed a big victory, which she did not get. Manning had started from a low base of voter support amid low expectations. Now that he was gaining strength rapidly, he had only to consolidate his position, which he did.

In the domain of advertising, Reform did well by doing little. The national campaign spent only the $400,000 extracted from the constituency associations during the summer. It stuck to the five ads that had been prepared in advance and did not attempt to fine tune or replace them. Nor did it bring out new ads during the course of the campaign in order to attack other parties or to respond to attacks on Reform. The ads caught the better side of Preston Manning and the Reform party — simple, unpretentious, with a quirky sense of humour.

Nothing indicates that the ads changed any votes, but they successfully avoided the mistakes that had marred Reform's advertising efforts during the referendum campaign. There were no more leader's talking heads, implying that Manning was the party. And there were no manipulative slogans like the "Mulroney deal." This may not sound like much, but it represented a positive achievement in a campaign in which for all parties the ads that had the greatest effect were ones that backfired, most notably the early NDP ads depicting people's alleged rage against Mulroney's policies and the last-minute Conservative attacks on Jean Chrétien. It is worth noting that Reform, without polling and advertising expertise, managed to avoid the blunders made by older parties with much more experience, money, and professional talent. Have we entered a new minimalist age in which less is more?

The Reform Party's leader's tour also proved remarkably successful in light of the meagre resources available to finance it. Until the final week of the campaign, Manning and his small entourage — usually about half a dozen people — flew by commercial airliner because the party could not afford to charter a jet.[38] Volunteers did almost all the organizational work, both locally and at the national office. The tour could have been a disaster, with daily stories about lost luggage, missed appointments, and late rallies, all accompanied by unflattering photographs. But none of this happened. Travel arrangements worked, meetings went off on schedule, and Manning attracted large crowds everywhere, even though admission was usually charged for his speaking engagements. Again, minimalism triumphed.

Another Reform success story was fundraising. As explained previously, the national office had a war chest of little more than $100,000 on the eve of the election. The party is philosophically opposed to going into debt, and in any case banks had refused to advance it any funds based on the rebates expected from Elections Canada. Thus, the national office canvassed the constituencies to pay for a minimal advertising campaign, and several well-to-do Calgary businessmen were discreetly approached for large contributions to create a fund for the leader's tour. But money started to pour in once the writ was dropped. On October 14, the party's daily bulletin reported that the national office had taken in about $1.7 million and the constituencies about $3.5 million and projected an overall fundraising total of about $6 million for the entire campaign.[39] The party, in fact, ended 1993 with a surplus of $1.03 million in the bank even before receiving its refund from Elections Canada.[40] This represented a remarkable achievement in view of the fact that Canada's other federal parties routinely go millions of dollars into debt to finance their campaigns. It seemed even more remarkable because there were few large donations from corporations and none from unions.

Although the Reform campaign went smoothly most of the time, on three occasions mistakes were made that required damage control. First was a meeting in Medicine Hat, Alberta, on September 25, when Manning responded to a question on the implications of Reform's health-care policy. He was reported as saying that the party "would remove federal roadblocks to provinces allowing private health-care insurance — and would open the door to extra billing, user fees and private hospitals."[41] This had to count as a serious mistake within the terms of the Reform campaign plan. The platform and the Zero in Three package had been designed to maintain federal transfer payments for health care at their present levels. The strategy was to deflect criticism on health care by presenting Reform as the only party willing to commit itself to making no further cuts in federal funding. When asked about the issue, Manning could have said as much and stopped. Reform was already running big risks by attacking federal programs such as OAS and UI; nothing required Manning to take additional risks by speculating in detail about what the provinces might do if a Reform government removed some of the constraints in the Canada Health Act.

Manning's response upset the other members of the campaign management committee, as well as many candidates, and they demanded that he repair the damage. But he made things worse in an interview with the *Globe and Mail* that generated new headlines: "Manning Targets Health Care," "Two-Tier Plan Would Allow User Fees, Private Programs," and "Reform Proposes Two-Tiered Health Care."[42] During the rest of the campaign, he was forced to spend much time repeating that Reform was not proposing an American-style system:

> We would let the provinces and the electors of those provinces make those decisions. But this idea that we are promoting American-style health care or deductibles or user fees is not correct.
>
> No province in their right mind would initiate an American-style health-care system.[43]

Although there is no evidence in the polling data that Manning's gaffe caused a loss of support, it may have contributed to the levelling off that took place at the end of September. At the very least, it gave the other parties a weapon to use against Reform by diverting Manning from the things he was supposed to be talking about. It could have been a major setback, particularly since damage control was so slow. That it did not do more harm was perhaps due to the fact that Campbell committed multiple errors in the same period, the most notable of which was her statement that an election was the wrong time to talk about social policy. At least Manning looked straightforward and honest by comparison.

The second episode resembled the first, except that it was less costly. Immediately after the leaders' debate, Manning told a reporter that he personally favoured taking Canada out of NATO and that the Reform Party would "quite possibly" adopt this position, even though the Blue Book offers unequivocal support for NATO and NORAD.[44] Given the low salience of foreign policy and defence matters in Canadian public opinion, this probably would not have had any measurable impact on voting intentions; but it had the potential to work mischief within the party, whose membership contains a sizeable number of retired military people, as well as many conservatives for whom NATO is an important issue. Moreover, it begged the question of how the leader of a populist party, whose agenda is supposedly contained in the Blue Book, could cavalierly differ with such an important policy, without warning and without offering a rationale. By comparison, in the period when Ed Broadbent differed with the NDP's policy of withdrawing from NATO, he dealt with the disagreement much more carefully.

In this instance, damage control was quicker and more effective than in the medicare episode. The very same day, Manning provided a clarification that what he really wanted was a formal review of Canada's defence policy to determine what priorities could be maintained. He admitted that he had made a mistake in speculating about leaving NATO, and that was the end of the affair.[45]

The third episode of damage control involved John Beck, Reform candidate in the Ontario riding of York Centre. When speaking at Osgoode Hall law school at York University on October 13, Manning was confronted by a student with evidence of Beck's racist remarks: "I feel the time has come for white Anglo-Saxons to get involved. . . . We're destroying ourselves hourly . . . and these people [immigrants] coming from another country, one evil is just as bad as another."[46] Within an hour, Beck had been contacted and had resigned under pressure.

The Reform constituency association in York Centre was very weak, and Beck had been nominated without opposition during the summer of 1993. To be more precise, he received 14 votes at a nomination meeting attended by 23 people on July 13. Contrary to some statements,[47] Beck had in fact filled out the candidate questionnaire and had been interviewed, but in the absence of a real contest his racist views had not come to light. According to Virgil Anderson, Beck must have deliberately concealed his true opinions because they did not surface in either the questionnaire or the interview.

As soon as the incident at Osgoode Hall took place, the Tories deluged journalists with collections of controversial quotations by other Reform candidates, the most damaging of which was a statement by Hugh Ramolla, the Reform candidate in Burlington, who had shouted "Hit her, Craig" at another Reformer when an NDP candidate would not yield the floor at a meeting.[48] Manning publicly rebuked Ramolla but did not force him to resign. (In an unrelated incident, Ramolla was convicted after the election of assaulting his wife.)

It is unclear whether the Beck/Ramolla episode caused Reform support to erode. The national polls consolidated in Figure 8-1 show an essentially flat trendline for Reform during October. The Environics tracking poll shows Reform moving upwards from 17% to 22% of the national vote during the seven days immediately following the incident, then falling off a few points thereafter.[49] The Canadian National Election Study tracking poll shows Reform climbing steadily in early October and reaching a peak of over 30% (in Canada outside Quebec) on October 16, then falling back. In the opinion of the researchers who analyzed this data, had the election been held on October 16, Reform "would certainly have formed the official Opposition."[50] With these discrepancies among polls, it would not be safe to make a hasty judgment, particularly since the Beck/Ramolla episode was only one, and not the most prominent, of the many stories being reported in the media. Further research may establish a clearer picture of the forces at play.

The results of the 1993 election can be used to evaluate the success of the various Reform strategies. Parties put together electoral coalitions by means of the policy positions and other signals that they transmit to the voting public; thus, by reversing the reasoning process, we can use the composition of the Reform coalition to judge the effectiveness of the various signals that the party sent out.

Something can be learned simply from looking at the pattern of Reform victories. Of the 52 seats won by Reform candidates in 1993, 35 had been won in 1988 by Conservatives, and 17 by New Democrats. Of the 17 seats that had previously belonged to New Democrats, 15 were in British Columbia; and at least five of these were in districts that had usually voted Conservative in the past but had elected NDP candidates in 1988 when Reform candidates siphoned off some of the previous Conservative vote.[51] Superficially, it may seem as if Reform appealed mainly to former Conservative voters but also had some ability to draw from the NDP; however, other sources of data show that, while the Conservative connection is valid, Reform actually attracted very few crossover voters from the NDP. Reform was able to take seats from the NDP because the NDP's support collapsed, but that does not mean that previous NDP voters themselves went over to Reform.

That Reform drew votes from the Conservatives is corroborated by a closer look at Ontario, where Reform won only one seat and did not come within 4,000 votes of winning any others. Reformers did finish second in 56 Ontario ridings, but many of these second-place showings were so far back as to be relatively meaningless. A more significant indication of Reform strength was to get at least half as many votes as the winner in that riding. This happened in 23 constituencies, of which 22 had been Conservative in 1988 and one had been NDP — Ed Broadbent's old riding of Oshawa.

Gross election results also yield some insights into the geographic composition of the Reform coalition. The party elected 24 members in British Columbia, 22 in Alberta, four in Saskatchewan, one in Manitoba, and one in Ontario; it did not come close to victory anywhere in Atlantic Canada; and it did not run candidates in Quebec. This was obviously a party based on strength in the West, particularly the prosperous provinces of Alberta and British Columbia.

This impression is substantiated by Reform's percentage of votes in the nine provinces in which it ran candidates, listed below from west to east:

British Columbia	36.1%
Alberta	52.0
Saskatchewan	27.3
Manitoba	22.4
Ontario	20.1
New Brunswick	8.5
Nova Scotia	13.3
Prince Edward Island	1.5
Newfoundland	1.0

Allowing for Reform's strength in its home province of Alberta, there was a definite west-to-east gradient in this distribution of votes, which must be explained by the party's history, since issues of western regionalism hardly played any role in the campaign.

There also was a rural cast to the Reform vote. Its only urban sweep occurred in Calgary, where the party won all six seats. No Reformers won in Victoria, Winnipeg, Regina, Saskatoon, or any of the major cities of Ontario; and only two out of six succeeded in Edmonton. The pattern was particularly obvious in metropolitan Vancouver, where Reform won all the suburban seats but lost seven inner-city ridings. It looks as if the Reform coalition brought together rural and middle- to upper-income suburban voters.

Again, the evidence from Ontario reinforces this view. In only one of 39 highly urbanized Ontario ridings[52] did a Reform candidate get at least half as many votes as the winner, whereas Reform candidates managed to reach that level in 22 cases out of the remaining 60. In relative terms, Reform did best in Ontario in the outer suburbs of Toronto, the cottage country of central Ontario, and the Niagara peninsula — all formerly Conservative bastions.

Based on these simple facts, we can make some preliminary judgments about the various strategic conceptions mentioned earlier in this book. Even though Manning hardly mentioned western issues in the campaign, The Party of the West does very well in explaining Reform's performance — 51 of 52 seats. The Party of the Right also does well; it seems as if Reform took over much of the traditional Conservative vote in Ontario and the West. Manning's notion of The Party of the People may also be of some importance in accounting for Reform's ability to attract minor but useful support away from the Liberals and NDP. These were secondary components of the Reform coalition but might be credited with supplying the margin of victory in a few close races. In contrast, Manning's notion of the Hinterland Party is not borne out by the evidence. There was, to be sure, abundant rural support for Reform, but not in remote, resource-producing regions. Reform did poorly in the Yukon, Northwest Territories, northern Ontario, and Atlantic Canada — all areas that should have been sympathetic to Reform under the hinterland hypothesis. Finally, if The Party of English Canada had been fully effective in this election, Reform should have been able to elect members, or at least pull votes, much more evenly across all provinces outside Quebec. As The Party of English Canada, Reform's vote should have looked much more like the No vote in the referendum than it actually did.

These preliminary assessments can be refined by looking at the data in a more systematic way. Table 8-2 displays the correlation coefficients between the 1993 Reform percentage of the vote in each constituency and the percentages of the votes obtained by the various parties in the same ridings in 1988. The correlations are calculated separately for each province (because of their small size, Saskatchewan and Manitoba are treated as if they constituted a single province) and then collectively for the five provinces together. Atlantic Canada is not included in the analysis because Reform contested only 20 of 32 seats in the region and nowhere finished higher than third place; its support in this region was too tentative for much profit to be derived from detailed analysis.

Table 8-2

Correlation of 1993 Reform Vote Percentages with 1988 Percentages of Various Parties by Constituency

1988 Percentages

1993 Reform %	Liberal %	NDP %	PC %	Reform %	(PC + Reform) %
B.C.	-.45*	-.20	.45*	.47*	.61**
Alberta	-.71**	-.79**	.52*	.63**	.86**
Sask./Man.	-.50*	-.20	.87**	.54*	.84**
Ontario	-.60**	-.14	.61**	____	.61**
All provinces	-.79**	-.07	.60**	.73**	.80**

* p < .01
** p < .001

SOURCE: Reform percentages for 1993 were calculated from returns printed in the GLOBE AND MAIL, October 27, 1993. Other data were taken from Monroe Eagles, James P. Bickerton, Alain G. Gagnon, and Patrick J. Smith, THE ALMANAC OF CANADIAN POLITICS (Peterborough: Broadview Press, 1991).

The correlation coefficient is a statistical measure that ranges between 1.0 and -1.0. A correlation of 1.0 means that the variations in one variable are exactly mirrored in another; where one is high or low, the other is also high or low. A positive correlation close to, but less than, 1.0 means there is a close, but not exact, relationship. In contrast, a correlation of -1.0 means that two variables are exactly but inversely related; one is low where the other is high, and vice versa. A correlation close to, but not reaching, -1.0 means a close but not exact inverse relationship. A correlation of 0 means that two variables are unrelated, that there is no pattern in the variation of their values.

The most striking finding is that in each province, as well as in all provinces taken together, a strong positive correlation exists between the 1993 Reform vote and the 1988 PC vote. It is also noteworthy that the correlation can be increased by treating the 1988 PC plus Reform votes as a single variable, i.e., two wings of an already dividing bloc of conservative-minded voters. The correlation of .80 for all provinces between 1993 Reform % and 1988 (PC + Reform) % is, as these things go, very strong; it means that 64% of the variance in the 1993 Reform vote can be explained by this relationship. Many well-accepted scientific findings are based on less robust statistical associations. In simple terms, Reform generally did well in the same ridings where the PCs used to do well.

Not surprisingly, there was an almost equally strong negative correlation (-.79) between the 1993 Reform vote and the 1988 Liberal vote. Again, in simple language, this means that Reform had trouble attracting support in Liberal ridings, which tend to be populated by Roman Catholics, Jews, francophones, and visible minorities. Interestingly, however, the correlation between the 1993 Reform vote and the 1988 NDP vote was strongly negative only in Alberta (-.79) and virtually zero overall (-.07). This probably reflects the fact that there are several distinct types of NDP voters — public-sector workers; unionized industrial and resource-extraction workers; Saskatchewan wheat farmers; the urban poor; ideological activists (feminists, environmentalists, gay rights, etc.) — distributed in a highly uneven way across the country.

We can use a similar approach to explore the demographics of the Reform electoral coalition. Table 8-3 displays the correlation coefficients between the 1993 Reform vote and several constituency-level demographic indicators. "Rural" represents a simple dichotomy: urban seats are Victoria, metro-Vancouver, Calgary, Edmonton, Regina, Saskatoon, Winnipeg, metro-Toronto, Ottawa, Hamilton, London, Windsor, Thunder Bay, and Sudbury; everything else is classified as rural. Hence "Rural" really is a composite of rural and suburban, i.e., outside the central city. "% French" refers to the percentage of people in the riding who speak mainly French at home. "% Immigrant" refers to the percentage of individuals in the riding born outside of Canada. "Average Family Income" is based on the 1985 income of husband, wife, and any unmarried children still living at home; it includes common-law unions. "% Low Income" refers to the percentage of families in the riding whose income is below the Statistics Canada low-income threshold; this figure varies from province to province and between urban and rural areas because it is adjusted for the local cost of living.

Table 8-3

Correlation of 1993 Reform Vote Percentages with Various Demographic Variables by Constituency

1993 Reform	% Rural	% French	% Immigrant	Average Family Income	% Low Income
B.C.	.70**	-.10	-.71**	-.11	-.59**
Alberta	.65**	.02	-.72**	.04	-.62**
Sask./Man.	.51*	.13	-.60**	-.22	-.20
Ontario	.40**	-.40**	-.24	-.05	-.48**
All provinces	.31**	-.26**	-.32**	-.09	-.07

* p < .01
** p < .001

SOURCE: Reform percentages for 1993 were calculated from returns printed in the GLOBE AND MAIL, October 27, 1993. Other data were taken from Monroe Eagles, James P. Bickerton, Alain G. Gagnon, and Patrick J. Smith, THE ALMANAC OF CANADIAN POLITICS (Peterborough: Broadview Press, 1991).

Interpretation of this table enriches our preliminary conclusions about the demographics of Reform support. Its non-urban character stands out clearly; the central city was not the place to go looking for Reform votes in the last election. Even more striking, and also not surprising, is the strong negative correlation of the Reform vote with the percentage of immigrants, who, of course, tend to be concentrated in urban areas. In Ontario, but not in the West, there is also a moderate negative correlation with the percentage of francophone voters — again not surprising in view of Reform's stand on bilingualism.

Table 8-4
Reform Support Indices for Various Groups

Geographic	Index of Support
Atlantic Provinces	31
Ontario	96
Prairies	229*
British Columbia	197*

Age	
18–25	87
26–35	102
36–45	96
46–55	125*
56–65	91
65+	91

Sex	
Male	122*
Female	78

Education	
Elementary only	80
Some secondary	94
Completed secondary	109
Some university	92
Completed university	93

Family income	Index of Support
<$20,000	75
$20–$40,000	81
$40–$60,000	121*
$60–$80,000	90
>$80,000	128*

Occupation

Homemaker exclusively	103
Student	27
Retired	90
Unemployed	92
Professional	109
Management/self-employed	107
Sales	150*
Clerical	93
Skilled labour	104
Unskilled labour	116
Farmer	156*

Community size

500,000+	89
100–500,000	104
30–100,000	96
10–30,000	135*
1–10,000	136*
Rural	96

The relationship with income is more complex. Overall, and within each province, virtually no relationship exists between the Reform vote and average family income. However, there is a fairly strong negative correlation, except in Saskatchewan/Manitoba, between the percentage of Reform vote and the percentage of low-income families (who tend to be concentrated in city centres as well as some remote rural areas). This combination is consistent with the findings from studies of the Reform party, which indicate that Reformers tend to come from the employed (or retired) middle class.[53] One meets few single mothers, welfare recipients, or unemployed people in the party; but one also meets few of the really well-to-do — executives of large corporations and professionals such as lawyers and doctors. People with very high incomes tend to prefer the Liberals or Conservatives. A similar table of correlations for those two parties (not printed here) would show moderate positive correlations for the Conservatives in British Columbia, Alberta, and Ontario, and for the Liberals in British Columbia and Saskatchewan/Manitoba, between vote percentage and average family income in the riding.

We can supplement the constituency data with data about individuals drawn from a national sample survey of 1,500 respondents conducted immediately after the election by Harold Clarke, who is an expert on Canadian voting behaviour.[54] Table 8-4 contains some of Clarke's data reworked to emphasize the tendency of various geographic and demographic groups to vote Reform. A support index of 100 means that the members of the group voted Reform at the same rate as the whole sample (18.7%). An index of 200 would mean that members of the group were twice as likely as the national average to vote Reform; an index of 50 would mean that they were half as likely to do so. An asterisk is placed after any index larger than 120 to highlight the groups that gave especially strong support to Reform.

The most obvious pattern in the data is the strength of the Reform Party in the West; beyond that, this looks like a typical profile of support for a conservative party, with some interesting populist variations. The strong support from those aged 46 to 55 — the period during which most people's lifetime earnings peak — makes sense in light of the Reform Party's message of economic independence and reduced reliance on government. A gender gap — greater support from men than women — is also typical for conservative parties in the late 20th century. But the educational, occupational, and income aspects of Reform support are not quite what one would expect from a conservative party. For example, support by educational group peaks with those who have completed secondary school and falls off for those who have attended university. Support tends to rise with family income but not in a straightforward way; it goes down for the $60,000 to $80,000 group. And the pattern of support from occupational groups is particularly complex. There is as much Reform support among skilled and unskilled workers as among managerial and professional groups. The occupational groups that are most strongly Reform are sales personnel and farmers — both highly individualistic occupations. Finally, there is a definite small-town character to Reform support; it is strongest in towns with a population of less than 30,000.

Although much more statistical analysis by survey-research specialists will be necessary, the data contain strong hints of the kind of coalition projected by Stephen Harper in his 1989 strategy paper. In the 1993 election, there were both middle-class and working-class Reform voters, and they could be found in both cities (especially suburbs) and rural areas. What held these disparate groups together? Probably a positive orientation towards the private-sector economy and traditional moral values, although this needs to be tested by further research.

The Clarke survey also asked respondents how they voted in 1988, which brings us to a final test of different models of strategy. Did Reform recruit its voters mainly from former Conservative supporters, as one would expect of The Party of the Right? Or were they more or less equally distributed among former supporters of all parties, as one would expect of The Party of the People or The Party of English Canada? Table 8-5 contains the answer:

Table 8-5
1993 Vote by 1988 Vote (Omitting Quebec)

1993 Vote	1988 Vote		
	Liberal	**PC**	**NDP**
Liberal	79	26	41
PC	3	33	5
NDP	3	3	43
Reform	15	38	11
	100%	100%	100%
n =	228	323	202

gamma = 0.67
Kendall's tau = 0.48
p < .0000

In 1993 the Liberals were successful in holding their 1988 support, but a mere 33% of those who voted Conservative in 1988 repeated that choice in 1993, as compared to 38% who moved to Reform. Voters from other parties also moved to Reform, but on a much smaller scale: there was a 15% defection rate from the Liberals and an 11% defection rate from the NDP. This shows that The Party of the Right offers a better explanation of the Reform vote than does The Party of the People or The Party of English Canada because Reform recruited much more heavily from the Conservatives than from the Liberals or NDP. On the other hand, recruitment from the Liberals and NDP was more than negligible; votes from these two parties proved essential to winning some close races. In that sense, Manning's depiction of Reform as more than a party of the right may have had some payoff if it encouraged even a minor degree of defection from the Liberals and the NDP.

It is also worth looking at retention and defection rates just in the four western provinces, where Reform won almost all its seats (Table 8-6):

Table 8-6
1993 Vote by 1988 Vote (Four Western Provinces)

	1988 Vote		
1993 Vote	**Liberal**	**PC**	**NDP**
Liberal	66	18	26
PC	4	23	4
NDP	2	6	61
Reform	28	55	9
	100%	100%	100%
n =	53	162	64

gamma = 0.67
Kendall's tau + 0.52
p < .0000

In the West, the Conservatives lost a massive 55% of their vote to Reform, and the Liberals 28%, as compared to only 9% for the NDP. Again, Reform recruited mainly from the Conservatives, but obtained a useful supplement from the Liberals and to a lesser extent the NDP.

The data can also be turned around to look at the Reform coalition in another way. Nationally, fully 70% of 1988 voters who chose Reform in 1993 had voted either Conservative or Reform in 1988. (In this survey, all respondents who had voted Reform in 1988 did so again in 1993, but the number was very small, only 11). For the West, the percentage of 1993 Reform voters who had voted Conservative or Reform in 1988 rises to 81%. The overall conclusion is inescapable. The Reform vote, especially in areas where the party was successful, was basically a secession movement from the Conservative Party, which started in a small way in 1988 and reached large proportions in 1993. Switchers from other parties were a useful supplement in tight races, but not numerous enough to affect the character of the coalition.

Finally, Clarke's data show that the shift from the NDP to Reform that allegedly took place in British Columbia was illusory. Only 9% of those in western Canada who voted NDP in 1988 changed to Reform in 1993 and in British Columbia the figure stood at only 8%. Almost three times more defecting NDP voters went to the Liberals than to Reform. True, the NDP lost 15 seats to Reform, but not through direct vote transfers. While the NDP in British Columbia was losing votes mainly to the Liberals, Reform was holding the vote it achieved in 1988, picking up more than half of the 1988 Conservative vote and about one-third of the 1988 Liberal vote, but adding less than a tenth of the 1988 NDP vote.

We have now accumulated enough evidence to make a reasonable assessment of the various models of new-party entry discussed in this book. They are listed below in declining order of their importance in the 1993 election.

• The Party of the West was crucial to electoral success, even though western issues did not figure prominently in the campaign. Being a western party gave Reform the territorial concentration necessary to win seats. Without that western base, it might have gotten 20% of the vote across the board, as it did in Ontario, and yet have won hardly any seats. The party must be ever conscious of its western base as it tries to sink deeper roots in Ontario and Atlantic Canada, and to enter Quebec for the first time. If it jeopardizes its western base, it threatens its very existence.

Ironically, however, being national also seems necessary to western success. As a purely western party in 1988, Reform did not elect anyone. As a national party in 1993, it elected 52 MPs, 51 of them in the West. It appears that both parts of Manning's original formula — a national party and a western base — are essential.

• Invading from the right worked in 1993. The Conservatives failed to meet the challenge, veered instead towards the centre, and virtually destroyed themselves. Reform now has a unique opportunity to replace the Conservatives as the main party of the right, at least in English Canada. To do so, it must broaden and deepen its policies by converting the Blue Book, which is a preliminary sketch, into a full-fledged conservative philosophy. If Manning's non-ideological bent interferes with this process, it could jeopardize the opportunity to establish long-term dominance of the right. However, initial signs in 1994 were that most members of the newly elected Reform caucus intended to go in a conservative direction.

• The Party of the People, although the major strategy in Manning's mind, was only a secondary factor in the 1993 election. It probably helped attract some support from the Liberals and NDP, but that was the icing, not the cake. Regardless of its relative importance, however, it will continue to dominate

Manning's thinking and will thus affect the way the Reform Party presents itself in the public arena.

• The Party of English Canada undoubtedly contributed to Reform's explosive growth during the era of the Meech Lake and Charlottetown accords. However, it had little to do with the 1993 election, which was fought, at least outside Quebec, on economic and ideological issues rather than ethnic and linguistic ones. Still, it could again play a larger role in the future once the question of Quebec's independence comes back to the fore. Reform has already attracted the support of those ex-Conservatives most opposed to bilingualism and special status for Quebec. Another national unity crisis could trigger a similar exodus among Liberal and NDP voters if they thought their basic interests were threatened by the separation of Quebec.

• The Party of the Hinterland did not prove a useful model. Reform did poorly in the most remote, rural, poverty-stricken areas of Canada such as the Territories, the Maritimes, and northern Ontario, whereas it did very well in the affluent areas of metropolitan Vancouver and Calgary, and got promising results in the outer suburbs of Toronto. The emerging Reform coalition, if it continues to develop, will unite the restive taxpayers of suburbia with the traditionalist inhabitants of small-town Canada. The poor, the dependent, and those engaged in declining industries will likely look to parties of the left or centre to offer them largesse from the state.

9

Countdown to Victory?

Examination of Preston Manning's career as leader of the Reform Party, from the founding of the party in 1987 to its electoral breakthrough in 1993, leads to three main conclusions: First, Manning is driven by a monistic, trans-ideological, populist vision, which stems from his need to avoid conflict. He expresses that need in a theory of conflict mediation based on self-sacrifice, but in practice he leans closer to conflict suspension through trust in the leader's vision. He has integrated the personal, the religious, and the political to produce this unique vision, which, though unrealistic in many respects, is still his greatest asset. It is a formidable political weapon that he can use against opponents who lack a comparable worldview to orient their actions.

Second, paradoxically, the nature of Manning's vision drives him to operate in some respects like a conventional politician. The key to understanding the paradox is to realize that he only sees ideology as a means to his larger ends. Thus principles and policies become dispensable; they are not ends in themselves but devices for getting the leader closer to the ultimate goal of putting himself into power at the head of his populist movement. Consequently, Manning's political strategy is mainly a matter of timing and communications. It is based on giving expression to currents in public opinion that established politicians ignore and riding those currents as they turn into waves. It also involves sensing new waves as they begin to swell.

Third, Manning's populist vision, as well as his conception of strategy as timing, requires a highly personalized style of political leadership, which consists essentially of using people as sounding boards and ratification bodies. His preferred procedure could be called Triple R — "react, revise, ratify." He presents a draft of a policy or a proposal for a course of action, asks for reaction, goes away and revises it if necessary, then comes back and asks for ratification. Although he pays attention to what people tell him, and he does make changes, he retains control of the process. He wants to be the author at every stage from setting the agenda through conceptualizing the problem to choosing the exact words of the final document.

When he runs into obstacles, Manning resorts to an alternate version of Triple R that might be called "react, re-route, release." That is, if he does not get a policy ratified by one body, he will find or create a more compliant one. This style of leadership accounts for the fluid decision-making procedures that have marked the Reform Party from the beginning. The one constant in the flux of advisers, committees, task forces, and straw votes is Manning himself.

Manning has not changed since the 1993 election; his worldview, strategy, and leadership style remain exactly the same. To see this, let us look more closely at four important developments for the Reform Party in the first half of 1994: its performance as an opposition party in the House of Commons, Manning's problems with the Reform caucus, his Countdown to Victory expansion plan designed to win the next election, and the repositioning of the party on the Quebec issue that he carried out in June.

Manning's task as leader of an opposition party is rather different from what it was as leader of a new party trying to break into the system. Then he could set his own agenda, but now he must participate in the day-to-day activities of the House of Commons. If he is to be effective, he must work with the agenda established by the government.

Unfortunately, he is not particularly well prepared for the task. He comes out of the non-partisan political tradition of Alberta, in which all successful premiers have acted as if the opposition were irrelevant.[1] He first learned the art of politics by observing his father, as premier of Alberta, leading a government to which opposition was almost non-existent. His subsequent political experience lay in founding and leading his own party, where again he could establish the agenda. Before being elected in 1993, he had never served in a legislature or worked for a party that functioned as a legislative opposition. Now that he is in the House of Commons, he does not seem to particularly enjoy the role; he seldom speaks on the floor, and he spends most Mondays and Fridays in Calgary attending to other business.

Reinforcing this personal experience is Manning's conception of the role of the opposition, which he describes as putting forth "constructive alternatives." He has also called this "demonstrating Reform principles in practice"[2] and "giving Canadians a preview of what a Reform government would be like."[3] After a few months of the new Parliament, it has become clear that this implies a narrower approach to opposition than Canadians are familiar with. Opposition parties of the past (and the BQ in this Parliament) have conceived their role as:

- stating their own positions in preparation for future elections;
- exposing corruption and incompetence with the aim of damaging the government politically or even forcing ministerial resignations;
- mobilizing political opposition to governmental measures, thus leading to changes in policy and amendments to bills;
- obstructing the government, using up legislative time and thereby forcing the government to abandon projects that it does not have time to get through Parliament.

Of these four roles, only the first fits Manning's conception of the "constructive alternative" and giving a "preview" of a Reform government. Of course, there have been occasions when individual Reform MPs managed to embarrass the government, as when Myron Thompson exposed the wasteful use of government jets,[4] and Chuck Strahl and Paul Forseth revealed that Revenue Minister David Anderson was suing the government even as he sat in the cabinet.[5] Manning, however, appeared little involved in these episodes and did not lead the Reform caucus in a coordinated way to embarrass, hinder, or otherwise influence the government. One exception was his threat to begin a taxpayers' revolt if Paul Martin's first budget contained major revenue increases, a gesture that may have had some practical effect in forestalling new taxes.[6] But otherwise Manning let the Liberals have things pretty much their own way in the House of Commons in the first months of 1994.

An excellent example of this is the story of C-18, a bill the Liberals introduced in March to suspend the process of redistributing House of Commons seats. Under existing legislation, seats are supposed to be redistributed after every decennial census. The process is cumbersome because a separate commission is appointed in each province to make recommendations and hold public hearings before submitting a final report to

Parliament. Because of the slowness of the process, the Conservative government suspended any attempt to carry out a redistribution based on the 1991 census before the 1993 election, which thus had to be held in ridings based on the 1981 census returns.

When preliminary reports from provincial commissions became available in early 1993, there was considerable unhappiness in the Liberal caucus because of changes to existing riding boundaries. Sitting MPs always dislike such changes as they require the creation of new poll organizations and fundraising networks, and sometimes even pit sitting MPs against each other for renomination in new constituencies. Also, the proposals would have increased the size of the House from 295 to 301, with four new seats in Ontario (all in the fast-growing outer suburbs of Toronto) and two new seats in British Columbia. Some observers suggested that the Liberals were unhappy to see new seats go to areas where Reform was strong and were unhappy that, for the first time, Quebec's share of seats in the Commons would fall below 25% (75 of 301). Whatever the motives, the Liberals brought in C-18 to suspend the process for two years while the House of Commons considered alternatives. A delay of this length probably meant that no redistribution could be carried out before the next election, expected for 1997 or 1998.

It looked initially as if Reform might go along with the Liberals' attempts to get all-party support for C-18. Many Reformers would have been inconvenienced by the proposed changes, most notably caucus chair Deborah Grey, whose Beaver River riding would have disappeared altogether, and Preston Manning himself, whose Calgary Southwest riding boundaries would have been redrawn in the process of giving Calgary an extra seat. But those opposed to the bill prevailed in caucus, and a few Reformers conducted a minifilibuster against C-18, arguing that it would waste the $5 million already spent by provincial commissions, that it encouraged Liberal manipulation of the process, and that it would jeopardize the achievement of any redistribution before the next election.[7]

Reform's actions produced a small tactical victory by delaying third reading until after the Easter recess, thus allowing the provincial commissions to go into the public hearings stage of their proceedings. They forced the Liberals to use time allocation (closure) to pass the bill, making them look undemocratic.[8] They drew a little public attention to the issue and generated editorials condemning the government.[9] And they primed the issue for the Senate by inviting the Conservative majority in that body to offer further resistance. If Reform had gone along with the Liberals and Bloc Québécois in supporting C-18, it would have been virtually impossible for the Senate

Conservatives to stand in the way of an all-party consensus in the House.

Such is the stuff of opposition politics. A party that systematically pursues such tactics — not on every issue but on matters that fit within its profile — can exercise real influence on the policy process by delaying the government and forcing it to accept changes. It can also build its own support for the next election. The Liberals should know. They fought the Conservatives relentlessly, opportunistically, sometimes even absurdly from 1984 through 1993; now they are government and the Conservatives are history.

The most interesting thing about Reform's effort to derail C-18 was that Manning did not participate in it. He did not speak on the floor of the House, did not raise the matter in Question Period, did not issue a press release or hold a news conference. In brief he did nothing to block the bill. This undermined the political effect of the struggle because the media still see Manning as the only reliable indicator of what really matters to Reform. If he is not involved in an initiative, reporters regard it as a sidebar. Thus, when C-18 was finally amended to overcome objections raised in the Senate, the political credit went chiefly to the Conservatives rather than to Reform, even though Reform had initiated the struggle.

Another example of Manning's tendency to undermine his own caucus occurred in June, when the Reform caucus tried to hold up three pieces of Indian Affairs legislation — one transferring some departmental functions to bands in Manitoba, two others enacting the Yukon land claims settlement. This would have been an excellent opportunity to expand and communicate Reform's position on native rights, which has never been very clearly articulated; but instead Manning worked at cross purposes with the caucus. While they were combatting the Manitoba bill, he met with Manitoba Grand Chief Phil Fontaine and said, "It's not our intention to obstruct anything but to ask questions."[10] Then, a few days later, he cut Reform MP Herb Grubel loose when Grubel got into trouble in the debate on the Yukon bills. In trying to explain how Canada's Indian policy has created a culture of dependence, Grubel said, "We have been misguided when in the past we have given in to the demands of the native community to give them more physical goods, to allow them to live on their South Sea island equivalent," and also compared Canada to a well-meaning parent giving "too much money to . . . your teenagers."[11] Without even telephoning Grubel, Manning quickly called his remarks unacceptable and said they did not represent party policy.[12] Obviously, Grubel had chosen his words for shock effect, and Manning obviously wanted to distance himself; but saying that Grubel's views did not represent party policy was another matter altogether. The culture of dependence among Indians is a troubling phenomenon admitted even by strong supporters of native rights, as in Menno Boldt's recent book *Surviving as Indians*.[13] Given its overall emphasis on personal responsibility and the private sector, how could Reform policy not be concerned about dependence among natives? Later, Manning clouded the issue still further by commenting about the Yukon bills: "We aren't opposed in principle to what they're endeavouring to do. . . . Right now, our concern is more just that this is being too hastily done."[14]

Of course, the Liberals have the votes to pass whatever they want in the Commons; the point of trying to obstruct legislation is to mobilize political opposition against it outside Parliament (and sometimes to encourage resistance in the Senate, although probably not on these bills), as well as to use up time in order to force the government to make choices. But Manning's actions undermined the purpose of the caucus actions. He did not lead the floor fight, did not articulate a clear policy, and at crucial moments cast doubt on the caucus's aims. As a result, no clear statement of purpose came through to the public, even though Reform MPs spoke in great detail about their objections to the bills.

The reason that Manning offered little strategic leadership to the Reform caucus in combatting the legislative agenda of the government was that his interests in the House of Commons lay elsewhere. His priority was to create a public impression that Reform MPs constitute what he has sometimes called a "new breed" of politicians. This led to numerous symbolic and procedural breaks with parliamentary tradition:

• Reform MPs took a voluntary salary reduction, offered to opt out of the parliamentary pension plan, and declined to take advantage of many perks and junkets.[15]

• Manning rejected the car and driver that he could have had as leader of a recognized party.[16]

• The caucus decided to call its whip "coordinator" because it sounded less coercive.[17]

• Many Reform MPs participated in a grassroots swearing-in ceremony in their ridings in which they recited a pledge of allegiance to their constituents.[18]

• Manning did not appoint the customary critics to be caucus spokesmen on specific issues. Instead there was a much looser system of clusters of members interested in five broad areas: economic affairs, public finance, social affairs, natural resources, and "other."[19] Cynics said this was done to prevent the emergence of authoritative voices other than Manning's own;

be that as it may, it certainly frustrated the media by making it hard for them to know whom to contact.

• Manning chose not to sit in the front row of Reformers on the floor of the House, even though it made bad television to have him speaking amidst a sea of suits.[20]

• A fax line was set up to allow members of the public to send in questions to be read during Question Period.[21]

• Reformers toned down their behaviour during Question Period. They eschewed desk-thumping and taunting; and initially they asked questions as if they actually cared about the answers, whereas the conventional practice is to ask only about matters on which you already know the answers, and you know that they will embarrass the government.

• Manning chose to ignore media expectations about timeliness. Before making a speech in the House of Commons on Paul Martin's first budget, he spent two weeks consulting the grassroots. By the time he got around to addressing the issue, the media were on to other issues and barely reported his speech.[22]

• Manning poured extraordinary effort and resources into organizing a forum on assisted suicide, televised in Calgary on April 17 and accompanied by several forms of polling to elicit the "consensus of the constituency" on this issue.[23] He temporized when it turned out that most respondents favoured legalization of assisted suicide under certain conditions. At first he appeared to say that the results were inconclusive; then, after a couple of weeks, he announced that he would vote for such a bill if the government introduced it, even though he personally opposes legalization; still later, he started to add conditions that might allow him to oppose a government bill.[24] At the time of writing, it is not clear what he will do when the issue arises in Parliament. The point of the exercise was to illustrate Reform's new approach to representation, but Manning's equivocations may create an impression that he is not serious about voting according to the consensus of the constituency.

Media reaction to Reform's efforts at opposition went through several stages. At first, they covered Reform as a novelty, speculating on what changes these western "rednecks" might cause in Ottawa. Then they were pleasantly surprised at the restraint and politeness exhibited by Reformers during Question Period.[25] But later, when reporters began to realize that Reform was having little impact on the government's agenda, they began to ask more probing questions about its performance as an opposition party.[26] Liberal ministers privately admitted that Reformers were causing them few problems in Question Period.[27] Manning's response to the criticism was both candid and illuminating. He admitted that Reform had been outperformed by the BQ, but said that it really didn't matter in the long run: "We're building to try to get a Reform government by the end of the 1990s, not just to score some temporary points in this session." He even predicted that Reform would soon displace the Bloc as the official Opposition by winning by-elections outside Quebec.[28]

The answers show that Manning is focused on future electoral success and regards playing the role of opposition as a lower priority. Now it is probably true that the ordinary voter pays little attention to the day-to-day activities of the House of Commons and has little conception of exactly what an opposition party should do. But to neglect the opposition role may be short-sighted even in Manning's own terms of electoral success because good performance in the House builds up a reputation for competence that can help attract popular support, and bad performance can lead to loss of support.

Manning's limited conception of the role of an opposition party reflects not only his personal dislike of conflict but also his populist worldview. For the sake of argument, accept his monistic vision of a society without profound conflicts of interest, his notion of the populist party that mirrors the demographic composition of the whole society, and his theory that MPs should be freed from party discipline so that they can discover and represent the "consensus" in their riding. Given these assumptions, all shades of opinion in society will be represented within the governing party by MPs in touch with their constituents, and there will be no need for parliamentary opposition in the usual sense, that is, parties whose role is to oppose for the sake of opposing. The only legitimate role of opposition is to showcase a future governing party, not to wage war in Parliament against the present governing party.

By the end of June 1994, when the House rose for its summer recess, most members of the Reform caucus were clearly not satisfied with their performance in the past session, although they did not publicly put the blame on Manning. Before leaving Ottawa, they adopted a plan to reorganize caucus activities, which was supposed to require Manning to designate critics for particular areas so that caucus would have consistent, visible spokesmen.[29] Moreover, proposals were now supposed to flow through an internal committee to ensure that caucus members had an adequate chance to develop a collective position; and caucus officers were supposed to be chosen by genuine election.

The details of the new plan were implemented in a special caucus meeting in late July. After that meeting, Ray Speaker said, the caucus "can now run their own show," and Stephen Harper added, "We've got to where we need to be."[30] In fact, however, Manning managed to retain much of his discretionary authority by astutely exercising his manipulative skills.

First, he saved two of his caucus officers through a clever manoeuvre. Those seeking internal reform had put together a full slate of candidates for an election, but Manning persuaded one of the central figures on that slate not to stand. In the end, members elected Jim Silye from Calgary Centre as the new coordinator and Stephen Harper as the new deputy coordinator, but they left Elwin Hermanson as house leader and Ed Harper as deputy house leader. Manning, moreover, won the right to appoint the chairmen of three caucus committees. This is important because those chairman will sit along with Manning and the caucus officers on the new administrative council, which is supposed to exercise control over the caucus agenda. Although he will now have to contend more directly with Harper, Manning will still be surrounded largely by people of his own choosing. Finally Manning did not fully carry out the requirement of appointing individual critics. In a dozen portfolios, including crucial ones such as finance, national unity, and foreign affairs, he left two or even three caucus members with the title of critics.[31] This weakens their prestige with the media and creates future possibilities for Manning himself to intervene at crucial moments in the public debate, if he wants to.

Manning's performance at this meeting shows that he will not easily be reined in by would-be internal reformers. His ability to control the agenda and manipulate situations is superb. If he is given time, he will always find a way to preserve his position and pursue his own objectives. The only way to impose anything on him is to catch him by surprise and push through a quick decision; and even then, since all decisions require subsequent implementation, Manning is likely to elude those seeking to tie him down.

To be successful in its opposition role, the Reform caucus must stick together, and here Manning's Triple-R leadership style faces major challenges. Triple R is effective when Manning is working with small groups of close advisers who feel that, as one once said, "Preston's political judgment is infallible." It also can work with large bodies, like Reform assemblies or other public audiences, where it is obvious that the group as a whole is incapable of coherent action. But it tends to break down in mid-size groups whose members want to share decision-making authority. Not surprisingly, there were severe clashes, which led to factionalism and expulsions, on the first three executive councils of the Reform Party, as team-building came into conflict with Manning's solitary nature and desire for personal autonomy.

After the 1993 election, Manning tried to lead the Reform caucus as he had led executive council. Although procedures called for caucus officers — chair, house leader and deputy leader, coordinator (whip), and deputy coordinator — to be elected, Manning in effect appointed them. First he held a straw vote in which members submitted written suggestions; then he tabulated the names and announced his own suggestions for ratification, just as he had always done for executive council officers.[32] It did not come out until much later that those whose names he put forward were not necessarily those who had been most frequently mentioned in the straw vote.

Manning started to run into internal resistance when he tried to get approval for his own policy statement on the Triple-P issues so vital to Reformers — the pay, pensions, and perks of MPs. Caucus instead voted to appoint a committee of three, chaired by Stephen Harper, to draft a position. Not long afterwards, Manning suffered another reverse when he nominated Reform House Leader Elwin Hermanson to be the party's representative on the House of Commons Board of Internal Economy, which deals with the Triple-P issues. Another caucus member nominated Stephen Harper, who was chosen on the ensuing ballot. The message was clear that Manning could not automatically count on getting his own way.

In March 1994, conflict began to spill out in public over Manning's attempts to get the caucus to adopt a code of conduct. Manning had long been concerned with such matters; he had written in *The New Canada* that

> the current pace and seeming futility of much parliamentary activity put severe strains on the MPs' personal and family relations. There are lobbyists in Ottawa whose starting premise is that one out of three MPs has a marital, financial or drinking problem that makes him or her ineffective or vulnerable to influence and direction by others.[33]

Manning had originally wanted the drafting of the code to be done by a joint caucus-party committee chaired by Cliff Fryers, but he had to make Ray Speaker the chairman in deference to caucus wishes. Then, several Reform MPs, most notably Jan Brown of Calgary Southeast, publicly criticized the draft code for dealing with matters of personal conduct such as sexual morality and the use of alcohol.[34] As a result of such criticism the code ultimately dealt only with official and political conduct.[35] Thus Manning was deprived of what would have become a powerful instrument of control over caucus members.

This minor public quarrel was quickly followed by a bigger and more damaging fight over Preston Manning's remuneration as party leader. To understand this episode, some background facts are essential. The details of Manning's compensation have varied over the years. He closed down Manning Consultants on January 1, 1988, and became a full-time employee of the party,[36] but at first there was little money for his salary. In 1989, he claims to have received only $12,200 in salary and benefits, including a $5,000 RRSP contribution.[37] As finances later permitted, the executive council aimed to compensate him on a level comparable to that of the leader of the New Democratic Party. There were various combinations of salary and allowances, plus some side benefits at different times, such as the royalties from *The New Canada*, payment for overdue dental work, and foreign travel only loosely connected with party business.

Immediately prior to his election as MP, Manning was receiving the following compensation from the Reform Party:

- an annual salary of $76,500
- a receiptable, non-taxable expense allowance of $18,000
- a taxable automobile allowance of $6,000
- a "special, non-accountable expense allowance of $25,000."[38]

This package could not continue after the election because the party constitution says that "the Leader and Chairman of the Executive Council of the Party, *so long as they are not Members of Parliament*, shall be offered remuneration in direct proportion to the amount of time given to the responsibilities of office, as determined from time to time by the Executive Council."[39] At their February meeting, the executive council voted to discontinue the salary and non-taxable allowance but to continue the two taxable, non-receiptable allowances, totalling $31,000 a year, and to give Sandra Manning a $12,000 non-receiptable allowance for her role as leader of the Partners' Program for MPs' spouses.[40] (She decided a month afterwards not to take the money and to terminate the Partners' Program.)[41]

Executive council does not seem to have looked closely at the party's constitution when it approved these allowances. The person making the motion said that "the Constitution prohibits payment of salary to the Leader";[42] but the word actually used in the constitution is "remuneration," which, incidentally, is the same word Revenue Canada uses to describe non-receiptable allowances.[43] Revenue Canada considers non-receiptable allowances as the equivalent of income and requires that withholding tax be deducted.[44] Thus the allowances, though perfectly admissible under Canadian law, conflict with the party's own constitution.

More important than these technicalities, approving the allowances was a political blunder because the Reform Party had long made a major issue of excessive pay, perks, and pensions of MPs. In December 1993, Manning's decision to send back the car and driver allocated to him as leader of a recognized party in the House of Commons had made the front pages of the nation's newspapers. Along with most other Reform MPs, he had also announced that he would give up 10% of his basic salary.[45] For him to take extra money from the party could not but make these gestures look hypocritical. Of course, many other Canadian leaders have had special financial arrangements with their parties, often far more lucrative than Manning's arrangement; but these other leaders had not made a major public issue of reducing MPs' compensation.

The mistake was costly at several levels. At the level of public opinion, it threatened to deconstruct the image of austerity that Manning and the Reform caucus had built up through their initial actions in Ottawa. At the grassroots level of party membership, it had a negative impact on fundraising, which depends on getting large numbers of small donations from repeat givers. This financial shortfall, in turn, undercut Manning's expansion plan, which we will examine further on in this chapter. The allowances affair also damaged Manning's reputation among the media. He has never had many supporters in Canada's left-liberal media, but those who regarded him as a right-wing threat to "progressive" values had at least feared the political ability he displayed in launching a new party. Now they saw him make an error of the most elementary kind, and they began to question his competence. For the first time, journalists began to question whether Manning had the political ability to become prime minister.

Within the caucus, there was still another problem because Manning had not discussed his private financial arrangements with members when they were working out their Triple-P position. He was already on shaky ground with some caucus members because he was skirting the Blue Book's opposition to "the practice of paying multi-salaries to those M.P.s who are also Cabinet Ministers, Committee Chairmen, and/or any other such parliamentary positions."[46] The caucus committee had originally recommended that Manning and the other caucus officers renounce the additional salary that the House of Commons offers to those in such positions.[47] Manning had persuaded a majority of caucus to vote against this recommendation but left some members wondering whether he was living up to the party's policy. Now, for them to learn three months later that he was getting additional money from the party was bound to make them feel that he had not dealt openly with them.[48] Moreover, the Reform caucus had publicly criticized non-receiptable allowances paid to members of the House of Commons,[49] so for Manning to accept one as leader of the party contradicted at least the spirit of their position.

When news of the allowances began to appear in the press in late March,[50] Manning and Cliff Fryers aggravated the damage by claiming that Manning needed the money for his wardrobe. "Our own media people," said Manning, "are always telling us you've got to dress properly." Fryers claimed that Manning had to have his suits dry-cleaned "after every function."[51] These ill-advised comments created a tag similar to Brian Mulroney's famous Gucci shoes, thus making it easier for critics to cite the issue without worrying about the complex details.

It is not clear whether the story was leaked by someone in the caucus opposed to the allowances or by someone close to Manning trying to turn it into a public test of loyalty for suspected dissidents. In any case, once the story got out, caucus members were inevitably asked for their reaction. Several made cautiously critical comments, but a real row did not ensue until Stephen Harper said flatly, "The whole idea of non-accountable expenses is not acceptable."[52] The *Calgary Sun* ran a cover story with the headline "Manning in Pay Perk Storm" and Harper's picture together with a further quotation: "The compensations are not consistent with what the party is asking of Parliament."[53] In this context, one must remember Harper's position as a member of the House of Commons Board of Internal Economy, where he was trying to advance Reform's Triple-P positions. His effectiveness on that body would have been undermined if he had let Manning's allowances pass without comment.

The day that Harper's comments were reported, the management and planning committee of executive council, with Manning's approval, addressed this letter to the caucus and released it to the media:

> We are appalled to read headlines such as "Reform MP (Stephen Harper) Blasts Boss Over Perks" (Calgary Sun, April 6/94). The article indicates that Mr. Harper is misinformed on how the Leader's accountability for expenses is handled.
>
> We accept that Mr. Harper disagrees with and questions our decisions, however, we are disappointed that he did not make use of the Constitutional mechanisms established by members at the last Assembly to deal with such issues. Mr. Harper did not even place a phone call to the appropriate Committee members to get the facts or to register his concerns prior to expressing himself in the media.[54]

Harper did not respond in public to this blast, although other caucus members, especially Jan Brown, came to his defence.[55] The issue was then fought out at a five-hour meeting on April 11. According to informal reports that later circulated, almost everyone spoke, and many members sided with Harper by criticizing various aspects of what Manning and the executive council had done.

Manning said that he would furnish receipts for his expenses,[56] thus producing an apparent compromise to resolve the matter, but this was only cosmetic. With or without receipts, Revenue Canada regards his allowances as taxable remuneration because he uses them for personal expenses and they thus represent a form of income. His genuine political expenses, such as air travel and hotel bills, are paid by the House of Commons or the Reform Party, depending on the nature of the business. A fundamental question remains unanswered: are Manning's allowances remuneration and as such in violation of the party's constitution?

Within the caucus, it seems that Harper emerged from this episode with the advantage. A telltale sign was that in early May he was elected, along with Ray Speaker and Sharon Hayes, to the ethics committee for Reform MPs,[57] and was then chosen as chairman by the other two members. Manning and executive council had wanted one of the members to be Bob Head, a defeated Reform candidate and retired RCMP officer, who would have had the title of ethics commissioner. He would have been "the investigating arms and legs of the Committee" and would have "report[ed] to council on cases requiring Party sanction; and furnish[ed] Council with summaries of actions taken by Caucus . . . in order to ensure general adherence to the Reform standard."[58] That the caucus rejected a non-MP for this key role was another setback for Manning in his campaign to assert the ascendancy of the party over the caucus. That the caucus put Stephen Harper on the committee further demonstrated that they would not simply follow Manning's lead.

Driven by concern over their performance as an opposition party in the House of Commons, caucus disillusion with Manning's leadership continued to build throughout the spring of 1994. One significant episode was Manning's quick criticism of the Canadian Legion's decision not to require its branches to open their doors to observant Sikhs or others wearing "religious headgear." At the end of a meeting, he told caucus what he was going to say without allowing any time for discussion. Some supported his course of action, but most would have preferred to avoid antagonizing the Legion. Another flashpoint was the Grubel episode. No one in caucus defended Grubel's choice of words, but most members were upset that Manning had not thrown him any sort of lifeline. Several Reform MPs later went out of their way to make public statements supporting the substance of what Grubel had said, and Manning had to endure considerable criticism in caucus over what he had done.

By the end of June, it was clear to careful observers that Manning's grip over caucus had weakened. The internal reorganization plan discussed above included provision for a nominating committee that would put forward names for caucus officers. In the future, there would be contested elections for house leader and coordinator, so that Manning could not simply select his own loyalists. Perhaps the strongest sign of change was a statement by Manning's old friend Ray Speaker, who, because of his long years of political experience as MLA and cabinet minister in Alberta, is an important figure in caucus. "Manning," said Speaker, "has to start to delegate things and put a priority on where he should spend most of his time."[59] Speaker also emphasized that "there will be a rededication to our very basic tenets or philosophic attitude along with some rededication to the policy that sent Reformers to Ottawa."[60] This was his polite way of saying that many caucus members disagreed with Manning's desire to broaden the Reform philosophy, as illustrated by his actions in the Legion episode and his nebulous statements on Indian policy.

Some of Manning's problems in acting as an opposition leader and holding his caucus together may have arisen because his mind was elsewhere. Almost immediately after the 1993 election, he announced his Countdown to Victory plan for the Reform Party. The plan centred on expanding into Quebec and nominating a full slate of 75 candidates there in the next federal election.[61] Underlying the plan was the goal of winning enough seats to form a majority government. Long gone are the days when Manning's objective was simply to elect enough Reform MPs to hold "the balance of power for the West and the North."[62] As mentioned in Chapter 3, Manning's new goal is to become Canada's next prime minister, but he knows that he must elect members from Quebec as long as Quebec remains in Canada with 75 of 295 seats in the House of Commons.

Building a majority outside Quebec is mathematically possible but extremely difficult because it requires winning 150 out of 220 seats. It would most likely happen in a situation of extreme regional polarization, such as the American election of 1860 when Abraham Lincoln, with 39.8% of the popular vote, won the presidency with 180 of 303 electoral college votes — all from the North. Lincoln won all but three of the electoral college votes from free states while failing to win even one from a slave state.[63] The closest parallel thus far in Canadian history was the election of 1917, in which Robert Borden's National Union government won 153 of 235 seats, with only three in Quebec; this was an unprecedented wartime situation in which most of the Liberal Party outside Quebec had made an alliance with the Conservatives. Apart from that unique case, Jean Chrétien's current government, with only 19 seats in Quebec, is the majority government with the lowest level of support from that province. Joe Clark formed a minority government in 1979 with 136 out of 282 seats, only four of which were in Quebec; but it lasted less than a year.

Manning could undoubtedly adapt to extreme regional polarization, but there is no sign at the time of writing that he is trying to bring it about. Thus, to reach his goal of becoming prime minister, he needs to develop political support in Quebec in time for the next election, which in turn presents him with a major strategic challenge. As leader of a national party, he has to have something relevant to say in the impending public discussion of Quebec's separation; but he does not want to say things that will make it impossible to win votes in Quebec, unless it becomes clear that Quebec votes won't matter because Quebec is leaving Confederation. In other words, Manning is now in the conflict-of-interest trap that he originally invoked as a reason not to organize in Quebec in the early 1990s.

If there is a No vote in a Quebec referendum, or if no referendum takes place, Manning will have to pursue his goal of developing some support in the province. Realistically, the main thing he could offer Quebec is the principle of territorial bilingualism ("recognition of French in Quebec and English elsewhere as the predominant language of work and society"),[64] which could be developed into an offer of provincial jurisdiction over language and culture more generous to francophones in Quebec than anything likely to be offered by other parties. Since Reform does not carry the baggage of promoting official language minorities, it can afford to propose a bolder alternative. However, this would require the party to clarify ambiguities in its present policy. In addition to territorial bilingualism, it is also committed to "a language policy based on freedom of speech." In the Quebec context, the phrase "freedom of speech" evokes the Supreme Court's 1988 *Ford* decision, which struck down the signage provision of Bill 101 because it violated the right of free expression entrenched in the Charter.[65] Thus, invoking freedom of speech in Quebec sounds like code for promoting the language rights of the anglophone minority. Reform cannot have it both ways. One cannot be simultaneously committed to the majoritarianism of territorial bilingualism and the minority-rights protectionism of freedom of speech.

Of course, the party could enter Quebec as an English-rights party, and if it did so it could probably get some support in the Ottawa Valley, the

Eastern Townships, and the West Island of Montreal, and perhaps even elect a few MPs. But in Montreal, many of the target voters would be allophones rather than anglophones, so Reform would have to confront the same sort of obstacles that it faces in Toronto, where multiculturalism and immigration policy are touchstones for ethnic voters. Also, an anglophone/allophone strategy would cut Reform off from the much larger francophone vote, which Manning needs if he is going to become prime minister — assuming that Quebec is still within Canada at the time of the next election.

Beyond language and culture, Reform could also accommodate, if not all, at least some of Quebec's other demands through decentralization to preserve the equality of all provinces. For example, greater provincial control over health care, which is frequently demanded by Quebec's politicians, is already part of Reform's program. Other areas of agreement could no doubt be found. Ironically, movement along these lines would tend to re-create a political alliance of conservatives in English Canada with nationalists in Quebec — the formula by which Sir John A. Macdonald, Robert Borden, John Diefenbaker, and Brian Mulroney managed to create majority Conservative governments. Indeed, it is the only formula that has ever brought long-term success to the Conservatives, and it was also the formula for making Social Credit a national party in the 1960s and 1970s. It would be logical for Reform, as the inheritor of Conservative support in English Canada, and for Manning, as heir to the Social Credit tradition, to follow the same formula (and to encounter the inevitable tensions between English conservatives and French nationalists that have broken up such coalitions in the past).

However, timing is everything in this scenario. Reform cannot hope to make significant progress in Quebec as long as the Bloc Québécois is riding high. In fact, very little happened by way of expansion into Quebec in the first half of 1994. The party hired Quebec organizers,[66] and Manning made a trip to the province where he appeared on phone-in radio shows. Speaking in English (although he announced he was now taking French lessons), he got a cool reception.[67] By the end of April 1994, there were only about 200 Reform members in the entire province of Quebec,[68] compared to about 100 at the time of the referendum, and there was little sign of the grassroots activity that had spontaneously developed at a similar early stage of expansion into Ontario.

Considered on its own merits, Manning's move into Quebec is beset with so many difficulties that one may wonder whether it is worth the effort. But it cannot be viewed in isolation, for it is part of his plan to enlarge the party "so Reform reflects the demographics of the Canadian population as a whole." His populist dream of a trans-ideological party-movement that embraces all sectors of society and transcends political cleavages by discovering "the common sense of the common people" is as much alive as ever. Thus the Countdown to Victory plan does not build on strength but calls for recruitment of new members and supporters in precisely those areas where Reform has been weakest: geographically, in the Atlantic provinces, Quebec, and urban Ontario; demographically, among women, youth, ethnics, and trade unionists; politically, among former supporters of the Liberals and NDP.

This is supposed to be a major initiative, on which $1.7 million will be spent in 1994 alone if the money can be raised.[69] The importance to Manning of this expansion plan is also shown by his choice of organization and personnel to implement it.[70] The expansion committee follows the concentric-circle model used for the referendum and 1993 election campaigns; that is, it is controlled by a smaller steering committee consisting of a tight group of loyalists: Preston Manning is, of course, leader; Cliff Fryers, chairman; Virgil Anderson, director of expansion; Bob Mills, caucus representative; Glenn McMurray, executive director of the party; Rick Anderson, adviser.

The reader will recognize most of the names from earlier campaigns. Of the new names, Glenn McMurray is an accountant who was hired to replace Hal Kupchak as director of finance and then promoted to be executive director of the party after Gordon Shaw's retirement; he is a managerial, non-political figure. Bob Mills, the MP for Red Deer, has old ties with Manning going back to the time when they were both Social Crediters. Other key positions, beginning with Virgil Anderson as director of expansion, are also reserved for loyalists. Rick Anderson will chair Quebec communications, Delcy Walker will chair the demographic advisory committee, and Allan McGirr will chair political realignment. Although a few members of caucus are scattered here and there, overall the network of expansion committees is set up so that it is very much under Manning's direct control. Indeed, it is almost a parallel party organization. Cliff Fryers is not eligible for another term on executive council and cannot serve as party chairman past October 1994, but he and Rick Anderson remain Manning's most trusted and competent lieutenants. Letting them run an expansion program supported by its own designated budget could put a new instrument at the leader's disposal to deal with new initiatives, leaving executive council with routine business.

Given Manning's earlier statements about changes in party membership leading to changes in ideology, this phase of expansion seems calculated to shift the party more to the centre. Certainly, some members perceived it this way, which caused Cliff Fryers to write an exclamatory letter denying this in the party newspaper:

Overall, you [members] told us that you favoured the Party expanding to attract more support, *but under no circumstances should the Reform principles and policies be compr[om]ised!* The Executive Council and Leader agree with you completely and that philosophy will govern any of our efforts to broaden our base of support!

Your comments also indicated a concern that the Party *not* pander to groups of people in various demographic categories, simply to win their political support. We agree! What we *should* do is at least make an attempt to bridge the communication gap between ourselves and people who do not understand what we stand for. . . .[71]

In line with this, Manning changed his terminology somewhat. Countdown to Victory became Broadening the Circle, which sounds less opportunistic; and "demographic expansion" became "bridge building," which is supposed to emphasize the fact that Reform policy will remain unchanged but be better communicated.[72]

Interestingly, members' responses to a questionnaire on party expansion showed that they want expansion to mean doing more of the same rather than making qualitative shifts. They picked Ontario, where Reform is already strong, as the most important geographic target. They placed it well ahead of Quebec, which was only fourth in their preferences. They chose youth as the most important demographic target, putting it ahead of women and ethnic groups. This is significant because youth is not a permanently distinct segment of society but a phase that everyone goes through. Explaining to young people the importance of Reform principles to their future lives does not involve group rights in the way that special appeals to women and ethnic groups might. Those who answered the questionnaire also saw former PC supporters as the most important political target, which again means sticking with what has worked well in the past. In light of these findings, Manning will have to be extremely careful and skillful if he expects this phase of expansion to produce the trans-ideological, all-encompassing movement of which he dreams. A great many current members and supporters would be alienated if Reform became something other than an anglophone conservative party.

In any event, Reform is likely to remain, like other political parties, a coalition of certain types of voters based on overlapping, identifiable interests. The emerging Reform coalition is composed of the following interrelated groups: the middle-aged, married middle class, especially those who work in the private sector; moral traditionalists; rural and suburban voters; economically independent voters in the affluent provinces of British Columbia, Alberta, and Ontario;

anglophone Canadians, especially Protestants, of western, northern, and central European descent; and so on. As the outlines become clearer, it becomes harder to add new elements. Unemployed fishermen in Newfoundland, anglophones in Quebec, Jamaican immigrants in Toronto, francophone minorities in eastern and northern Ontario — all have objective interests that come into conflict with those already assembled in the Reform coalition.

The difficulty was illustrated by the reception Manning got when he spoke at a Canadian Federation of Labour convention in early May 1994. He was booed by the delegates when he said that Reform did not favour legislation banning the use of replacement workers during strikes.[73] Strictly speaking, his answer was not compelled by the Blue Book, but it followed the spirit of the text: "The Reform Party supports the rights of all Canadians, particularly the young, to enter the work force and achieve their potential. Unions and professional bodies may ensure standards, but should not block qualified people from working in a trade or profession or from gaining the necessary qualifications."[74] Perhaps more importantly, Manning would have created a row within the Reform Party, in which farmers and small businessmen are numerous, if he had come out in favour of banning replacement workers. The simple fact is that some objectives of organized labour are antithetical to those of other interests in society. In the end, politics means taking sides.

In terms of conventional politics, the Liberals' prospects for winning the next election are good. A recent statistical analysis of federal election results from 1953 through 1988 has shown that two factors suffice to make an accurate prediction of a party's showing: the presence or absence of a leader from Quebec, and a decreasing rate of unemployment if the party is already in office (or an increasing rate if it is out of office).[75] The first factor is derived from the tendency of Quebeckers to vote as a bloc when a federal party is led by a fellow Quebecker. Other things being equal, having a leader from Quebec is worth five to six points of the national popular vote if the other parties do not have leaders from Quebec.[76] The Liberals' advantage in having Chrétien as their leader in the next election may be neutralized to some extent by the presence of Lucien Bouchard and Jean Charest, but it remains to be seen whether the BQ and PCs will still be major parties at that time. The importance of unemployment derives from the understandable, if not wholly justifiable, tendency of people to hold the government responsible for the performance of the economy. Other things being equal, an increase or decrease of 1% in measured unemployment means a corresponding increase or decrease of 2% in popular vote.[77] Since Canada is slowly coming out of a major recession, the Liberals may be well positioned in this respect. With luck, Chrétien should be able to time the next election to take place when the unemployment rate is at least 1% or 2% lower than it is now.

However, it is dangerous to assume that the future will always resemble the past. Who would have predicted in 1988 that the Reform Party would win 52 seats in 1993, and that the Bloc Québécois, which did not even exist in 1988, would win 54? As the progress of the Reform Party has shown, things can depend very much on the "waves," and there are two great wavemakers on the horizon.

The first is the Quebec situation. The PQ won the October 1994 provincial election. It is committed to pursuing an aggressive separatist strategy, beginning with a declaration of sovereignty in the Quebec National Assembly and culminating in a referendum on sovereignty within a year. Thus the whole complex of ethno-linguistic and constitutional issues symbolized by Meech Lake and Charlottetown is almost certain to surface again.

If there is a Yes vote for sovereignty in a Quebec referendum, will that not discredit the Liberals' claim that they are the party of national unity? And will voters in Canada be content to have a prime minister from Quebec negotiating with the premier of Quebec on the dismemberment of Canada? Or will they demand a more authentic voice from English Canada? On the other hand, if there is a No vote on sovereignty, will the BQ not be discredited, opening a space for the Reform Party as the best option in Quebec for those seeking more provincial power, especially over language and culture? There are many scenarios, not all equally favourable to Reform. At this point, no one can say what will happen. But Reform will clearly have opportunities to grasp, or grasp at.

The other great wavemaker is the federal deficit. One can imagine a scenario highly favourable to the Liberals and unfavourable to Reform: Canada's sluggish recovery picks up steam over the next two or three years; the unemployment rate falls to 8% or 9%; federal revenues grow; the deficit falls to about $25 billion, where most media commentators no longer regard it as a pressing problem; and the Liberals dole out federal largesse, say a national child-care program, in time for the next election. Posing simultaneously as the party of fiscal responsibility and the party of social welfare, the Liberals would be likely to win another majority government.

However, several things have to fall just right for this Liberal utopia to be realized:

• There must be no Quebec secession crisis to destabilize the economy.
• The United States boom must continue.
• Economic growth in Canada must accelerate.

- The higher interest rates that result from faster growth cannot come back too soon.
- The Canadian dollar must remain reasonably stable even in the face of rising interest rates in the United States.
- As promised, the government must successfully reorganize Canada's hugely expensive social programs.

If these things do not happen, the deficit could remain over $40 billion or even grow beyond that level, which in turn could create international repercussions: a fall in the Canadian dollar, downgrading of Canadian debt, rising interest rates on federal and provincial securities, and, at the extreme, intervention by the International Monetary Fund. In this scenario, the Liberals could find themselves even more discredited by debt and deficits than the Conservatives were at the end of the Mulroney years, and Reform would be the logical alternative for voters concerned about these issues. This, particularly in combination with waves coming out of Quebec, could put Reform over the top in the next election.

On the other hand, if the Liberals succeed in dealing with the deficit, they may alienate many of the NDP defectors who voted for them in 1993. The Liberal sweep in Ontario, as well as their patchy pattern of victories in the West, was only possible because of the great decline in NDP support in 1993 as compared to 1988. The New Democrats went from having 20% of the popular vote and 43 seats in 1988 to 7% of the popular vote and nine seats in 1993. According to Harold Clarke's survey, of those previous NDP supporters who changed their vote in 1993, 72% switched to the Liberals. It is no exaggeration to say that the NDP collapse made the difference between a majority and a minority government for the Liberals in 1993. But the more the Liberals pursue fiscal responsibility, the more they will resemble the Mulroney Tories in power, and voters on the left may decide to return to the NDP — particularly if Bob Rae's Ontario government is just a distant memory by 1997–1998.

Finally, it is quite possible that the two waves may coincide and reinforce each other. Polls that show a likely Yes vote for sovereignty in a Quebec referendum could trigger a run on the Canadian dollar as investors seek to avoid the risks of political crisis. Canada is now so heavily indebted that there is no cushion against uncertainty. Real interest rates might have to go much higher than they are now to prevent the collapse of the dollar. Economic problems would be even more acute if Quebec issued a unilateral declaration of independence, announced that it would not take over any of the national debt, or embarked on some other radical course.

Against this backdrop, the crucial challenge for Manning in 1994 was to get ready to ride the waves. Already well-positioned on the deficit, he needed a position on Quebec that, while flexible enough to cope with Quebec remaining part of Canada, had the potential to make Reform the voice of English Canada in the worst-case scenario of a secession crisis. The way he dealt with this dilemma provided a fascinating example of his political style in action.

When the Commons first met after the 1993 election, Manning insisted that there was no need to discuss Quebec, and he reproved Lucien Bouchard and Jean Chrétien for dragging Parliament into a "constitutional swamp" and engaging in a "family feud."[78] He did refer to Quebec a couple of times in speeches in April and early May 1994, but he delivered these speeches outside of Ottawa and drew little attention. He continued this policy of near silence through mid-May even though Bouchard, by visiting Alberta and British Columbia, provoked reactions from provincial premiers Mike Harcourt, Ralph Klein, and Roy Romanow, as well as from Ron Irwin, the federal minister of Indian Affairs. Indeed, Manning criticized their statements as being overly provocative towards Quebec.[79]

However, during a parliamentary recess in mid-May when Manning and other Reform MPs were in their ridings, they heard their constituents saying that politicians should start standing up to Quebec separatists. Consequently, upon his return to Ottawa, Manning suddenly changed course. During Question Period on May 24, he challenged Jean Chrétien to come up with a "visionary and futuristic" Quebec policy.[80] The next day, he gave a briefing in which he told a dozen members of the Ottawa Press Gallery that it was time for the prime minister to sketch out a new vision of federalism, and also to expound on the difficulties of separation, so Quebec would realize that "it ain't that simple."[81] As well, he suggested that the prime minister should call a national election in case of a Yes vote in a Quebec referendum.

Manning got caucus to agree to use one of their allotted supply days to introduce the following motion:

> That this House strongly affirm and support the desire of Canadians to remain federally united as one people, committed to strengthening our economy, balancing the budgets of our governments, sustaining our social services, conserving our environment, preserving our cultural heritage and diversity, protecting our lives and property, further democratizing our institutions and decison-making processes, affirming the equality and uniqueness of all our citizens and provinces, and building peaceful and productive relations with other peoples of the world.[82]

Leading off the debate, Manning said he perceived "a growing vacuum on the national unity issue, a leadership vacuum,"[83] which he proposed to fill in two ways. First, he would appoint "a new Canada task force" to consult people on their ideas about federalism; it would be supported by "a major teledemocracy effort on this subject in the early fall."[84] Second, he would begin to raise all the hard questions concerning territory, citizenship, the debt, and so on that would have to be answered in case of a separation crisis. Manning spelled these out two days later in a letter published in the *Globe and Mail*, which contained a list of 20 questions for the prime minister to answer.[85]

Readers will recognize numerous characteristics typical of Manning in this performance:

• He repositioned himself very rapidly. After having insisted for months that one should not talk about national unity, he moved that question to the top of the agenda within a couple of weeks. Also, his actions contained a deeper inconsistency. Previously, Manning had maintained that the way to keep Canada together was to "push the separatists onto their own ground," that is, to take away third options so that Quebec voters would be confronted by the stark choice between Canada as it is and independence with all its risks. As long as third options existed, Quebec politicians would have a strong incentive to use the threat of separation to force constitutional change in Canada. Now Manning seemed to be putting forward his own third option at a time when the prime minister, by eschewing third options, had succeeded in "pushing the separatists onto their own ground."

• As always, he gave populist reasons for his shift: "This thing is boiling up whether we like it or not [and people are asking] 'why aren't you guys responding?'"[86] But he had really made the decision on his own. Manning had hardly consulted with caucus at all before he gave his press briefing on May 25. He himself decided to start talking about national unity, just as he had decided not to talk about it previously.

• The position pointed in two directions at once. Manning's "New Federalism" was supposed to induce Quebec to stay in Confederation, while his questions about the terms and conditions of separation were supposed to engender negative thoughts in Quebec about the costs of secession. (In another context, I once asked Manning whether he wanted to be reassuring or confrontational, and he unhesitatingly answered, "Both!")

• The position depended heavily on a slogan — New Federalism — which was ambiguous in a calculated way. Sounding somewhat like the promise of "renewed federalism" that Pierre Trudeau made during the 1980 referendum campaign, it hinted at the prospect of constitutional change; and in fact Manning did mention a few constitutional changes in his House speech: "a constitutional requirement to balance government budgets, a strengthening of the federal commerce power and a new division of responsibilities on education and training."[87] But these would hardly address Quebec's long-standing demands for additional powers; indeed, they point in the opposite direction, since Manning favours increased federal activity in education and job training, as well as the dismantling of provincial barriers to trade. While sounding vaguely like an offer to Quebec, the New Federalism was just the latest in Manning's line of futuristic slogans, following the New Canada and the New Economy.

• Much of the exercise depended on what might be called "vicarious positioning." Manning actually put forward few ideas of his own; almost everything was a demand for Chrétien to act — to offer a new federalism, to spell out the terms and conditions of separation, to call an election, to hold a referendum. Vicarious positioning satisfies Manning's need to avoid overt conflict; it also encourages the media to attribute positions to him that can later be repudiated if necessary. In tandem with vicarious positioning, Manning made heavy use of a technique he has always used with aboriginal affairs — asking questions without offering any answers. This makes him seem to be part of a debate without really taking sides, a tactic that again avoids overt conflict. It also amounts to playing for time while waiting to see which way the waves will roll.

• The questions were couched in curiously abstract language. Manning's list of 20 questions did not even mention the words *Quebec* or *referendum*. His first question is an example: "How would the Government of Canada respond to a formal request from the government of any province to secede from the Canadian federation?" The wording did not take into account the fact that only Quebec is likely to make such a request, and that such a request is far more compelling when backed by a referendum vote.

• In spite of the careful dialectical balance and the abstract wording of the position, a radical subtext was readily apparent. Calgary MP Jim Silye told a reporter immediately after the special debate in the House that the Reform Party was positioning itself to become the official voice of English Canada.[88] This is obviously what Reform's position will amount to in the event of a real secession crisis. In the meantime, Manning's New Federalism serves essentially as a shield against charges of brinkmanship.

• There was a devious political edge to the strategy. The prime minister could not engage in public debate over the terms and conditions of separation in the spring of 1994. To do so would undercut the chances for re-election, however remote they might be, of the Quebec Liberals, who would be running on a federalist platform. It would also cause the Canadian dollar to sink like a stone. Formulating everything in terms of questions for Chrétien to answer recalls the way Manning tried to politicize the Charlottetown Accord both before and during the referendum campaign. First he personally challenged Brian Mulroney to get Quebec to agree to the Pearson Accord; then, when Mulroney succeeded to a degree in that endeavour and the Pearson Accord became the Charlottetown Accord, Manning branded it the "Mulroney deal."

• Manning floated trial balloons. At one point he suggested that Chrétien would have to call a federal election in case of a Yes vote in a Quebec referendum; at another point he said that Chrétien ought to consider holding a pre-emptive referendum in Quebec under federal auspices.[89]

At the time many observers criticized Manning's repositioning; one even called it "amateurish."[90] Yet it would be a mistake to overlook two further aspects of the exercise that in the end may cause all criticism to be forgotten:

• Manning was following the basic Reform formula of giving voice to concerns that other politicians could not or would not raise. With the Liberals in government, and the NDP and Conservatives reduced to marginal players in Parliament, only Reform could start to lead a public debate about the terms and conditions of separation. There was a pressing need for discussion precisely because the political class in English Canada had always regarded these questions as taboo. The Conservatives, Liberals, and NDP had agreed in effect that one could make offers to Quebec as a response to threats of separation, but that one could not discuss the terms of separation as an alternative to yielding to the threat. Manning's instinct was sound — he could once again represent the unrepresented, that is, the large and growing number of Canadians who were willing to contemplate the departure of Quebec but who wanted to be assured that someone would represent their vital interests in the secession.

• He planned to run these issues through the grassroots of the party. The June 1994 issue of *The Reformer* contained a questionnaire that dealt with both the New Federalism and with "contingency planning." There would be a national teledemocracy session in the fall, and Manning promised to deliver a major speech on October 15 at the upcoming Reform Assembly in Ottawa.[91] Manning takes initiatives without consulting the party more often than other political leaders do; but, on an issue of major importance, he seldom neglects to consult the party. He may do so in a manipulative manner, since he always retains control of the agenda; but the process does give party members a real source of power.

Ultimately, timing will be critical to Manning's project of forming the government by the end of the decade. If a unity and/or fiscal crisis stirs up major waves, it would be possible for Reform to become the major party in Canada outside Quebec. But if the waves do not roll in, or if they do not carry Manning far enough towards power, the Reform Party will not be able to endure indefinitely in its present form. At least two major factors make it temporary, even without the sunset clause in the party's constitution.

One is the nature of the wave strategy. While paddling around between waves, Manning inevitably goes back and forth on certain issues; he cannot commit himself until he knows which way the wave is going. But every time a leader repositions his party he loses credibility, and these losses accumulate over time. Thus the wave strategy is a race against time. If the big wave is too long in coming, the leader may no longer have the ability to ride it when it arrives. The problem is particularly acute in the case of a new party like Reform, whose reputation depends critically on being different from the traditional parties. At a certain point, all the repositioning involved in the wave strategy will make the new party seem just as compromised as the traditional ones, and the advantage of newness will be lost.

A second problem is the nature of the populist party as Manning conceives it. Although Reform possesses the organizational structure of a conventional political party, it has the psychological dynamics of a social movement. It depends on zeal, urgency, and intensity of effort — not just during election campaigns, but all the time. Thus the need for other kinds of campaigns, such as Save Canada or Broadening the Circle, between elections. But this kind of effort cannot be sustained over the long term unless there is some great and obvious crisis to foment a sense of urgency.

If there are no giant waves in the next couple of years, or if they do not carry Manning to power, one of two things will happen to the Reform Party.

1. Like the Progressives of the 1920s, it may disintegrate, undone by lack of competence in conventional politics. The fate of many populist movements in Canada and other countries has been to burst upon the scene, exercise great influence upon the political agenda, and then disappear.

2. Like the CCF/NDP, Reform could choose to occupy a certain point on the ideological spectrum, which in this party's case would mean becoming

The Party of the Right. By displacing or absorbing the fragments of the Progressive Conservatives, Reform could conceivably become a new conservative party dedicated, not to a sudden surge to power, but to representing certain interests in the never-ending process of politics. Every democratic polity requires at least one viable party of the right, and Canada's first-past-the-post electoral system probably does not leave room for more than one over the long term. If Reform does not become that party, another party will, and Reform will fade away.

At the present juncture, therefore, two big questions arise for Reform: Will Manning's wave strategy succeed in bringing him to power at the head of a populist party-movement that is essentially a personal vehicle for the leader? And, if not, can Reform convert itself into a stable, enduring conservative party that is not a personal vehicle for Manning? The worry for those, like me, who would like to see a new conservative party is that Manning's commitment to the first option may make the second one impossible because the two involve different conceptions of the future. For the first option, the key is to read the waves and pick the one that leads to success in the next election; everything else is trivial. For the second option, the key is to build up a party that can survive by giving voice to conservative interests and binding them into a lasting coalition. At the present time, this would mean initiatives such as:

- mastering the opposition role in the House of Commons, thus showing that the Reform Party can actively promote the interests for which it speaks
- broadening Reform's portfolio of policies and filling in the many gaps, thus helping to consolidate and extend its emerging coalition
- allowing members to form provincial parties, thus further undercutting the Progressive Conservatives as Reform's major competitor on the right.

These are all initiatives on which Manning puts little emphasis or would prefer to avoid altogether; yet, if they are not taken soon, the chance for Reform to consolidate its position on the right may vanish. The opening on the right may disappear while Manning waits for the populist wave.

10

Postscript

Although the manuscript of the book was completed in July, correcting the page proofs provided an opportunity to add this postscript at the end of October 1994. It contains comments on recent developments affecting the four main themes of Chapter 9, as well as some reflections on the Ottawa assembly, which took place in mid-October.

1. *Performance as an opposition party.* The caucus reorganization carried out in the summer of 1994 brought obvious improvements in performance. Designating specific critics, even if there were still two or three critics for some portfolios, made them better briefed and more visible to the media.[1] There were also improvements in Question Period due to better planning and coordination. Reformers' questions became more pointed, better delivered, and more effectively clustered around strategic themes; and Reformers got better at repartee and heckling. As a result, their questions broke into the news more frequently, sometimes even eclipsing the replies given by the Liberal ministers.

Reform was still missing some chances, as illustrated by the affair of the $34 million payment to Quebec for the cost of the 1992 referendum. When this came up in the House, Manning was away on a speaking tour, and no one in Ottawa wanted to take the lead. As a result, the Reform caucus did not offer any serious objection to the payment until after Chrétien had caved in to the pressure exercised by the Bloc Québécois, and by then it was too late to have any real effect.[2] However, Reform did make excellent use of its next opportunity, which arose when it was learned that Heritage Minister Michel Dupuy had written to the CRTC on behalf of a campaign contributor in his riding, asking the commissioners to consider this constituent's request for a radio licence. In pursuing this in a coordinated way over several days, Reformers managed to bring out not only Dupuy's mistake but also Jean Chrétien's incompetence in handling the affair.[3] An encouraging development was that Manning participated effectively in the attack along with other caucus members; because of his long years of work with regulatory commissions when he was a consultant, this issue would have been of particular interest to Manning.

On November 1, Immigration Minister Sergio Marchi announced a reduction in the annual intake of immigrants, as well as tighter rules for family reunification. Ever since the 1993 election, Reform immigration critic Art Hanger had waged a dogged battle against Marchi, both in and out of the House, so Reformers could consider this a victory, even if larger social forces had been more important than anything said in the House of Commons.[4] Even when Reform has not always shone in the House, it has had a substantial effect on the government's political agenda simply by existing and giving voice to a segment of public opinion that otherwise would lack representation. Why did the second Mulroney government start to change social programs from universality to a needs basis? Why is the Chrétien government now talking about deficit reduction, reform of social programs, tighter immigration rules, and a tougher approach to criminal justice? The existence of the Reform Party is not the only answer, and maybe not even the most important answer, but it is certainly a significant part of the answer. Ask anyone on the left whether Reform has had an impact on public policy in the last seven years, and the answer will be a resounding yes. Delays in learning to use the House of Commons as a political forum do not mean that the party has been ineffective overall.

2. *Caucus harmony.* After their well-publicized disagreements of the spring, Manning and his sometime opponents in caucus seemed anxious to avoid public conflict. Yet an incident took place at the end of October showing that internal problems had not entirely disappeared. It was revealed in the press that Manning and Herb Grubel, one of the designated finance critics, wanted to delay releasing specific ideas for cuts to the federal budget, while Ray Speaker, the other finance critic, was ready to present an updated version of Zero in Three.[5] It was odd, to say the least, to see public disagreement among the leader and his two finance critics over a tactical question of this type. No doubt, both points of view had their merits: why discuss them in the newspapers rather than in a caucus committee?

3. *Expansion*. Expansion into Quebec has moved forward slowly. Six voting delegates as well as another 40 observers from Quebec attended the Ottawa assembly, and the first representative from Quebec was elected to the party's executive council. At the end of October, membership in Quebec was between 400 and 500, two constituency associations had been recognized, and officials were hoping to organize a constituency association and field a candidate in an impending by-election in Brôme-Missisquoi.[6] With Reform standing at about 1% in the Gallup poll in Quebec, a victory hardly seemed likely, but just running a credible francophone candidate would enhance Reform's standing in the province.

Behind these gradual steps forward lay a strategic debate not visible to the public. Within the Quebec Staff Group chaired by Rick Anderson, there were opposing views on how expansion should proceed. Not surprisingly, in view of his background, Anderson wanted to emphasize the Liberal voters of the Montreal area, capitalizing on their federalist sentiments. Others would have preferred to emphasize rural, nationalist francophone voters, in effect trying to re-create the western-populist/Quebec-nationalist alliance of the federal Social Credit party in the 1960s.[7] Anderson, as chairman, made his view prevail in the short term; but if the pace of progress in Quebec does not accelerate, the party may have to consider other alternatives.

4. *Positioning towards Quebec*. On the all-important Quebec question, Manning continued to maintain his "New Federalism" posture. In response to the Parti Québécois victory in the Quebec provincial election, he called for a "complete overhaul of the federal system."[8] He then spent $100,000 in a nationally televised forum with phone-in questions designed to elicit a show of support for his strategy.[9] In his address to the Ottawa assembly, he again discussed his "third option," arguing that Quebeckers, as well as all Canadians, would respond to a program of equality of the provinces, decentralization, balanced budgets, and enhanced criminal justice. He also claimed that his third option would not require constitutional change, at least in the short term:

> There's a role for constitutional amendments in rebuilding the national house, but it's at the end of the process, not the beginning. In other words, the process that I am describing for rebuilding our national house is the exact opposite of the process that was used in developing the Charlottetown Accord, the Meech Lake Accord, and the 1982 Constitution.[10]

While continuing with the third option, Manning was also quietly preparing for a more confrontational policy in case the separatist side appeared to be gathering strength. Working over the summer with national unity critic Bob Ringma, a couple of staff members, and his father, he developed answers to the 20 questions he had posed to the prime minister in June. For now, these answers remain locked in his filing cabinet; but they are there to be used in case a secession crisis threatens.

In the meantime, Manning added a little edge to his position by launching an attack on the Bloc Québécois. "We're going to take you on," he declared in his address to the assembly, by which he meant that Reform would displace the BQ as the official Opposition.[11] This, he said, might happen either by winning by-elections or by a vote in the House of Commons if the BQ should endorse a sovereignty resolution passed by the Quebec legislature.

This attack on the BQ got an enthusiastic response from the assembly delegates, as Manning knew it would; the theme had already been successfully previewed as a fundraising appeal under the name of Jim Silye.[12] For the time being, it sufficed to satisfy the desires of party members for a more active policy towards Quebec. As a political manoeuvre, it was vintage Manning — a cautious step forward, pre-tested, burning no bridges, and diverting attention from other issues on which he was not ready to speak.

The Ottawa assembly will be remembered for passing strongly conservative resolutions on various social and cultural issues. The most controversial of these resolutions are printed below with some comments in brackets:[13]

> If elected, a Reform Government will introduce legislation by which the criminal misuse of firearms will be severely punished, and the right of law-abiding citizens to own and use firearms will be protected. [This was a carryover from Winnipeg, where Stephen Harper had intervened to table it.]

> Resolved that the Reform Party support the idea of requiring recipients of Unemployment Insurance and Welfare, capable of doing so, to perform community service, job training or education while receiving benefits [i.e., workfare].

> Resolved that the Reform Party supports the addition of a new definition to the Criminal Code of Canada making any person who commits on two or more separate occasions a serious personal injury offense be deemed a dangerous offender the Criminal Code of Canada Section 753 and subject to an indeterminate period of jail. [This wording was put

forward by Reform justice critics Val Meredith, Paul Forseth, and Myron Thompson to replace the original motion, which had been modelled on the currently fashionable American idea of an automatic life sentence after three offences.][14]

Resolved that the Reform Party support the right of citizens to protect themselves and their property, against criminal acts using all reasonable means, and that their right to do so has priority over the offender's rights. [This, together with the first resolution, came close to endorsing a right to bear arms. A more moderate and carefully worded resolution on gun control was defeated.]

Resolved that the Reform Party support the repeal of the Official Languages Act.

Resolved that the Reform Party support limiting the definition of a legal marriage as the union of woman and a man, and that this definition be used in the provision of spousal benefits for any program funded or administered by the federal government.

Resolved that the Reform Party support amending the Immigration Act so that to qualify for Social Services or Healthcare, a sponsored immigrant must become a Canadian Citizen. [The original resolution called for a five-year waiting period for social benefits, longer than the three years required to become a citizen.][15]

Resolved that the Reform Party supports [that] immigration levels be established at a maximum of 150,000 per year in any year where the unemployment rate exceeds 10%, with increases in immigration as the unemployment rate falls below 10%.

Resolved that the Reform Party support the right of all job applicants to be evaluated solely on the basis of merit. [Intended as a rejection of affirmative action programs.]

Resolved that the Reform Party support a revision of the Federal Income Tax regulations to end discrimination against parents who provide child care at home. [A long-standing demand of Reform-friendly groups such as Kids First and REAL Women.]

Resolved that the Reform Party support an immigration policy requiring children born in Canada to take the citizenship of their parents except that children born in Canada to legal landed immigrants will be Canadian citizens.

Resolved that the Reform Party promote the freedom of the Canadian cultural community to develop and grow without needless protection and government regulation, encouraging a free cultural market which offers choice while lowering costs to consumers as services are provided by those sectors which are able to do so most cost-effectively. [Stemming from Canadian Heritage critic Jan Brown, this implied at least partial privatization of the CBC plus an end to subsidies for cultural industries.]

The process that led to this spate of social and cultural resolutions was notably different from what had prevailed at previous assemblies. Almost all of these motions, as their sometimes awkward wording suggests, came straight from constituency associations. The resolutions committee had collated them, weeding out redundancies and obvious non-starters, but had not attempted to improve the wording, propose alternative resolutions, or supply reasons pro and con. During the assembly, there were no warnings from the head table to remain moderate; indeed, chairman Cliff Fryers encouraged outspokenness in his opening remarks.[16] Some MPs exercised their influence in the debate on particular points, but neither Preston Manning nor Stephen Harper tried to play any guiding role. Harper had originally been appointed to the resolutions committee but had resigned during the summer. For his own part, Manning stayed away from the policy debates and later commented with an apparent lack of enthusiasm: "I don't see anything there to apologize or back off from."[17]

In practical terms, Manning must have sensed there was little he could do to hold off these resolutions, even though he had always tried to avoid the topics of many of them. In 1989 the Edmonton assembly had ended in confusion over what had been passed and not passed; and in 1991, at the Saskatoon assembly, Manning had manoeuvred to defeat almost all resolutions from constituency associations. He had then decreed that the 1992 Winnipeg assembly would craft an election platform out of existing policy, not make new policy. With much media commentary about the gulf between his moderation and the conservatism of party members, the delegates could not be denied a chance in 1994 to take a stand on contentious social issues.

The most obvious effect of these resolutions was to position the party unshakeably on the right. Ted Byfield's *Alberta Report*, which had been rather cool towards Manning ever since the referendum campaign, greeted the result

triumphantly with a smiling picture of Manning on the cover and the headline "Back on Track."[18] In contrast, shortly after the assembly, Denis Boucher,
Manning's assistant press secretary, publicly quit his job. A former aide to
Conservative cabinet ministers from Quebec and later a protégé of Rick
Anderson, he explained that the assembly had disillusioned him because he
had been led to believe that, under Manning's leadership, the party would
move to the left.[19] With these resolutions on the record, it is now much harder
for anyone to believe that Manning and Anderson have the power to turn the
Reform Party into a non-ideological populist movement.

As one who has repeatedly called for Reform to assume a more coherent
conservative identity, I welcome this development, but not without reservations about the way things were allowed to happen. At this assembly, the
party leadership virtually abdicated its responsibility for guiding policy
development. As mentioned, several of the resolutions from the constituencies were quite badly worded and, even though approved enthusiastically by
the delegates, could never be implemented by a Reform government. For
example, in a world context, the right to bear arms is an American pecu-
liarity, not a general tenet of conservatism, and it will not make headway
in contemporary Canada. Also, the idea of denying social benefits to
legally admitted sponsored immigrants (as worded, this includes spouses
and children) is inconsistent with the conservative ideals of equality before
the law and legal support for families; there are much better ways to deal
with the problems of sponsored immigrants. Although these and certain
other resolutions express genuine concern about genuine issues, they badly
need to be refined. This was something that Manning and Harper had
done very well in the party's earlier years, and that function was sorely
missed at this assembly.

In another instance — the resolution opposing legalization of homosexual marriage — there is nothing wrong with the wording, but the debate
was rife with immoderate language. "I do not hate homosexuals; I hate
homosexuality," Myron Thompson said to loud applause.[20] The old religious adage, "hate the sin and love the sinner," may be valid in its own
sphere; but in the political realm it is the language of zealotry, not of pru-
dence and moderation. There are any number of excellent arguments
against homosexual marriage that have nothing to do with hate.

Two MPs — Jan Brown and Stephen Harper — distanced themselves
publicly from the resolution on homosexual marriage, not so much for its
content as for the way it was put forward.[21] Both said they would vote
against a bill to legalize homosexual marriage, but they did not want it
made a party matter. "Those are not partisan issues. Those are moral issues,"

said Harper. "People have to be able to belong to political parties regardless of their views on those issues."[22] In categorizing gay marriage as a moral issue, Brown and Harper were saying that it should have come under the Reform Party's formula for "moral decision making." That is, in the absence of a referendum law, MPs should declare their personal views, consult their voters, and vote according to the "consensus of the constituency" if one can be found. That is the way Manning and the party had previously handled abortion and euthanasia. Most members of caucus had made no secret of their pro-life stance on these issues, so the party was perceived to have a position, or at least an orientation; but it was not formalized in the Blue Book and thus allowed dissenters to remain with dignity in the party. Ironically, Manning had arrived at this view of moral decision making even before founding the Reform Party, but he now found himself unable to make it prevail.

Not too much should be made of one meeting. In all parties, delegates to national conventions pass eccentric, extreme, or badly worded resolutions doomed to languish in quiet obscurity. However, the tendency at the Ottawa assembly indicates a potential trap for the Reform Party. Morally super-charged issues like gun control, gay rights, abortion, and euthanasia encourage single-issue zealotry; they easily become litmus tests for supporting the party. The emotions they generate hinder wider coalition building because these issues produce a crazy quilt of cross-cutting cleavages. Some of those opposed to abortion have a pro-life philosophy that also leads them to oppose capital punishment and support gun control, and so on. Obsession with such issues will promote fractiousness and hinder Reform from dominating the moderate right of the political spectrum.

One of Preston Manning's greatest achievements as leader of the Reform Party has been to maintain the party's focus on issues having broad coalition-building potential on the right: balanced budgets, provincial equality, and direct democracy. Social and cultural issues can play a supporting role, but they should not supersede the broader themes. The way to handle such issues is to exercise leadership, to get out in front with solid but responsible positions, rather than to say little and then be overwhelmed by immoderate demands from the grassroots. Manning has done this successfully on some social issues, such as bilingualism and multiculturalism; he will now have to do it on other issues — particularly in the realm of sexual politics — in which he has shown little interest in the past. It will be one more step in Reform's maturation as a political party.

11

Update 2009

Preston Manning always declared that the Reform Party's goal was not merely to exert influence on the agenda of other parties but to win an election and form a government. He hoped that Reform would displace at least one of the existing parties and thus become a contender for power. The 1993 election seemed like a promising first step in that direction, reducing the PCs to two seats and driving them deeply into debt. The NDP was also in big trouble, falling to nine seats and losing official-party status. Initially, it seemed plausible to think that Reform could become a contender for government by picking up former PC support across the country and perhaps adding some populist but not really left-wing NDP voters. However, it quickly became apparent that things would not be so easy. Reform showed no signs of advancing in the polls, and the Tories regrouped under a new leader, Jean Charest. It began to look as if Reform would be permanently defined by its initial success as a Western party and would never be able to break out of that mould. Rather than displacing any of the existing parties, it, along with the Bloc Québécois, had further fragmented the party system, moving it from a three-party to a five-party configuration in which the Liberals were the only party able to win races in all regions of the country.

In May 1996, at the initiative of columnists David Frum and Ezra Levant, about a hundred conservative writers and political activists attended the "Winds of Change" meeting in Calgary to discuss a possible rapprochement between Reform and the Progressive Conservatives.

High-ranking Reformers, including Cliff Fryers and Stephen Harper, were there, as were some influential provincial Conservatives from Alberta and Ontario; but federal Progressive Conservatives were notable by their absence. The meeting led to a concrete proposal for a joint Reform-PC candidacy in one Ontario riding as a start on a broader program of cooperation; but Jean Charest rejected any collaboration, and the plan went nowhere. The PCs simply weren't ready at this point to concede that they had been irrevocably damaged and would have to deal with Reform. For his part, Manning, while not dismissing out of hand the idea of cooperation with the Tories, continued to insist that Reform could win the next election by itself.

In historical perspective, the most important thing that happened at the Winds of Change conference was a speech by Stephen Harper outlining what I later dubbed the "Three Sisters" theory of Canadian conservatism. Harper argued on the basis of historical evidence that conservatives could win only when they brought their traditional Tory support in Ontario and Atlantic Canada together with the populists of the prairies and the Francophone nationalists (but not separatists) of Quebec.[1] Broadly speaking, that had been the formula of success for Robert Borden, John Diefenbaker, and Brian Mulroney — the only Conservative leaders in the twentieth century to win more than one election. Harper went on to make that speech his road map to power as he united the Western populists and the traditional Tories in the 2003 Conservative merger, and then worked tirelessly to make inroads in Quebec until he finally won ten seats there in the 2006 election.

Reform improved its standing in the 1997 election, winning sixty seats and becoming the Official Opposition, but it was not a breakthrough. Reform lost its only Ontario seat and was thus more than ever defined as a Western party. The PCs bounced back somewhat, winning twenty seats, mostly in Quebec and Atlantic Canada, and increasing their vote share from 16 percent to 19 percent, almost equal with Reform's. Meanwhile, Jean Chrétien's Liberals obtained another majority government in spite of getting only 38 percent of the vote. With Reform and the PCs splitting the conservative vote in Ontario, the Liberals won 101 of 103 seats in that province, providing a solid base for their majority. It was becoming depressingly apparent that the Liberals could go on winning indefinitely if Reform and the PCs did not somehow get together.

In his second autobiographical memoir, *Think Big*, Manning relates that he started work the day after the 1997 election on a plan to enlarge

Reform's support by reaching out to other parts of the political spectrum. At the May 1998 Reform Assembly in London, Ontario, he admitted it was unlikely that Reform, as presently constituted, could win a national election. He unveiled, and persuaded delegates to endorse, a plan for transforming the party. He put together a planning committee consisting half of Reformers and half of representatives from other parties, including members of several provincial parties as well as a few prominent federal Conservatives, such as Rod Love, former chief aide to Alberta Premier Ralph Klein, and Peter White, former top fundraiser for the federal Tories.[2]

This project, known as the "United Alternative" (UA), was seriously handicapped from the start by the absolute refusal of the federal Progressive Conservatives, under both Jean Charest and Joe Clark after he replaced Charest, to take part. With the obvious partner unwilling to talk, Manning had to scramble. He defined the United Alternative not as an attempt to "unite the right" but as an appeal to all who shared "four fundamental principles: fiscal responsibility, social responsibility, democratic accountability, and reformed federalism."[3] In practice, this meant conducting talks with a few renegade federal PCs but mostly with people active in various provincial parties of the right: Progressive Conservatives in Alberta, Manitoba, Ontario, and the Atlantic provinces; Liberals in British Columbia; members of the Saskatchewan Party; and a few refugees from various parties in Quebec.

The next step was the United Alternative assembly held in Ottawa in February 1999, attended by about 1,500 delegates, about two-thirds from Reform and one-third from other parties. This group voted to found a new party with a new name, constitution, policy manual, and leadership race that might result in choosing a new leader. In a mail referendum held in May 1999, the members of the Reform Party supported the UA proposal by a vote of 60 percent to 40 percent.[4] About a quarter of the Reform caucus publicly opposed the UA during the referendum campaign, fearing that Reform might lose its distinctive identity as a western-based party adhering to fiscal, social, and moral conservatism, but Manning forged ahead.

Referendum approval led to a second United Alternative assembly, held in late January 2000. The delegates voted overwhelmingly to found a new party officially named the Canadian Reform Conservative Alliance. They modified Reform's constitution and policies slightly to remove some items, such as opposition to official bilingualism, which seemed difficult to sell outside the West. However, the Canadian Alliance would not become functional until the Reform Party merged with it, and that required approval of the necessary constitutional amendments by Reform Party members voting in another mail referendum, whose results would be announced 25 March 2000. That hurdle was cleared easily; 92 percent of the Reformers who voted, with a majority in every province, supported converting Reform into the Canadian Alliance.[5]

Two days later, Manning resigned as Leader of the Opposition to launch his "PM 4 PM" (Preston Manning for Prime Minister) campaign for the leadership of the new party. The leadership race emphasized that the party really was a new entity; for Preston to simply carry on as leader would have confirmed what the detractors were saying, that the Canadian Alliance was just Reform under a new name.

Manning's major opponent was Stockwell Day, the treasurer of Alberta, who as a Pentecostal Christian appealed strongly to the social conservatives whom Manning had always tried to keep at arm's length or under strict control, fearing that to let them define the party would render it unelectable. Day's campaign, managed by Reform MP Jason Kenney, emphasized the recruitment of new members to the party, especially from religious groups and social conservative organizations. Another serious opponent was Tom Long, former campaign organizer for Mike Harris. Long appealed strongly to Ontario Tories, and he could raise lots of money to finance membership sales through telemarketing agencies. Reform MP Keith Martin also entered the race, but he had always been a maverick and attracted no support from caucus colleagues and little from elsewhere in the party. Finally there was an unknown fringe candidate, John Stachow, who proved to be a non-factor.

The race was structured as a two-stage run-off, with the top two candidates proceeding to the second ballot if no one got more than 50 percent on the first round. When the first ballots were cast on 24 June 2000, Day got 44 percent, Manning 36 percent, Long 18 percent, and Martin and Stachow less than 2 percent.[6] It would be Manning against Day in the run-off vote. Manning had gotten into the second round, but he had to be tremendously disappointed. The whole Canadian Alliance project was his idea, and yet the interloper Stockwell Day had gotten more votes than he had. Manning knew that he didn't have as much sales potential as Day and Long, who appealed to potential new blocks of members, but he thought he could mobilize long-term Reformers on his behalf. Yet I know from talking to many members at the time that a substantial number of those on whom Manning was counting had concluded that he was not the one to lead the new party, that he could not carry it to victory against the

Liberals, that a fresh face was needed. Indeed, I supported Stockwell Day, and Stephen Harper supported Tom Long. Unfair, to be sure, but no one ever said politics is fair.

Manning did what he could, making an alliance with Tom Long to try to secure the latter's supporters, but it didn't work. When the second ballot was counted on 8 July, Day had won with 64 percent of the vote to 36 percent for Manning.[7] The magnitude of the victory showed that it didn't stem just from the religious and social conservatives that Day had brought into the party. Day had the advantage of freshness; he looked younger and more athletic than Preston; he spoke at least some French, in contrast to Preston; and he had a controversial but still creditable executive record as a minister, culminating with the Finance portfolio, in Ralph Klein's Alberta Government. After years of leadership, Manning's weaknesses were all out in the open, whereas Day's were largely unknown but would soon be brutally exposed to public view.

The Alliance leadership race had certainly gathered a lot of attention, and experienced fundraisers such as Peter White and Gwyn Morgan had promised (and would deliver on their promises) to raise enough money in corporate donations that the Alliance would be able to go toe to toe against the Liberals.[8] Day, therefore, conducted himself boldly when Parliament opened, joking about a "new sheriff in town" and virtually daring Jean Chrétien to call an early election — rash behaviour, considering that Day hadn't had time to assemble an experienced campaign team and weld it into a cohesive whole.[9] That gave Chrétien cover for calling the election he wanted to head off Paul Martin's subterranean challenge to his own leadership.

An even bigger mistake on Day's part (judged with the wisdom of hindsight) was to announce that his signature policy would be a "flat tax" of the kind he had introduced when he was Finance minister of Alberta, i.e., a single rate of personal income tax on all income over a healthy personal deduction, accompanied by far fewer tax credits and deductions for specific purposes. That single rate had been 10 percent for provincial income tax in Alberta and would be 17 percent for federal income tax. As a result of criticism, Day modified his scheme from one rate to two, adding a second rate of 25 percent for income over $100,000 a year.[10] I supported that decision on fairly abstruse policy grounds,[11] but it did political damage to Day by making him look weak and indecisive. The far greater damage, however, was to alert the Liberals that the Alliance wanted to fight the coming election over the details of the personal income tax. Thus warned, the experienced and cunning Jean Chrétien produced his own tax-reform package. It was not a flat tax (neither was Day's by that time), but it lowered marginal rates significantly. The Liberals' proposed structure involved four rates — 16 percent, 24 percent, 26 percent, and 29 percent — compared to Day's two rates, 17 percent and 25 percent.[12] It was no longer tax reform against the status quo, but two versions of tax reform, each of which would put substantial dollars back in taxpayers' pockets. Thus deprived of his best issue, Day limped toward the election that Chrétien called for 27 November 2000.

Day ran like the Energizer Bunny during the campaign, but his performance was uneven. At times he seemed poorly organized and badly briefed, as when he said the St Lawrence River ran south rather than north,[13] and then threatened to punish the staffer who had misinformed him. Effectively utilizing a misstatement by Jason Kenney, the Liberals attacked Day for allegedly favouring private health care, leading him to hold up a hand-lettered sign saying "No 2-Tier Health Care" during the English-language leaders' debate.[14] The gesture made his point, but it also drew criticism for violating the debates' prohibition on using props. But even more damaging than that, the Liberals, with a lot of help from the media, were able to subject Day's allegedly creationist views to ridicule. Warren Kinsella hit a high note of campaign showmanship when he held up a purple Barney dinosaur on television and said: "I just want to remind Mr. Day that the *Flintstones* was not a documentary.... And this is the only dinosaur that recently co-existed with humans."[15]

The election was a disappointment for the Canadian Alliance. Under Day's leadership, it increased its vote share from to 19 percent to 26 percent, and its seat total from sixty to sixty-six, but these gains were much less than hoped for at the beginning of the campaign. Also, the Alliance did not achieve any strategic objectives: electing two members in Ontario did not amount to a breakthrough; it failed to defeat any senior Liberal ministers, such as Anne McLellan in Edmonton or Ralph Goodale in Regina; it did not defeat Progressive Conservative Leader Joe Clark in Calgary; and it allowed the PCs to elect the minimum number of twelve members required to achieve official party status in the House of Commons.[16]

Then, with his position already weakened by the election results, Day's past came back with a vengeance. In 1999, when he was minister of Finance in Alberta, he had publicly criticized a Red Deer lawyer and public school trustee, Lorne Goddard, who was defending a convicted pedophile accused of possessing child pornography. Day wrote to the *Red*

Deer Advocate that Goddard's (unsuccessful) defence of his client suggested "that he actually believes the pedophile has the right to possess child porn."[17] Goddard launched a libel suit for $600,000 in damages. With his legal defence paid for by the Alberta Risk Management Fund, Day dug in to prepare for trial; but, as the legal bills mounted, the Alberta Government finally convinced him to settle out of court. On 16 January 2001, word got out that the settlement had cost Alberta taxpayers $800,000, and Day had to endure weeks of remorseless criticism in the media.

His hold over the Alliance crumbled quickly in the next few months. Almost all senior staff in the Opposition Leader's Office and the party quit or were fired. In May, members began to resign or be suspended from the Alliance caucus — thirteen of them at the peak. They formed themselves into the Democratic Representative Caucus (DRC) and started merger talks with Joe Clark's Tories. This group contained some of the most prominent Reformers, such as Deborah Grey, Chuck Strahl, and Monte Solberg, most of whom had close ties to Preston Manning. Although Preston himself remained enigmatically neutral,[18] he announced his resignation from Parliament; and several of his most senior staffers, including Cliff Fryers, Rick Anderson, Ian Todd, and Morten Paulsen, also got involved in the DRC, making it look like a Prestonian plot to bring Day down. With supporters of Manning and Day attacking each other in intemperate terms, it was a painful time for Alliance supporters. It looked as if the party would tear itself apart and Joe Clark would pick up the pieces.

Predictably, party fundraising tailed off badly. There were many other imbroglios, too many to mention. Not all of them were Day's fault, but they all fed the impression of a leader who had lost control of his party. Under threat of a non-confidence vote at a caucus meeting scheduled for 17 July 2001, Day promised to resign as leader ninety days before any scheduled leadership vote. National Council then quickly announced there would be a leadership race with the vote to be held 20 March 2002, about nine months hence. Day could continue as leader until 20 December 2001.[19]

At that point the story shifts to the Alliance leadership race won by Stephen Harper in March 2004 and the subsequent merger with the Progressive Conservatives completed in December 2005. Readers are referred to *Harper's Team* for the full account of how the trials and tribulations of the Canadian Alliance eventually led to the establishment of the Conservative Party of Canada and the election of a Conservative government in January 2006.

THE LEGACY OF REFORM

In its thirteen years of existence, the Reform Party exerted a remarkable influence upon Canadian public policy and political institutions. That influence was not exactly what Preston Manning had in mind; the "cunning of reason," as Hegel called it, ensures that we never achieve precisely what we set out to do. Politics is a world of action and reaction, giving rise to uncontrollable chains of unintended consequences. Nonetheless, Manning deserves to be remembered as one of the most influential Canadian politicians who never became prime minister.

1. *Political Parties.* Reform never fulfilled Manning's original hope of creating a new governing party based in the West. Rather, after morphing into the Canadian Alliance, it merged in 2003 with the Progressive Conservatives to form the Conservative Party of Canada, which has in fact become a governing party with its political centre of gravity in the West. Preston Manning was the Moses who glimpsed the Promised Land, while Stephen Harper became the Joshua who took possession of it in bloody political warfare.

In terms of the models of political competition described in the first edition of *Waiting for the Wave*, Reform's gambit of Invasion from the Margin did not displace the Progressive Conservatives entirely, but it weakened them so much that accepting Harper's merger offer ultimately became their best bet. This result is consistent with the views of Anthony Downs, who first developed spatial models of political competition. Based on the US experience of new parties trying to enter the system, Downs argued that Invasion from the Margin would most likely have the effect of pulling one of the existing major parties away from its previous position.[20] That is essentially what happened in this case.

From a conservative point of view, it was beneficial that the Conservative Party of Canada was a bit more ideologically conservative than the old Progressive Conservatives, as symbolized by Harper's one non-negotiable demand — to get rid of the word "Progressive" in the party's name. The cost of splitting the conservative vote was three elections — 1993, 1997, and 2000 in which the Liberals coasted to victory because the right was divided. That led to conservatives missing out on lots of patronage opportunities while they were out of power, but the effect on public policy was not particularly harmful. As described in more detail below, Jean Chrétien's Liberal Government, pushed from the right by Reform and without much pressure from the weakened

NDP on the left, was at least as conservative in practice as Brian Mulroney's Progressive Conservatives.

Reform also had significant influence on the way political parties operate, especially in the area of fundraising. The Progressive Conservatives had introduced grassroots fundraising into Canadian politics in the 1970s, using the new technology of computerized direct mail; but they also continued to draw heavily on corporate support.[21] Continuing that tradition of direct mail and complementing it with telephone solicitation, Reform became the first national party to depend almost entirely on grassroots fundraising, in contrast to the corporate support of the Liberals and Progressive Conservatives and the union support of the NDP. Today, the Conservative Party maintains a large financial edge over its competitors by combining direct mail and telephone solicitation with mass voter identification to expand its donor lists.[22] The Conservatives' financial achievements rest squarely on the pioneering efforts of Reform.

In other respects, however, Manning's vision of a neo-populist grassroots party has not been realized. The Conservative Party has a large membership and donor base, but in other respects it is even more strongly controlled from the centre than the Liberals or NDP. This is a legitimate part of Manning's legacy, for he constructed Reform as a party with few intermediate structures, such as regional or provincial wings, between the leader and the members. The Conservative Party follows the same model, with no intermediate organizations based on region, ethnicity, gender, or philosophical interest. As I argued in the first edition, this is not a surprising outcome for a populist movement; populism is intellectually incoherent and can only be made to work through the leader's control of decision-making processes within the party. Harper doesn't bother with Manning's populist rhetoric, so he doesn't need to be as subtle in his control as Manning; Harper is just "the Boss," as many in his inner circle call him, and his word is law within the party.

2. *Democracy.* I know from the time I spent working with Preston that his vision of Reform as a neo-populist revival was very near to his heart. Sadly, however, this is an area where the Reform movement has had relatively little impact on Canadian institutions.

Manning's agenda for reform of the House of Commons has vanished with little trace. He wanted MPs to be more like delegates of their ridings, expressing the "consensus of the constituency" in their votes, especially on moral issues. That would have implied looser party discipline and more independent or crossover voting by caucus members. When Manning was Reform leader, he and other caucus members conducted various forms of constituency consultation to guide their votes in the House — town hall meetings, surveys, even in one case a televised town hall discussion with phone-in voting; but that impulse has died away. Conservative members today, like the members of other parties, almost always toe the line adopted in caucus, with rare deviations for personal reasons.

Manning also wanted to dial down the adversarial nature of Commons proceedings, to replace shouting and taunting with reasoned debate. Toward that end, he introduced a number of novelties when Reform members first came to Ottawa, such as seating the leader (himself) in the second row, appointing critic groups rather than individual critics, and taking time to consult before responding to the government's budget. But none of these innovations took root; in fact, Manning had to back away from most of them while he was still Reform leader, and he ended up expelling more members from his caucus than most leaders have ever had to do. Today, Harper's Conservative caucus is a tightly disciplined, almost military formation that uses all the old methods of political combat as enthusiastically as any other party. Although unfailingly supportive in public, Preston is probably glad not to be part of it.

Senate reform has not gotten much traction. In practice, the Conservative position has gone from Triple-E to Double-E, dropping the demand for an equal number of senators from each province, which cannot be achieved without constitutional amendment. In his first years in office, Harper made a genuine attempt to bring in legislation for fixed terms and election of senators, but it was blockaded by the other parties in both the House and the Senate. Consequently, he appointed eighteen senators in late 2008, though they have pledged to resign and run if an elective procedure ever becomes available. If Harper can stay in power long enough to appoint a Conservative majority to the Senate (early 2010), it is possible that federal legislation for Senate elections may someday pass, but that will be far from the end of the matter. Provincial enthusiasm, except in Alberta and Saskatchewan, has been notably lacking, and Ontario and Quebec will probably challenge any reform attempt in the courts if legislation gets to the point of passing.

Reform's direct democracy proposals also went almost nowhere. Parliament never adopted referendum, initiative, or recall legislation (BC did adopt initiative and recall legislation in 1994).[23] And the Conservative Party voted at its 2005 Montreal policy convention to leave these items out of its policy book. The one sub-area where progress occurred was with respect to amending the constitution. Brian Mulroney's government introduced legislation authorizing submission of constitutional amendments to a referendum after Alberta, British Columbia, and Quebec did the same in their sphere of provincial jurisdiction — all of which enabled the defeat of the Charlottetown Accord.

But with that one exception, Canadian democracy is still pretty much the same as it was in 1987, when Manning founded the Reform Party: strongly disciplined parties, a highly adversarial House of Commons, an appointed Senate, and no consultation with the people through the mechanisms of direct democracy.

3. *National Unity.* Broadly speaking, three ill-assorted blocs of voters came together to defeat the Charlottetown Accord in the 1992 referendum: separatists in the province of Quebec; Reformers, i.e., populist conservatives, chiefly in the West and in rural Ontario; and Trudeau Liberals, scattered across the country. Reformers played no role in Quebec, where the Accord would have been defeated in any case by the odd-couple votes of separatists and Trudeau Liberals; and the other provinces and the federal government would never have adopted the Accord against the wishes of Quebec, because the main point of the Accord was to respond to demands from Quebec. But if only Quebec had opposed the Accord, and if it had passed elsewhere in the country, there would have been a clamour to revise it to make it more palatable in Quebec, and then Canada would have been back in the mug's game of bargaining with those who used separation as a threat. By ensuring that the Accord was defeated in the West and barely passed in Ontario, Reform drove a stake through the heart of the Charlottetown Accord, so that it could never be resurrected.

That, in my view, was a signal contribution to national unity. The Charlottetown Accord was, above all, an agenda for never-ending future negotiations. If it had passed, Canada would still be bargaining with Quebec over jurisdictional issues, or (more likely in my opinion) Quebec would be long gone from Canada, leaving behind a disproportionate share of the national debt. Constitutional negotiations developed in Quebec an appetite for concessions that only grew with the eating, and they had to be stopped,

Reform made another major contribution to national unity after the close call of Quebec's 1995 separation referendum. In the wake of that near-death experience, Stephen Harper introduced a private-member's bill,

C-341, whose short title was the "Quebec Contingency Act (referendum conditions)." [24] The bill not only upheld the rule of law by rejecting the validity of a unilateral declaration of independence, it also prohibited recognizing the results of a Quebec referendum "if the question is ambiguous or unclear."[25] Harper's bill began the discussion that ultimately led to the Supreme Court's ruling in the Quebec secession reference and the Liberal Clarity Act of 2000.[26] In this area, as in others discussed below, Reform played the essential role of running interference for controversial proposals eventually enacted by the Liberals.

Finally, Reform contributed to reducing the mood of alienation that sprang up in Western Canada, particularly in Alberta, in the wake of Pierre Trudeau's National Energy Program. With its inspired motto "The West Wants In,"[27] Reform provided a focus for Western political efforts within, rather than outside, the constitutional framework of Canada. Then, after the 2006 election, Stephen Harper became prime minister while representing Calgary Southwest, Preston Manning's old riding. As Harper said on election night, 23 January 2006, "To the people of the West, let me say one thing and let me be clear: the West is now in. Canada will work for all of us."[28]

4. *Fiscal Responsibility.* Progress towards fiscal responsibility was one of Reform's greatest triumphs. Initially, the Liberals expressed little concern for balanced budgets after the 1993 election, but Finance Minister Paul Martin was convinced by the Mexican peso crisis of late 1994 that a run on the Canadian dollar might be next unless our chronic federal deficit was brought under control.[29] The result was the landmark 1995 budget, which initiated reductions in the size of the federal civil service as well as in fiscal transfers to the provinces. After three years the federal budget was back in balance without raising taxes, just as Manning had said was possible when he ran on his "Zero-in-Three" proposal in the 1993 election campaign.

Jean Chrétien and Paul Martin were in power, and they deserve credit for balancing the budget, but Reform deserves some credit as well. Reform had run interference, taking the political heat for introducing a concept — balancing the budget by reducing spending — that was initially unpopular. Reform Finance Critic Herb Grubel recorded how Paul Martin encouraged him to keep up the pressure: "He said he needed me and Reform to demand very drastic spending cuts to eliminate the deficit. The demands would allow him and his rather substantial cuts to seem moderate by comparison."[30] It was indeed a favourable political configuration for the Liberals; with Reform exerting pressure from the right and the NDP defending deficit-spending from the left, the Liberals could take drastic action while still appearing moderate. It was, however, only possible because Reform had moved the whole political spectrum to the right on this issue.

Of course, nothing in politics is ever permanent. After eleven years of balanced budgets, the Harper government was led, partly by the international financial crisis, to go into deficit in 2009–10 and probably for several years thereafter. But thanks to Manning and Reform, the conventional wisdom accepted by both Conservatives and Liberals was now that deficits might be required temporarily but should not become "structural," i.e., permanent even in times of relative prosperity. The government's budget brought down on 27 January 2009, contained a plan for getting out of deficit within five years. It may not happen that way because nothing is ever straightforward in government and politics; but at least the Canadian people now realize, thanks largely to the Reform movement, that deficits and debt are dangerous instruments of public policy.

5. *Lower Taxes.* Reform worked for lower taxes from the beginning, opposing Mulroney's GST not because it was a bad tax but because it was not accompanied by spending reductions. But the real battle for tax reform could not begin until the budget had been balanced, shortly before Stockwell Day defeated Manning in the leadership race for the new Canadian Alliance. Day almost immediately made lower taxes his signature policy, calling for a single-rate personal income tax at the federal level, similar to what he had introduced when he was treasurer of Alberta. It might have become a winning issue in the 2000 election except that Day announced it ahead of time, giving the crafty Chrétien time to develop a counterproposal for a reduction in most of the personal income tax brackets. Paul Martin also announced tax reductions when he was prime minister, but did not get a chance to put them into effect. In the years 2006–08, Stephen Harper reduced the GST from 7 percent to 6 percent and then to 5 percent, took a point off the lowest marginal rate of personal income tax, announced a multi-year schedule of cuts to the corporate income tax rate, and enacted a variety of tax cuts targeted at particular demographic and professional groups. There was also a further modest reduction in the personal income tax in the 2009 budget.

Again, nothing is ever permanent in politics, but for the time being the need for lower, or at least not higher, taxes has become an article of conventional wisdom. The Liberals criticized Harper's GST reductions not because they were tax cuts as such but because they were allegedly the *wrong* cuts — the Liberals claimed to prefer personal income tax cuts. Liberal Leader Stéphane Dion also campaigned in 2008 on lower corporate income taxes. Personally, I'm not too concerned about which tax gets cut. I'll take my stand with Milton Friedman: "I never met a tax cut I didn't like — though I would go on to say that I like some better than others."[31]

6. *Social Conservatism and Family Values.* A social conservative agenda was not part of Preston Manning's original plan for the Reform party; he was far more concerned about constitutional, institutional, and fiscal issues. In fact, Preston's theory of representation was designed to prevent Reform from becoming identified as a socially conservative party; he wanted to let individual MPs oppose abortion or support capital punishment without committing the party to a collective position. But many of those who changed their support from Progressive Conservative to Reform in the early years were very concerned about abortion, capital punishment, and gay rights. These issues had all been hotly contested during Brian Mulroney's years as prime minister, and many erstwhile Progressive Conservatives thought he had neglected their point of view. In practice, then, the Reform Party became known for social conservatism and support for "family values." That posture was strengthened rather than weakened when it became the Canadian Alliance because the new leader, Stockwell Day, and some of his key lieutenants such as Jason Kenney, were strongly identified with that position.

But in spite of strenuous efforts, Reform and its successors lost every battle over high-profile issues of social conservatism. The most recent example was gay marriage, which Harper opposed both as Alliance leader and as Conservative leader in the 2004 election campaign. Probably the most that can be claimed in this area is that the Reform/Alliance/Conservative presence has perhaps prevented other issues, such as euthanasia and legalization of mind-altering drugs, from coming to the fore.

In another sense, however, Reform's pro-family position has led to real results. Reform, the Canadian Alliance, and the Conservative Party always opposed creating a national system of childcare. In the 2004 election campaign, Harper ran against Paul Martin's plan to do that, proposing instead a "Child Care Allowance" of $100 per month per child under six. This appears to be a permanent innovation; the other parties still talk of instituting a national system of childcare, but they don't propose taking back the Child

Care Allowance. During his time in office, Harper has also modified the tax code in numerous ways to put more money in the pockets of parents: increasing tax credits for spouses and parents, allowing limited income splitting, and creating tax credits for some of the expenses of raising children, such as sports and arts participation, school books, etc. The pattern of innovations is rather messy, but taken together they have helped to make the Canadian personal income tax system more generous to those who undertake the responsibility of being parents.

Reform's legacy in this area consists not only of amendments to the tax code but also of changes to the way in which public debate in conducted. Today all parties, of the left as well as the right, routinely talk about families. Jack Layton is just as likely as Stephen Harper to propose policies allegedly designed to help "hard-working Canadian families." Of course, Conservative and NDP approaches to helping families are very different, but it is significant that the concept of family is now normally included in public debate.

It is hard to be precise about such things, but Reform may have had a greater influence in a relatively short time than any other Canadian "third party." Remember that Reform existed only thirteen years (1987–2000), or sixteen years if want to include its reincarnation as the Canadian Alliance. In that short period of time, it was no small achievement to have steered federal politics in the direction of balanced budgets, lower taxes, and stiffer resistance to Quebec separatism. By way of comparison, the only great achievement at the federal level that the CCF could claim at the end of its first thirteen years (1932–45) was to have pushed the Liberals into enacting the baby bonus during World War II.

But over the longer time span of more than seventy-five years from its founding to the present, the CCF/NDP has exercised greater influence than Reform. Louis St Laurent called the CCF "Liberals in a hurry," and indeed they and their NDP successors were in the forefront of pushing for the welfare state, the rights of women, environmental concern, and many other policies that Canadians today take for granted. Without being in power for a single day at the federal level, the CCF/NDP has shaped the profile of Canadian public policy in all sorts of ways.

From the very beginning, however, Manning rejected the notion of building a party of influence, which he derided as a "right-wing NDP eternally destined to opposition status."[32] He wanted to build a national party with wide enough support to win elections and form the government of Canada. Thus he designed the Reform Party with a sunset clause to terminate its existence in the year 2000 and led its transformation into the Canadian Alliance in an attempt to broaden its support. Reform exercised a powerful influence in its opposition years, but Manning was never satisfied with that; he wanted to govern. Ironically, he never achieved that objective for himself, but the dream did come true for Stephen Harper. Even more ironically, Harper was hampered by the minority status of his government once he was in power and could never make more than relatively minor incremental changes to federal policies. The exigencies of politics led him away from the hard right in some respects. So, Manning and Harper accomplished only a small part of what they dreamed, and what they did achieve looks different than they ever could have envisioned. But without the dreams they wouldn't have accomplished anything at all.

Where there is no vision, the people perish: but he that keepeth the law, happy is he.

Proverbs 29:18, King James Bible

Appendix

Models of Party Competition

The description of Reform Party strategies in Chapter 3 was written for general readers. This Appendix contains a further discussion for political scientists interested in the rational-choice approach to strategy.

From 1867 until the election of 1993, no party except the Liberals and Conservatives formed either the government or the official Opposition in the Canadian House of Commons (the Progressives had enough seats to form the official Opposition in 1921 but chose not to and quickly disintegrated as an effective force). After 1935, the CCF/NDP more than once occupied second or even first place in public opinion polls but never did better than third in seats. Thus the 1993 results, which established the Bloc Québécois as the official Opposition with 54 seats, and the Reform Party close behind with 52 seats, are unique in Canadian history for propelling two new parties into the system on a large scale.

Canada's single-member-plurality or first-past-the-post electoral system is chiefly responsible for screening out would-be new parties. No proposition in political science is better documented than that the first-past-the-post method of voting tends to reduce political competition to a contest between two large parties.[1] Other parties exist and even elect representatives, but they hardly ever take control of the government. Plurality voting tends to reduce political competition to two main parties surrounded by a fringe of "also-rans" because it is a winner-take-all system within each constituency and offers no consolation prizes. Under these rules, voters are reluctant to "waste" their votes on candidates from small parties who have little chance of success. Thus barriers to entry of new parties are high.

However, the effects of plurality voting operate in the first instance at the constituency level, which opens the door for a form of multi-party competition amounting to the simultaneous co-existence of two or more two-party systems. A multi-party system at the macro-level can emerge from the aggregation of two-party systems at the micro-level.

This interaction between territorial constituencies and plurality voting also creates an avenue for the entry of new parties into a two-party system. A new party's chance of success depends on the extent to which it can appeal to groups of voters who have sufficient territorial concentration to constitute local pluralities. This can even lead to the displacement of an existing party and participation in government. Within this century the Labour Party replaced the Liberals as one of the two main parties in Great Britain, showing that it can be done. Labour rode to power on the votes of the workers who were first enfranchised in the electoral reform of 1882 and were not yet attached to either of the existing parties.[2] In Britain, as in every other country, residential segregation between the working class and middle class allows a workers' party to take advantage of local pluralities and thereby win victories in those constituencies.

New parties may also enter the system at times of constitutional crisis or economic catastrophe when existing parties are massively discredited. The rise to power of the Gaullists in France following the collapse of the Fourth Republic provides one example of this phenomenon. The rise of the Republicans in the American secession crisis and of Social Credit in Alberta in 1935 at the height of the Depression provide two others. The last two examples are highly relevant to Preston Manning. He comes out of Alberta Social Credit; and as those who follow his career will know, he has closely studied the American secession crisis; he refers to it frequently in his writings and speeches, and likes to quote Abraham Lincoln. Manning's own model of how a new party breaks into the system owes much to crisis scenarios.

In Canada, a number of new parties have successfully entered provincial politics and their success has not always depended on a crisis scenario. Every province between British Columbia and Quebec has been governed by three or even four different political parties during the course of the 20th century. And in Canadian federal politics, parties other than the Liberals and Conservatives (chiefly the Progressives, Social Credit, and CCF/NDP) have won seats in every general election since 1921. In fact, the role of new parties, or third parties, is quite striking in Canadian politics as compared to most countries with plurality voting.

The main reason for the greater importance of new parties in Canada is the existence of cross-cutting cleavages in Canadian politics.[3] In every industrial democracy, there is an ideological dimension of political conflict over the role of government in the economy, and parties take positions on a spectrum from left to right. But in Canada, politics also has an identity dimension of ethno-linguistic conflict; and the demographic differences that fuel this conflict are also reflected in territorial patterns of residence. The primary ingredient here is the linguistic tension between French and English, which has been interlaced over the years with related cleavages between Catholics and Protestants, whites and "ethnics," or visible minorities, and western and eastern Canada. The economic dimension and identity dimension of Canadian politics cut across each other in a way that promotes the fission of parties. For example, many western free-trading Liberals bolted their party during World War I when the Quebec Liberals seemed lukewarm about prosecuting the war; the westerners ended up in the Progressives. Francophone social democrats in Quebec never seem to feel at home in the federalist NDP and so have ended up in the separatist Parti Québécois. And so on.

The importance of new parties in Canada led Maurice Pinard to write his well-known book, *The Rise of a Third Party*, which combined a broad historical overview with a case study of Social Credit's entry into Quebec federal politics in 1962. Pinard's original hypothesis was that a new party was likely to succeed when two conditions coincided: (1) the system was so dominated by a single party that support for its traditional rival had fallen below one-third of the votes; and (2) the system was beset by a crisis, such as a depression or deep recession, which shook people's trust in established parties.[4] While this hypothesis seemed to fit many cases, such as the emergence of provincial Social Credit in Alberta in 1935 and federal Social Credit in Quebec in 1962, it could not account for all cases, including very important ones such as the rise to power of the Parti Québécois in the 1970s.[5]

Such evidence led Pinard to reformulate his model in more general terms: "A one-party-dominance system is only one type of a more general condition of structural conduciveness, that of *the political non-representation of social groups through the party system*."[6] From this perspective, the PQ's success can be explained by the fact that the Quiet Revolution created a relatively well-educated urban class of francophone voters whose nationalist, but socially liberal, values were not well represented by either the Liberals or the Union Nationale. Alain Gagnon and Brian Tanguay, the most recent authors on minor parties in Canada, accept Pinard's reformulated view that "the non-representation of interests by the traditional parties" is "probably the most important factor in the creation of minor parties," particularly when accompanied by "a sudden deterioration of economic conditions."[7]

This line of Canadian research converges with studies on third parties in the United States. It has been noted in American history that third parties have tended to arise at times when the two main parties have drawn together on crucial issues:

> The Liberty and Free Soil parties arose only after the refusal of either of the major parties to call for the abolition of slavery. The Populists were unhappy with the hard money policies of both the Democrats and Republicans, which they felt benefited Eastern creditors at the expense of debtors in the West. The Progressive Party arose in 1924 only after being faced with the conservatism of both the Democratic presidential candidate, John W. Davis, and the Republican President, Calvin Coolidge. Henry Wallace established the Progressive Party in 1948 in protest to the hard-line foreign policy stand taken by each of the major parties.[8]

On a more general note, the authors of *Third Parties in America* conclude: "Major party failure is the primary force motivating third party voting in America. When the two major parties deteriorate — when they neglect the concerns of significant blocs of voters, mismanage the economy, or nominate unqualified candidates — voters turn to a third party alternative."[9]

Ernest and Preston Manning made essentially the same point in *Political Realignment*, published in 1967: "Once the major political parties have converged to the point that they are distinguishable from one another only on the grounds of superficialities and the personalities operating, the period of inadequacy has begun. Voters no longer have the opportunity to choose between legitimate alternatives."[10] The Mannings at this time advocated the ideological realignment of existing parties, not the creation of a new party, but the basic insight is the same: if the views of large numbers of voters are not adequately represented, the situation is ripe for political entrepreneurship to present new alternatives.

Even when minor parties fall by the wayside, as most do sooner or later, they arguably play a crucial role in keeping the major parties responsive to voters. The smaller parties bring new ideas to the surface; they tug the larger parties in their direction by threatening to take away votes, money, and volunteers; and they occasionally obtain great leverage in periods of minority government, as in 1972–1974, when the NDP kept the Liberals in power.

Although this understanding of the place of new parties is essential, it is rather like studying the earth's surface in terms of plate tectonics. It deals mainly with long-term, impersonal causes, such as demographic tendencies, economic cycles, and secular trends in public opinion that operate systemically and are not under anyone's control. It is useful to political scientists who are content to explain the inevitability of events, but not very useful to political activists who would like to promote or fend off the entry of new parties into the system.

At this point, the methodology of *rational choice* comes into play. Rational-choice analysis assumes that political actors at all levels, from voter to prime minister, are rational in the instrumental sense of that term, that is, they know what ends they would like to attain, they wish to attain them at the least cost, and they are capable of choosing the most effective means of achieving those ends. Fundamentally, rational-choice analysis is the study of strategy. As such, it represents an exciting and liberating advance in political science because it goes beyond abstract, impersonal causes into the real world of political actors, whose daily business involves making strategic choices.

The pioneering effort in applying rational-choice methodology to the competition of political parties was made by Anthony Downs in *An Economic Theory of Democracy* (1957). Downs's best-known result is his analysis of the simplest case, where competition is restricted to two parties. Legally, there is always the possibility of more than two parties in a liberal democracy; but the actual situation is often very close to the two-party case because of the high barriers to entry erected by plurality voting and reinforced by legislation handicapping new parties (regulation of funding, advertising, ballot format and so on).[11] In addition to the typical rational-choice assumption that all political actors act rationally, Downs assumes that there is only one relevant dimension of political cleavage in the society, which for convenience we can think of as ideology, since that factor operates in all democratic systems. Also for convenience, Downs assumes that there is a normal distribution of ideological positions among voters, although the shape of the distribution does not actually matter in the simplest case. The result is the famous median-voter hypothesis, illustrated in Figure A-1.[12]

Assume that rational voters will vote for the party whose location on the ideological spectrum is nearest to their own location, and that rational party leaders will seek to position their party so as to get more votes than their competitors. Under these conditions, both parties will approach the position of the median voter, the mid-point of whatever ideological spectrum prevails in the society. The reason is that if a party were to move either

Figure A-1
Simplest Model Of Two-Party Competition

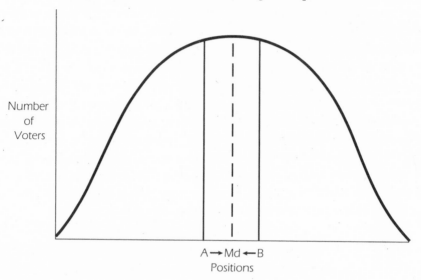

to the right or the left, it would allow its competitor to position itself closer to a majority of voters, thereby garnering their support.

This model is, of course, highly simplified. Voters do not respond to parties solely on the basis of ideology; they are also concerned with the character and personality of candidates, especially of party leaders. Many voters, moreover, are only vaguely aware of the ideological positions that parties assume. Rational-choice theory predicts, in fact, that most voters will follow a strategy of rational ignorance; that is, they will not invest heavily in acquiring information about politics, preferring rather to follow cues given by the much smaller number of politicians, journalists, and other observers who have strong incentives to become knowledgeable.[13] But even with all these qualifications, party positioning can still be expected to make a difference at the margin; and marginal gains and losses make all the difference to parties contesting for power. Hence we must expect party leaders to think strategically about positioning as a way of maximizing their support.

Although Downs's first model is admittedly simplistic, it correctly predicts the "tweedle-dee-tweedle-dum" competition between two large centrist parties that generally characterizes politics in Britain, Canada, New Zealand, Australia, and the United States. Also, it is not hard to build greater degrees of realism into the model. For example, the ideological position taken by a party is more like a line segment than a point. That is, it cannot be perfectly precise; and, in a world of imperfect information, having a broader position may allow one to overlap with the competition and thus attract some of that party's support. Moreover, party leaders are not at complete liberty to position the party wherever they wish in order to attract votes; they also have to pay special attention to the views of the people who volunteer time and money to keep the party going. These volunteers and donors tend to be more extreme, in one direction or another, than the median voter; it is the very fact that they are off centre, so to speak, that creates an incentive for them to volunteer time and money to modify the "natural" equilibrium at the position of the median voter. Volunteers and donors, therefore, tend to pull their parties away from the centre, and leaders must balance that pull against the imperatives of vote maximization.[14] Adding all of this to the simplest model gives a more realistic one in which two parties compete with overlapping but discernibly different positions (Figure A-2).

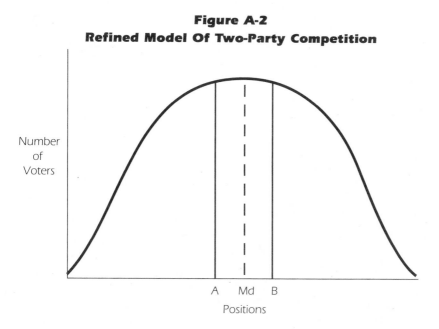

Figure A-2
Refined Model Of Two-Party Competition

Now relax the constraint that there can be only two political parties. Is there a winning strategy by which a third party can enter the system or even displace one member of the duopoly? Assume that a new party C is trying to break into a system dominated by old parties A and B. One obvious move would be for new party C to position itself just to the right of old party B (to the left of A would amount to the same thing).[15] If such a move were possible, C would be closer than B to most right-wing voters and should attract their support, thus finishing ahead of B. How many members C would elect would depend upon the geographical concentration of the conservative voters for whom it was contesting with B. If such voters were evenly dispersed across many constituencies, it is possible that C's challenge would do nothing but produce a landslide for A, whose left-wing support would be unaffected. But whether or not C can elect many members the first time, the model suggests that it should be able to outflank and finish ahead of B, thus positioning itself to enter the duopoly in the future (see Figure A-3).

Figure A-3
Brams/Landry Model of Third-Party Entry

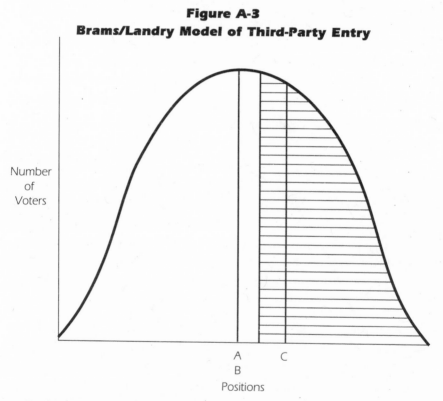

In this simple form, Invasion from the Margin is a patently unrealistic model. It predicts wave after wave of successful invasions from both left and right, which would lead to a virtual kaleidoscope of parties. In fact, politics does not look like that anywhere in the world; the tendency is always for a small number of parties to achieve long-term dominance.[16]

This is particularly true under plurality voting, in which a party will go nowhere unless it can find supporters who are territorially concentrated in order to create local pluralities. But even if that can be achieved, two other factors blocking Invasion from the Margin are inertia and imperfect information. Like any purveyor of goods and services, an established political party has a huge advantage in reputation, credibility, and name-recognition over a new competitor. To have any hope of success, the recent entrant must differentiate itself from the established party. That requires not only putting in a lot of hard work but also assuming a position not too close to the duopoly; for if C is only slightly different from B, why should voters who are used to B take the risk of supporting C, about which they know very little? But taking a position far out towards the tail of the opinion distribution in order to promote clear differentiation carries its own risks. The ends of the spectrum harbour extremists whose active support can be counterproductive for winning elections: communists and anarchists on the left, racists and fascists on the right.

For all these reasons, positioning for a new party playing Invasion from the Margin is highly sensitive. It must find a position far enough away from its main competitor so that it can differentiate itself, but not so far away that it appeals only to the small number of voters on the tail of the opinion distribution; and it must draw an effective line beyond itself so that it does not get discredited by extremists.

Finally, even if the new party finds a workable position, its main competitor can respond by moving towards it somewhat. Since the established party is by hypothesis operating in the region of the opinion distribution where voters are most numerous, it needs to take only a relatively small step away from the centre to win back a substantial number of voters who might be attracted to the new party. For this reason alone, Downs dismissed Invasion from the Margin as unworkable. In his opinion, it would not allow a new party to break into the system, though it might succeed in moving the position of an existing party, at least for a time.[17] Downs's view should be kept in mind as one possible scenario for the ultimate fate of the Reform Party. However, his rejection of Invasion from the Margin is untenable as a general proposition, for there is at least one modern example of its success in Canada — the CCF/NDP.

The CCF/NDP established itself in Canadian politics by outflanking the Liberals on the left. Whether they were offering qualitatively different positions known as democratic socialism or social democracy, or whether they were merely "Liberals in a hurry," they were always to the left of the Liberals.[18] As the model predicts, they had problems with extremists on the far left, but they eventually managed to drive out the communists and fellow-travellers. They vaulted over the barrier of first-past-the-post voting by relying upon the votes concentrated in the working-class areas of major cities (Vancouver, Winnipeg, Toronto); manufacturing centres (Windsor, Hamilton, Oshawa);

and unionized natural-resource-extraction areas (mining, forest products). They concentrated their resources by appealing mainly to English-speaking Canadians, although they also made an effort to compete in Quebec. They never managed to displace the Liberals in the federal governing duopoly, but Ed Broadbent mused about this publicly early during the 1988 election campaign when the NDP was leading the Liberals in public opinion polls.[19] The federal New Democrats are in disarray at the time of writing; but given that they have formed governments in four provinces and Yukon, it would be presumptuous to say that their positioning will never turn into a winning strategy at the federal level.

Political conflict along a single dimension, combined with the high barriers to entry erected by plurality voting, tends to produce an equilibrium outcome of stable competition between two large centrist parties. But as a general rule, the tendency to equilibrium vanishes when more than one dimension of conflict exists.[20] Imagine a society with two ideologies, left (L) and right (R), and two social groups, pink (P) and blue (B). To simplify matters, do not worry about matters of degree; assume that political parties may recruit support by advocating one of the four possible pairs of positions: left-pink (LP), left-blue (LB), right-pink (RP), and right-blue (RB). Each voter will have his own preferred ordering of these four possibilities. Let us say that conservatively minded pinks will order RP>RB>LP>LB and conservatively minded blues will order RB>RP>LB>LP. A political leader who can keep voters' attention focused on ideological conservatism may be able to hold together a coalition of pink and blue conservatives; but such a coalition is always vulnerable to appeals from a political entrepreneur who draws attention to ethnicity in hopes of creating, say, a pink party embracing both liberals and conservatives. Political scientists refer to such a situation as cyclical. Regardless of what position a party assumes in two-dimensional issue space, there is always the possibility that it can lose part of its support to another party that outflanks it along one or the other of the relevant dimensions.

Several authors have pointed out that parties can follow "preference-shaping" as well as "preference-accommodating" strategies.[21] That is, leaders are not bound by the existing distribution of public opinion. On established issue dimensions, they can try to move the median position in one direction or the other; and they can also seek to highlight new dimensions that were previously not the subject of overt political conflict. William Riker argues that political entrepreneurs on the margins are constantly trying to raise new issues, seeking dimensions of cleavage that will pry apart existing coalitions. He sees a "natural selection" of issues in which most such attempts fail but an occasional one succeeds in bringing about a major realignment.[22]

Ideological conflict is ubiquitous in democratic politics, and ethno-linguistic conflict is quite common, but they are not the only possibilities; in principle an unlimited number of potential issue dimensions exist. Although the number of potential dimensions of political conflict is unlimited in theory, it is rather constrained in practice. Arend Lijphart claims to have found seven different issue dimensions exemplified in the 22 democracies he studied. The parenthetical numbers in the following list denote the number of cases out of 22 where Lijphart found the particular dimension to have high or medium importance:[23]

1. Socioeconomic   (22)
2. Religious   (13)
3. Cultural-ethnic   (5)
4. Urban-rural   (8)
5. Regime support   (5)
6. Foreign policy   (9)
7. Postmaterialism   (3)

In his view, the cultural-ethnic cleavage has high significance, and the socio-economic dimension medium significance in Canada, while the others are not relevant. Lijphart's view of Canada is reasonable enough for the period he studied (1945–1980), but a longer historical perspective might have suggested to him the political possibilities of regionalism. Another possible dimension of politics is the conflict between masses and elites expressed in populist parties. Although Lijphart did not include populism in his list of seven dimensions salient to post-World War II democracies, it has been important in earlier periods of history and has surfaced recently in Canada as in many other countries.

Reform strategy has been, in effect, a series of attempts to exploit the multidimensional potential of Canadian politics. Creating a Party of Western Canada was a way of cutting across existing ideological cleavages to solicit the support of a broad cross-section of western voters. Becoming The Party of English Canada was another way of cutting across ideological lines of division to create an electoral coalition, and the same could be said of Manning's vision of Reform as The Party of the People.

As pointed out in Chapter 3, Manning has never fully committed the Reform Party to any one of these new dimensions but has highlighted them all at various times while "waiting for the wave." Ultimately, his strategy for coming to power depends on crisis scenarios and systemic shocks strong enough to swamp all existing partisan alignments. But while waiting for those waves to break, raising new dimensions that cut across existing cleavages is a highly rational undertaking for a political entrepreneur who seeks to carve out a niche in the system. However, one may question the wisdom of experimenting with three new dimensions, plus conventional conservative positioning, in such a short period of time. Trying out new identities may preserve flexibility, but it also raises doubts about what the party stands for, and indeed whether it stands for anything other than putting the leader into 24 Sussex Drive.

Notes

INTRODUCTION

1. Murray Dobbin, *Preston Manning and the Reform Party* (Toronto: James Lorimer, 1991), 215.

CHAPTER 1

1. Sydney Sharpe and Don Braid, *Storming Babylon: Preston Manning and the Rise of the Reform Party* (Toronto: Key Porter, 1992), 2.

2. Preston Manning, *The New Canada* (Toronto: Macmillan Canada, 1992), 96.

3. Ibid., 97.

4. Preston Manning, "National Spiritual Revival: A Centennial Project for Canadian Christians" (Edmonton: "Canada's National Back to the Bible Hour" [1967]).

5. Manning, *The New Canada*, 97.

6. Ibid., 100–101.

7. Ibid., 95–102.

8. Preston Manning, "The Reconciliation of Parties in Conflict: The Theory and Application of a Model of Last Resort," *Crux* 21 (1985): 10–18, reprinted in Donald M. Lewis, ed., *With Heart, Mind and Strength: The Best of Crux 1979–1989* (Langley, B.C.: CREDO Publishing, 1990), 237–51.

9. Ibid., 250.

10. Manning, *The New Canada*, 102.

11. Radio address no. 813 on "Canada's National Bible Hour," entitled "Christians and Politics," n.d.

12. Manning, *The New Canada*, 104.

13. Ibid., 94–109.

14. Preston Manning, "Moral Decision Making in the Political Arena," transcript of radio address 1008 on "Canada's National Bible Hour," September 1985.

15. Ibid., 8.

16. See Manning, *The New Canada*, 321–22.

17. Reform Party of Canada, *Principles and Policies*, 1991, 11, 39; Manning, *The New Canada*, 108.

18. Preston Manning, "Constituent Consensus Rules," *Calgary Herald*, May 1, 1994.

19. Dobbin, *Preston Manning and the Reform Party*, 115.

20. Ibid., 215.

21. Ibid., acknowledgements.

22. Preston Manning, "Choosing a Political Vehicle to Represent the West," in *Act of Faith*, ed. Ted Byfield (Vancouver: British Columbia Report Books, 1991), 172.

23. Preston Manning, "Building the Reform Team: The Hockey Analogy"; George Koch, "Looking Leftward: Manning's Search for New Members Angers the Party's Right Wing," *Alberta Report*, February 5, 1990, reprinted in Byfield, *Act of Faith*, 89–90.

24. E.C. Manning, *Political Realignment: A Challenge to Thoughtful Canadians* (Toronto: McClelland and Stewart, 1967). Preston's role is mentioned in the acknowledgements.

25. Ibid., 62.

26. Daniel Bell, *The End of Ideology: On the Exhaustion of Political Ideas in the Fifties* (New York: Free Press, 1962/1960), 402–40 3.

27. Of all these names, the only one to appear in *The New Canada* is Thomas Sowell (315) in a section that I drafted for Manning. He bought one of Sowell's books, *Preferential Policies*, on my recommendation, but his subsequent statements on race show no sign of being influenced by Sowell.

28. Ernest C. Manning, *The White Paper on Human Resources Development* (Edmonton, 1967), 25; John J. Barr, *The Dynasty: The Rise and Fall of Social Credit in Alberta* (Toronto: McClelland and Stewart, 1974), 146.

29. Reform Party of Canada, Official Record of Assembly 1992, plank 6 — Agriculture.

30. News release, "Reform Party Releases Comprehensive Agriculture Plan," June 22, 1993; Jim Romahn, "No Big Reform," *Kitchener-Waterloo Record*, June 29, 1993.

31. Reform Party, *Principles and Policies*, 1991, 25.

32. Kenneth Whyte, "Preston Manning: PM or Post Mortem," *Saturday Night*, July/August 1993, 16.

33. For example, the Zero in Three package of budget-balancing reforms called for an intensified OAS clawback beginning at the average family income ($54,000 at the end of 1992).

34. Geoffrey York, "Leader Says Reform Policy on Defence Might Change," *Globe and Mail*, October 6, 1993.

35. Principle no. 6, in Manning, *The New Canada*, 360.

36. Dobbin, *Preston Manning*, 165.

37. *Haig and Birch v. Canada* (1992), 9 O.R. (3d) 495.

38. Thomas Flanagan, Reform Party Policy Interpretation Bulletin, October 30, 1992; Virgil Anderson to all Reform candidates, December 18, 1992.

39. Canadian Press, "Manning Angers Gays," *Calgary Herald*, June 17, 1993.

40. Preston Manning, letter to Vancouver *Sun*, June 24, 1993.

41. "Pick Me! Pick Me!" *Canadian Living*, September 1993, 120.

42. Sheldon Alberts, "Manning Favours Limited Protection of Gay Rights," *Calgary Herald*, May 17, 1994.

43. Hugh Winsor, "Manning Draws Big Crowds, But Little National Attention," *Globe and Mail*, June 15, 1992.

44. Issue statement no. 9, November 20, 1991, in the Reform Party of Canada, Green Book (a binder collection of issue statements). Manning inserted this paragraph into my draft.

45. Preston Manning, covering circular letter for the draft speech, June 1, 1993.

46. Nuala Beck, *Shifting Gears* (Toronto: HarperCollins, 1992).

47. Preston Manning, "The Reformer's Guide to the New Economy," draft speech, May 31, 1993, list based on section headings from pp. 28–42.

48. Preston Manning, interview with Professor R. A. Young, June 13, 1991, in London, Ontario, recounted by Young to me, February 28, 1994.

49. Conversation with Ken Whyte, March 2, 1994.

50. Preston Manning, candidate questionnaire, March 18, 1991, 27.

51. Melanie Verhaeghe, "Fight for the Right to Party," *Winnipeg Sun*, February 12, 1992.

52. Peter Stockland, "Presto and his Friendly Fire Zones," *Ottawa Sun*, May 26, 1993.

CHAPTER 2

1. Manning, *The New Canada*, 6.

2. Ibid., 7.

3. Reform Party constitution, October 29, 1992, 1. See also Manning's Vancouver speech in Byfield, *Act of Faith*, 166–67. Although they did not use the term *reform tradition*, Manning's friends John J. Barr and Owen Anderson constructed a similar genealogy in *The Unfinished Revolt: Some Views on Western Independence* (Toronto: McClelland and Stewart, 1971), 36–39.

4. Manning, *The New Canada*, 26.

5. Ibid., 25.

6. Ibid., 26.

7. Ibid., 260.

8. Ibid., 27.

9. Preston Manning, interview in *NeWest Review*, April/May 1989, 23–24.

10. Reform Party constitution, October 30, 1987, s. 11(c).

11. Manning, *The New Canada*, 148.

12. Kenneth Whyte and Mike Byfield, "A Constitution with a Difference," *Alberta Report*, November 9, 1987, in Byfield, *Act of Faith*, 40.

13. Jim Cunningham, "Spreading the Word; Manning Takes His Message to the People," *Calgary Herald*, September 26, 1993.

14. E.C. Manning, *Political Realignment*, 18.

15. Ibid., 64–68. There is a similar list of 10 items in the *White Paper on Human Resources Development*, 18.

16. Manning, *The New Canada*, 147.

17. Reform Party, *Principles and Policies*, 1990, 4. The Triple-E Senate was added to the list at the Saskatoon Assembly, so this item is now second in the current list of 21 principles.

18. Manning, *The New Canada*, 360–61.

19. The Marxist literature on populism is summarized in David Laycock, *Populism and Democratic Thought in the Canadian Prairies, 1910–1945* (Toronto: University of Toronto Press, 1990), ch. 1, especially 14–19, and 308–9, n. 13. But apart from Sinclair, cited below, I have not found this Marxist literature helpful and have not drawn upon it.

20. Peter R. Sinclair, "The Case of Western Canada," *Canadian Journal of Sociology* 9 (1975), reprinted in George Melnyk, ed., *Riel to Reform: A History of Protest in Western Canada* (Saskatoon: Fifth House, 1992), 200.

21. Ibid., 199–200.

22. Preston Manning, "The New National Agenda," November 1992.

23. Paul Wilson of Toronto, one of Havel's English translators, could not locate it for me.

24. Reform Party, *Principles and Policies*, 1991, 11.

25. Manning, *The New Canada*, 326.

26. Ibid.

27. Thomas Flanagan, "Reform of Canada's Parliamentary Institutions," June 1991, 45–47.

28. Manning, *The New Canada*, 325–26.

29. Green Book, issue statement no. 37, July 16, 1992.

30. Sinclair, "The Case of Western Canada," 199.

31. Reform Party, *Principles and Policies*, 1991, 39.

32. CBC, "The World at Six," March 30, 1994, segment regarding preparations for euthanasia forum in Calgary.

33. Reform Party, constitution, October 29, 1992, s.5(e).

34. I saw this first-hand at the organizational meeting of the newly elected executive council in May 1991, and have been told by insiders that it is always done this way.

35. Peter C. Newman, *The Distemper of Our Times: Canadian Politics in Transition* (Toronto: McClelland and Stewart, 1968), 126ff.

36. Dobbin, *Preston Manning and the Reform Party*, ch. 6, "Managing the Membership."

37. Constitution, 1992, ss.1(b) and 1(c).

38. Ibid., s. 1(d).

39. Reform Party, *Principles and Policies*, 1991, 14, has a vague paragraph on the development of skills. There is nothing on higher education as such.

40. Reform Party news release, "Manning Advocates Advanced Education Vouchers," January 21, 1992.

41. Official Record of Assembly 1992, Plank 17.

42. Official Record of Assembly 1992, Additional Planks.

43. Official Record of Assembly 1992, Plank 6.

44. Preston Manning, "A New National Agenda for October 27" (Keynote speech at Winnipeg Assembly, October 24, 1992), 7.

45. David Laycock, "Institutions and Ideology in the Reform Party Project," Canadian Political Science Association, Ottawa, June 1993, 6.

46. Manning, *The New Canada*, 24.

47. Preston Manning, "The Road to New Canada," Address to the Saskatoon Assembly, April 6, 1991.

48. Reform Party, *Principles and Policies*, 1991, 18.

49. Thomas Flanagan and Faron Ellis, "A Comparative Profile of the Reform Party of Canada," at Canadian Political Science Association, Charlottetown, June 1992.

50. Geoffrey York, "Reform Plans to Broaden Base, Including Foray into Quebec," *Globe and Mail*, December 9, 1993.

51. I Corinthians 9: 20–22.

CHAPTER 3

1. George Melnyk, "Waiting for the Wave," interview with Preston Manning in *NeWest Review*, April/May 1989, 23–24.

2. Ibid.

3. Joan Bryden, "Reform's 'Ship' Dead in the Water," *Ottawa Citizen*, February 8, 1993; Preston Manning, "Fireside Chat" to all candidates, audiocassette, Feburary 12, 1993.

4. Dobbin, *Preston Manning*, 66–70.

5. Manning, *The New Canada*, 126–27.

6. Sharpe and Braid, *Storming Babylon*, 5.

7. Machiavelli, *The Prince*, trans. George Bull (Harmondsworth: Penguin, 1961), 130.

8. Ibid., 151.

9. On the "sacred trust," see David Bercuson, J. L. Granatstein, and W. R. Young, *Sacred Trust? Brian Mulroney and the Conservative Party in Power* (Toronto: Doubleday Canada, 1986), 93–121. On Air Canada, see N. J. Baxter-Moore, "Ideology or Pragmatism? The Politics and Management of the Mulroney Government's Privatization Programme," *British Journal of Canadian Studies* 7 (1992): 793.

10. Keith Archer and Faron Ellis, "Opinion Structure of Reform Party Activists," Midwest Political Science Association, Chicago, April 1993, Table 4.

11. Shawn Henry, "The Bases of Support for the Reform Party of Canada: Riding a Populist Wave or Providing a Conservative Alternative?" (University of Calgary, Department of Sociology, MA thesis, 1993), 133.

12. Neil Nevitte, "Electoral Discontinuity: The 1993 Canadian Federal Election," Israel Association for Canadian Studies, Jerusalem, May 1994, appendix.

13. E.g., in the Angus Reid Group, Options for Western Canada Study, Spring 1991 (four western provinces), about 60% of those who said they planned to vote Reform claimed they had voted PC in 1988.

14. Thomas Flanagan and Faron Ellis, "A Comparative Profile of the Reform Party of Canada," Canadian Political Science Association, Charlottetown, June 1992, 8.

15. Graham Fraser, *Playing for Keeps: The Making of the Prime Minister, 1988* (Toronto: McClelland and Stewart, 1989), 48; Jeffrey Simpson, *Faultlines: Struggling for a Canadian Vision* (Toronto: HarperCollins, 1993), 276.

16. Reform Party, *Principles and Policies*, 1990, 7; Paul Bunner and Peter MacDonald, "A National Agenda: Manning Calls Quebec's Bluff," *Alberta Report*, November 6, 1989, reprinted in Byfield, *Act of Faith*, 76–78.

17. "Manning Can Live with Loss of Quebec," *Globe and Mail*, July 27, 1992.

18. Diane Francis, "A Man Worth Getting to Know," *Maclean's*, March 2, 1992, 13: David Steinhart, "Manning's Tour de Force," *Calgary Herald*, April 22, 1994.

19. Miro Cernetig, "Reform Party May Contest Quebec Ridings," *Globe and Mail*, February 8, 1993.

20. Richard Mackie, "Next Time Quebec, Manning Promises," *Globe and Mail*, September 20, 1993.

21. Preston Manning, "Countdown to Victory," audiocassette, December 2, 1993.

22. Preston Manning to constituency presidents, candidates, area organizers, memo, August 29, 1988.

23. Manning, *The New Canada*, 126–29.

24. Angus Reid Group, Options for Western Canada, June 1991, 96.

25. Mel Hurtig, *A New and Better Canada: Principles and Policies of a New Canadian Political Party* (Toronto: Stoddart, 1992), 30.

26. Byfield, *Act of Faith*, 172.

27. Reform Party constitution, October 30, 1987, s. 11.

28. Manning, *The New Canada*, 230–33; Byfield, *Act of Faith*, 91–92, 106.

29. Byfield, *Act of Faith*, 172.

30. Margaret Canovan, *Populism* (London: Junction Books, 1981), 265.

31. Ibid., 271.

32. Reform Party, *Principles and Policies*, 1991, 3, Statement of Principles, no. 14.

CHAPTER 4

1. The title of this chapter was taken from a subheading in Preston Manning's memo to executive council, March 25, 1989.

2. Manning, *The New Canada*, 125–44.

3. Byfield, *Act of Faith*, 170, 172.

4. Ibid., 170.

5. Ibid., 168.

6. Ibid., 172.

7. Ibid.

8. Ibid., 173.

9. Ibid., 179.

10. Steve Weatherbe, "Proposing Policy Alternatives," *Alberta Report*, June 8, 1987, reprinted in Byfield, *Act of Faith*, 27.

11. Stephen Harper and John Weissenberger, "Political Reform and the Taxpayer," n.d.

12. Printed with a few deletions as "A Question of Fairness: The Makings of a New Majority," *Alberta Report*, November 16 & 23, 1987, reprinted in Byfield, *Act of Faith*, 43–48.

13. Ibid., 46.

14. Ibid., 43–44.

15. Ibid., 48.

16. Manning, *The New Canada*, 149.

17. Reform Party of Canada, *Platform and Statement of Principles*, August 1988, 16–17.

18. Ibid., 19.

19. Ibid., 4.

20. Preston Manning, circular letter of August 29, 1988.

21. Ibid.

22. Preston Manning to Stephen Harper, memo, November 8, 1988.

23. "Reform Party Commentary on Free Trade Agreement," October 18, 1988.

24. "An Open Letter to Free Trade Liberals," n.d.

25. Stephen Harper to Preston Manning, memo, March 10, 1989.

26. Ibid.

27. Stephen Harper and John Weissenberger, unpublished ms., n.d., ch. 2, "The Political Class."

28. James Q. Wilson, *American Government: Institutions and Politics*, 3rd ed. (Lexington, Mass.: D.C. Heath, 1986), 118.

29. Harper to Manning, memo, March 10, 1989.

30. Ibid.

31. Preston Manning to environmental policy task force, draft, April 17, 1989.

32. Preston Manning to members of executive council, March 25, 1989; Manning to Reform Party members, June 26, 1989.

33. Preston Manning to Reform Party members, June 26, 1989.

34. Ibid., Attachment A.

35. Reform Party news release, "Leadership Lacking in Federal Budget," May 9, 1989.

36. Reform Party of Canada, *Platform and Statement of Principles*, August 1988, 16.

37. Preston Manning, "Reorganizing Via Rail," text of radio address, June 21, 1989.

38. See, for example, the policy committee's remarks on a resolution to abolish the GST immediately, Exposure Draft of Policy Resolutions for Saskatoon Assembly, January 13, 1991.

39. Official Record of Assembly 1992, Winnipeg, October 23–25, 1992, amendment to plank 3 on tax reform.

40. Preston Manning to constitutional task force, February 13, 1989.

41. Preston Manning, "Leadership for Changing Times," Address to the Edmonton Assembly, October 28, 1989, 6–7.

42. Reform Party, *Platform and Statement of Principles*, August 1988, 23.

43. Paul Bunner and Peter MacDonald, "A National Agenda: Manning Calls Quebec's Bluff," *Alberta Report*, November 6, 1989, reprinted in Byfield, *Act of Faith*, 76–79.

44. *House of Commons Debates*, April 12, 1989, 413.

45. 1987 constitution, s. 11(b).

46. "Key Resolutions on the Expansion of the Reform Party," n.d., appended to Stephen Harper, "Expansion to the East — The Time Is Now," April 25, 1990.

47. Kenneth Whyte, "Under Attack: Suddenly, the Major Parties have Discovered the RPC," *Alberta Report*, October 29, 1990, in Byfield, *Act of Faith*, 115.

48. Manning, *The New Canada*, 293.

49. Robert Matheson to constituency presidents, June 9, 1989.

50. Official Record of Saskatoon Assembly, April 4–7, 1991, 22.

51. Official Record of Saskatoon Assembly, April 4–7, 1991, 23.

52. Stephen Harper, "Some Thoughts on the Eastern Expansion Situation," and "Expansion to the East — The Time Is Now," both April 25, 1990.

53. Stephen Harper, "The Reform Vision of Canada," April 5, 1991, 8.

54. Official Record of Saskatoon Assembly, April 4–7, 1991, 3.

55. Official Record of Saskatoon Assembly, April 4–7, 1991, 5.

56. Compare the 1990 Blue Book, 23, to the 1991 Blue Book, 35.

57. Robert Matheson to constituency presidents, June 9, 1989.

58. Preston Manning, "The Road to New Canada," April 6, 1991, 2.

59. Ibid., 7.

60. Ibid., 8.

61. Ibid., 9.

62. Ibid., 14.

63. Ibid., 15.

64. Ibid., 16–17.

65. Simpson, *Faultlines: Struggling for a Canadian Vision*, 125.

66. "The Road to New Canada," 16.

CHAPTER 5

1. In attendance were Preston Manning, Cliff Fryers, Stephen Harper, Diane Ablonczy, Alan Wiggan, Randy Lennon, and myself.

2. This is approximately what was said; I did not write down Fryers' and Manning's exact words.

3. I attended a rally in Calgary in fall 1991 when Don Leier, vice-chairman of the party, said more or less, "The other parties expect Preston to be flying Air Canada, but we'll make sure he has his own jet."

4. Minutes of executive council meeting, June 15–16, 1990; Strategic planning committee to executive council, July 26, 1990, *re* "Restructuring Party Operations."

5. Reform Party news release, "Reform Council Nullifies Gamble Nomination," April 2, 1993.

6. Frank I. Luntz, *Candidates, Consultants, and Campaigns: The Style and Substance of American Electioneering* (Oxford: Blackwell, 1988). Foreword by Richard Wirthlin.

7. Robert Mason Lee, *One Hundred Monkeys* (Toronto: Macfarlane, Walter and Ross, 1989), 133–34; Fraser, *Playing for Keeps*, 131, 320, 376.

8. Frank I. Luntz and associates, "A Telephone Survey of Voter Attitudes in Canada: Presentation Materials," September 19, 1991.

9. John Laschinger and Geoffrey Stevens, *Leaders and Lesser Mortals: Backroom Politics in Canada* (Toronto: Key Porter, 1992), 80–87.

10. John Sawatsky, *The Insiders: Government, Business, and the Lobbyists* (Toronto: McClelland and Stewart, 1987), 208.

11. Christina McCall-Newman, *Grits: An Intimate Portrait of the Liberal Party* (Toronto: Macmillian of Canada, 1982), 455.

12. Sawatsky, *The Insiders*, 152–56.

13. Ross Howard, "Cabinet Dispute Holds Up Ethics Package," *Globe and Mail*, March 18, 1994.

14. Communication from Robert Harper, who helped to organize the dinner in his role as assistant to Deborah Grey.

15. At a media-briefing session that Anderson arranged for me in Ottawa, he became quite upset when I told a group of reporters that Quebec had too much power in Confederation. "Canadians Are Fed Up with Quebec: Reformer," Montreal *Gazette*, December 4, 1991.

16. Rick Anderson to Preston Manning, Tom Flanagan, Stephen Harper, April 8, 1991.

17. Rick Anderson to Preston Manning, Tom Flanagan, Stephen Harper, January 10, 1992.

18. Rick Anderson to TEAC members, December 16, 1991.

19. George Koch, "The Real Fight Begins," *Alberta Report*, November 4, 1991, 13.

20. Dick Harris, "Proposal: National Corporate Fund Raising Initiative for 1992," January 17, 1992.

21. Miro Cernetig, "Manning Turns Battle against Deal into Election Campaign," *Globe and Mail*, September 19, 1992.

22. Suzanne Zwarun, "Women and the Reform Party," *Chatelaine*, March 1992, 46.

23. Lorne Gunter, "A Growing Alberta Tidal Wave," *Alberta Report*, March 23, 1992, 15.

24. George Koch, "The RPC Counter-Attacks," *Alberta Report*, February 3, 1992, 9–12.

25. Melanie Verhaeghe, "Fight for the Right to Party," *Winnipeg Sun*, February 12, 1992.

26. William Walker, "Reform Party Ponders Expulsion of Brockville Worker," *Toronto Star*, January 17, 1992.

27. Reform Party news release, "Reform Council Requests LeGrand's Resignation," January 18, 1992.

28. Conversation with Bill Dunphy, the reporter for the *Toronto Sun*.

29. Reform Party news release, "Reform Party Executive Expels Racist Members, Plans Further Steps," March 10, 1992.

30. Rose DiManno, "Ex-mercenary Aims for Country 'Uniquely' White," *Toronto Star*, June 19, 1991.

31. Alan Muxworthy to Diane Ablonczy, July 24, 1991. Copy furnished by Muxworthy when the original could not be found.

32. William Walker, "Reform Party Is Racist as Duke, Copps Says," *Toronto Star*, November 20, 1993.

33. Ron Csillag, "Orthodox Jew Follows Reform," *Canadian Jewish News*, December 5, 1991; Norm Ovenden, "Reform's 'Invisible' Minorities Speak Up," *Edmonton Journal*, December 7, 1991.

34. William Walker, "Reform Party is Racist as Duke, Copps Says," *Toronto Star*, November 20, 1993.

35. Excerpts from a press scrum with Brian Mulroney, December 12, 1991, attached to Reform Party news release, [December, 1991].

36. William Walker, "Reform to Probe Morality of MPs," *Toronto Star*, February 6, 1992.

37. E.g., "Digging the Dirt," Victoria *Times-Colonist*, February 12, 1992.

38. Judith Lavoie, "Reform's Life Insurance Scheme to Raise Money Shocks Party Renegade," Victoria *Times-Colonist*, February 29, 1992.

39. Zena Olijnik, "Reform Seeks Loyalty from Beyond the Grave," *Winnipeg Free Press*, March 1, 1993.

40. Sean Durkan, "PCs Claim Reform Plan's Illegal," *Calgary Sun*, March 12, 1992.

41. "Taxman Wrong about Reform," *Calgary Sun*, March 27, 1992.

42. Reform Party news release, "Reform MP Releases Public Letter from Party Members Who Donated Life Insurance Policy," March 18, 1992.

CHAPTER 6

1. Rick Anderson to Preston Manning, Tom Flanagan, and Stephen Harper, memo, April 8, 1992.

2. Miro Cernetig, "Manning Targets Welfare System," *Globe and Mail*, June 8, 1992.

3. Reform Party news release, "No Constitutional Deal Better Than a Bad Deal, Says Manning," June 22, 1993.

4. Reform Party news release, "Canadians More Concerned about Economy Than Constitution, Manning Declares," June 25, 1992.

5. Ibid.

6. Reform Party news release, "Reform Party Encouraged by Premiers' Agreement," July 8, 1993.

7. Reform Party news release, "Manning Says Mulroney Must Act on Constitutional Deal and Support Senate Reform," July 22, 1993.

8. James Parker, "PM Wants Unity Talks to Fail: Manning," Saskatoon *Star-Phoenix*, August 7, 1993.

9. John Geddes, "Equal Senate May Bring Manning to Ottawa," *Financial Post*, August 26, 1992.

10. Miro Cernetig, "Reform Party a House Divided," *Globe and Mail*, October 23, 1992; David Roberts, "Manning Under Attack at Reform Convention: No-Side Campaigner Said to Have Supported Parts of Deal," *Globe and Mail*, October 24, 1992.

11. Leader's letter to members, September 8, 1992.

12. Rick Bell, "Reform Callers Oppose Accord," *Calgary Sun*, September 8, 1992.

13. Miro Cernetig, "Saying Yes to the No Side: Manning Chooses High-Risk Campaign," *Globe and Mail*, September 3, 1992.

14. Brian Laghi, "Reform Party Faces a Fight for Its Soul," *Edmonton Journal*, August 29, 1992.

15. Tom Flanagan to Preston Manning, August 26, 1992.

16. Gordon Shaw, executive director, to constituency presidents and candidates, October 30, 1992. Percentages based on 28,826 responses out of about 130,000 mailed out.

17. Miro Cernetig, "End Constitutional Wrangling by Voting No, Manning Says," *Globe and Mail*, September 11, 1992.

18. Special issue of *The Reformer*, fall 1992.

19. Reform Party of Canada, Department of Research, "The 'Consensus Report on the Constitution' of August 28, 1992: Analysis for Reform Party Candidates," September 20, 1992.

20. "Manning Reserves Judgment on Deal," *Globe and Mail*, August 25, 1992.

21. David B. Magleby, "Opinion Formation and Opinion Change in Ballot Proposition Campaigns," in Michael Margolis and Gary A. Mauser, eds., *Manipulating Public Opinion: Essays on Public Opinion as a Dependent Variable* (Pacific Grove, Calif.: Brooks/Cole, 1989), 112.

22. Mark Lisac, "Manning's Criticism of Deal Flawed," *Edmonton Journal*, September 11, 1992.

23. *Calgary Herald*, editorial, September 11, 1992.

24. Hugh Winsor, "Reform Leader Traps Himself," *Globe and Mail*, September 16, 1992.

25. William Walker, "Sit on Fence, Manning Urges Ontario," *Toronto Star*, September 18, 1992; Walker, "Manning Reveals Reform's Real No Agenda," *Toronto Star*, September 19, 1992.

26. Reform Party of Canada, news releases, December 3, 1992; December 15, 1992; January 26, 1993.

27. Sean Durkan, "PM Will Pick Senators," *Calgary Sun*, December 15, 1992.

28. Miro Cernetig, "Reform Party a House Divided," *Globe and Mail*, October 23, 1992; David Roberts, "Manning Under Attack at Reform Convention: No-Side Campaigners Said to Have Supported Parts of Deal," *Globe and Mail*, October 24, 1992.

29. Jim Morris, "PM Cuffs Reform Leader at Home," *Winnipeg Free Press*, October 25, 1992.

30. Miro Cernetig, "Money Running Low for Reform Party," *Globe and Mail*, September 18, 1992.

31. Miro Cernetig, "Reform Party a House Divided," *Globe and Mail*, October 23, 1992.

32. See the draft referendum campaign plan of September 10, 1993, which lists Anderson as a member of the committee. It is not signed, but the reference initials show it was written by Manning and typed by his secretary.

33. Statement by Rick Anderson at meeting in Calgary, January 15, 1993.

34. Reform Party of Canada, "Constitutional Referendum Campaign," September 15, 1992.

35. Statement by Rick Anderson, January 15, 1993, confirming my earlier conversation with Miro Cernetig.

36. Statement by Rick Anderson, January 15, 1993.

37. Peter Morton, "Hard Sell," *Financial Post Magazine*, October 1992, 19.

38. Preston Manning, "Statement for the Official Launch of the Reform Party of Canada's Referendum Campaign," September 18, 1992, Calgary, 4.

39. Robert Sheppard, "Western Challenger Wins Round 1 on Points," *Globe and Mail*, October 7, 1992.

40. Ibid.

41. William Gold, "Manning Lost Ground in Defeat to McLaughlin," *Calgary Herald*, October 7, 1992.

42. Rick Salutin, *Globe and Mail*, November 13, 1992.

43. Joan Bryden, "Media May Not Be Negative Enough," *Calgary Herald*, January 6, 1992.

44. Rick Anderson to Preston Manning, Tom Flanagan, and Stephen Harper, April 8, 1992.

45. Canada West Foundation, "Public Opinion and the Charlottetown Accord," January 1993, 6.

46. Graham Fraser, *Playing for Keeps*, 129.

47. Reprinted in *The Reformer*, fall 1992.

48. "Statement by Preston Manning for the Official Launch of the Reform Party of Canada's Referendum Campaign," September 18, 1992.

49. Charlie Anderson, "Deal May Be Mulroney's, But the Choice Is Yours," Vancouver *Sun*, September 21, 1992.

50. Gordon Shaw to candidates and constituency presidents, memo, October 2, 1992, with attached ad mats.

51. Reform Party of Canada, "For the Love of Canada, No: Why You Should Vote NO on October 26," pamphlet.

52. Cliff Fryers to candidates and constituency presidents, November 4, 1992.

53. Mark Miller, "Reform Ads Rapped," *Calgary Sun*, October 14, 1992.

54. Bob Bragg, "Manning Is Surely a Politician Now," *Calgary Herald*, October 21, 1992.

55. Larry Johnsrude, "Reformers Set Leader on the Defensive," *Calgary Herald*, October 24, 1992.

56. Brian Laghi, "Manning Takes Flak for TV Commercials," *Edmonton Journal*, October 24, 1992.

57. Ibid.

58. Larry Johnsrude, "Reformers Set Leader on the Defensive," *Calgary Herald*, October 24, 1992.

59. Jim Cunningham, "Clark Blasts Reforms' [sic] TV-ad 'Gutter Tactics,'" *Calgary Herald*, October 23, 1992.

60. *The Reformer*, January 1993; "Manning Would Change Label of Accord from 'Mulroney Deal,'" *Vancouver Sun*, March 11, 1993.

61. Angus Reid news poll, released September 14, 1992.

62. Richard Johnston et al. "The People and the Charlottetown Accord," in Ronald L. Watts and Douglas M. Brown, eds., *Canada: The State of the Federation 1993* (Kingston, Ont.: Institute of Intergovernmental Affairs, 1993), 30.

63. Chart furnished by Neil Nevitte from the Canadian Referendum Survey conducted by Richard Johnston et al. The graphic representation is slightly misleading because there are only 13 cases (1% of the sample) in the 81–100 category, but the relationship is still strong. Pearson's $r = 0.22$, $p < .01$.

64. Byfield, *Act of Faith*, 172.

65. Ibid., 173.

66. Paul Nesbitt-Larking, "Patterns of Protest in the 1992 Referendum and the 1993 Federal Election," Canadian Political Science Association, Calgary, June 1994, 8.

CHAPTER 7

1. John Yerxa Consumertrak, March 1993, had Reform in third place in both Calgary and Edmonton. Angus Reid placed Reform at 24% in Alberta in May 1993, again in third place.

2. Reform Party news release, "Alberta Reformers Throw Down Senate Gauntlet," January 26, 1993; Ashley Geddes, "Klein Thawing Toward Federal Tories," *Calgary Herald*, February 5, 1993.

3. Ad in the *Globe and Mail*, October 30, 1992.

4. Preston Manning, "The New National Agenda," November 1992.

5. Reform Party news release, "Manning Proposes Cutting Cabinet to Sixteen Ministers," June 24, 1993; Marina Jimenez, "Manning Wants to See 16-member PC Cabinet," *Calgary Herald*, June 25, 1993.

6. Norm Ovenden, "Manning Would Slash Federal Jobs," *Edmonton Journal*, November 10, 1992.

7. Kenneth Whyte, "Reformers Feeling Frisky after Polls Show Surge in Popularity," *Globe and Mail*, May 22, 1993.

8. Reform Party of Canada, Election Platform, January 29, 1993, printed in the Blue Sheet.

9. The speeches were to take place on March 29, 1993 in Toronto; April 12 in Vancouver; April 22 in Ottawa; April 26 in Calgary.

10. "Proposals for Stimulating the Canadian Economy by Eliminating the Federal Deficit," draft, April 14, 1993.

11. Ibid.; Reform Party, *Principles and Policies*, 1991, 33.

12. Reform Party, *Principles and Policies*, 1991, 29.

13. Michael Walker and Isabella Horry, "March's Solution: How to Effectively Cut Federal Spending," *Fraser Forum*, March 1993, 5–14.

14. Reform Party, *Principles and Policies*, 1991, 28.

15. "Reform's Empty Promise," *Edmonton Journal*, April 5, 1993; Karen Hall, "Just When You Thought It Safe . . . ," Vancouver *Province*, April 4, 1993; Leonard Shifrin, "No Monopoly on Stupid Social Policy," Saskatoon *Star-Phoenix*, April 5, 1993.

16. Jim Stott, "Herald's Coverage of Reform Inadequate," *Calgary Herald*, May 9, 1993.

17. Jonathan Ferguson, "Manning Manoeuvres into Spotlight of Fiscal Fever," *Toronto Star*, April 3, 1993; Brian Lewis, "Only Manning Talks Sense on Budget," Vancouver *Province*, May 2, 1993.

18. "The Fat That Remains," *Globe and Mail*, April 29, 1993.

19. Preston Manning, covering circular letter for the draft speech, June 1, 1993.

20. "Fireside Chat No. 6," audiocassette, April 29, 1993.

21. John Flanders, "Stockbroker Sold on Reform," *Hamilton Spectator*, June 25, 1993.

22. Reform Party of Canada, campaign organization chart, July 6, 1993.

23. Kenneth Whyte, "Nice Guys Finish Last," *Saturday Night*, July/August 1993.

24. Kenneth Whyte, "Ottawa Insider Surprise Choice to Manage Reform Campaign," *Globe and Mail*, July 17, 1993.

25. Thomas Flanagan to Preston Manning, letter, July 19, 1993.
26. Preston Manning to Thomas Flanagan, letter, July 27, 1993.
27. Joe Woodward, "The RPC's Controversial Key Man," *Alberta Report*, August 6, 1993.
28. Stephen Harper to Cliff Fryers, letter, August 9, 1993.
29. Ted Byfield, "Reform Party Must Return to Former Policy to Win," *Calgary Sun*, August 9, 1993; "Shift in Strategy Dooms Reformers," *Calgary Sun*, August 15, 1993; "Is Reform Wooing Ottawa at West's Expense?" *Financial Post*, August 28, 1993.
30. Brian Laghi, "Reformers Fear Softer Policies May Hurt Their Showing at Polls," *Edmonton Journal*, September 7, 1993.
31. Cliff Fryers to candidates, September 7, 1993.
32. Reform broadsheet, fall 1993, "This Election Don't Just Buy the Packaging — Look at What's Inside."
33. Preston Manning, "Fireside Chat No. 10," audiocassette, July 20, 1993; "Fireside Chat No. 11," audiocassette, August 24, 1993.
34. Preston Manning to Reform Party candidates, July 22, 1993, covering letter for draft of an "Open Letter to the Electors of Quebec."
35. Preston Manning, draft, "Open Letter to the Electors of Quebec," July 21, 1993, 1.
36. Ibid., 3.
37. Preston Manning to all candidates, August 6, 1993, enclosing both drafts.
38. On public service strikes, see Issue Statement no. 6, October 30, 1991, "Should Federal Employees Have the Right to Strike?"
39. Allan McGirr to all candidates, memo, July 29, 1993.
40. Mitchell Grey to CMC, memo, August 24, 1993.

CHAPTER 8
1. "Grits, Tories Start Race in Virtual Tie," *Calgary Herald*, September 11, 1993.
2. Sean Durkan, "PM Begins Race in Lead," *Calgary Sun*, September 9, 1993: "Grits, Tories Start Race in Virtual Tie," *Calgary Herald*, September 11, 1993.
3. Edward Greenspon and Jeff Sallot, "How Campbell Self-Destructed," *Globe and Mail*, October 27, 1993.
4. Susan Delacourt, Murray Campbell, and Edward Greenspon, "Liberal Hopes on the Rise," *Globe and Mail*, September 21, 1993.
5. Jeff Sallot and Hugh Winsor, "PM Won't Touch Key Issue," *Globe and Mail*, September 24, 1993.
6. Joe Sornberger, "PM Promises More Info on Cuts," *Calgary Herald*, September 25, 1993.
7. David Steinhart, "Deficit Plan Unveiled," *Calgary Herald*, September 28, 1993.
8. Edward Greenspon, "Tories' Supposed Strong Point Turning Out to Be Anything But," *Globe and Mail*, September 29, 1993.
9. Warren Caragata, "Debate: Insults Outweigh Ideas," *Calgary Herald*, October 5, 1993.
10. Ross Howard, "Tories Rush to Attack with New Ads," *Globe and Mail*, October 6, 1993.

11. Sean Durkan and Bill Kaufmann, "Heat's on Reform," *Calgary Sun*, October 10, 1993.

12. Tim Naumetz, "Cuts Made on the Run," *Calgary Sun*, September 29, 1993.

13. "The Voters Speak," *Globe and Mail*, October 25, 1993.

14. Edward Greenspon, Ross Howard, and Susan Delacourt, "Tories Try to Recover from Goof," *Globe and Mail*, October 16, 1993: Julian Beltrame, "Kim Targets Tories," *Calgary Herald*, October 17, 1993.

15. Edward Greenspon and Jeff Sallot, "How Campbell Self-Destructed," *Globe and Mail*, October 27, 1993.

16. Reform Party news release, "Manning Says: 'Let the People Speak!'" Calgary, September 8, 1993.

17. Doug Ward, "Reform Leader's Trying to Reform Own Image to Appeal to Mainstream," Vancouver *Sun*, September 14, 1993.

18. Jim Cunningham, "Manning's Campaign Under Fire," *Calgary Herald*, September 16, 1993.

19. Preston Manning, "Let the People Speak," September 18, 1993.

20. Norm Ovenden, "Manning Outlines Deficit Plan," *Calgary Herald*, September 21, 1993.

21. "The Only Deficit Plan We've Seen," *Globe and Mail*, September 23, 1993.

22. Preston Manning, "Fireside Chat No. 10," audiocassette, July 20, 1993; "Fireside Chat No. 11," audiocassette, August 24, 1993.

23. Preston Manning, circular letter, June 1, 1993.

24. Reform Party news release, "Manning Points to Light at the End of the Economic Tunnel," Carman, Manitoba, September 23, 1993; Reform Party news release, "Manning Points the Way to a More Hopeful Future for Saskatchewan Farmers," Yorkton, Saskatchewan, September 24, 1993.

25. Preston Manning, "Toward the New Economy," October 8, 1993.

26. "Manning Pitches Scheme for Rich," *Calgary Herald*, September 26, 1993.

27. "A Voter's Guide to the Issues," *Globe and Mail*, October 2, 1993.

28. Reform Party news release, "Manning Calls for Parole Board Reform and Accountability," Vancouver, September 30, 1993.

29. Geoffrey York, "Leader Says Reform Policy on Defence Might Change," *Globe and Mail*, October 6, 1993.

30. Hugh Winsor, "Liberals Near Majority, Globe Poll Finds," *Globe and Mail*, October 16, 1993.

31. Environics tracking poll, October 14, 1993, three-day average.

32. Hugh Winsor, "Liberals Near Majority, Globe Poll Finds," *Globe and Mail*, October 16, 1993.

33. Reform Party news release, "Manning Says Liberals Don't Deserve a Majority Government; Minority Parliament Is Best for Canada," Cambridge/Sarnia, October 12, 1993.

34. Reform Party news release, "Manning Offers Canada New Federalism," Toronto, October 1, 1993.

35. Richard Johnston, Neil Nevitte, Henry E. Brady, "Campaign Dynamics in 1993: Liberals, Conservatives, and Reform," Canadian Political Science Association, Calgary, June 1994, 13–15.

36. "Reform in Their Sights," *Globe and Mail*, October 6, 1993.

37. Bob Fife, "How They Did," *Calgary Sun*, October 5, 1993.

38. Jim Cunningham, "Reform Flying on New Note," *Calgary Herald*, October 20, 1993.

39. Reform Party, *The National Informer*, October 14, 1993, 1.

40. "Reform Fund Canada Report," *The Reformer*, vol. 2, issue 3, May 1994.

41. "Manning Pitches Scheme for Rich," *Calgary Herald*, September 26, 1993.

42. Miro Cernetig, "Manning Targets Health Care," *Globe and Mail*, September 29, 1993.

43. Jim Cunningham, "Manning Insists Health Plan OK," *Calgary Herald*, September 29, 1993.

44. Geoffrey York, "Leader Says Reform Policy on Defence Might Change," *Globe and Mail*, October 6, 1993.

45. Mark Miller, "Manning Wants Study of Canada's Military," *Calgary Sun*, October 6, 1993.

46. Hugh Winsor, "Reform Candidate Quits," *Globe and Mail*, October 14, 1993.

47. Edward Greenspon, Miro Cernetig, and Ross Howard, "Tories Hunting Flawed Reformers," *Globe and Mail*, October 15, 1993.

48. Ibid.

49. Environics tracking poll, October 14 to October 21.

50. Richard Johnston, Neil Nevitte, Henry E. Brady, "Campaign Dynamics in 1993: Liberals, Conservatives, and Reform," Canadian Political Science Association, Calgary, June 1994, 2.

51. Monroe Eagles, James P. Bickerton, Alain G. Gagnon, and Patrick J. Smith, *The Almanac of Canadian Politics* (Peterborough: Broadview Press, 1991), 583.

52. Twenty-three in metro-Toronto, 4 in Ottawa, 4 in Hamilton, 3 in London, 2 in Windsor, 2 in Thunder Bay, and Sudbury.

53. Thomas Flanagan and Faron Ellis, "A Comparative Profile of the Reform Party of Canada," Canadian Political Science Association, Charlottetown, June 1992, 7–8.

54. Harold Clarke, "The Dynamics of Support for New Parties and National Party Systems in Contemporary Democracies: The Case of Canada," funded by the National Science Foundation (United States). Data courtesy of Harold Clarke.

CHAPTER 9

1. Leslie A. Pal, "The Political Executive and Political Leadership in Alberta," in Allan Tupper and Roger Gibbins, eds, *Government and Politics in Alberta*, (Edmonton: University of Alberta Press, 1992), 23.

2. Preston Manning, "Leader to Presidents," audiocassette, January 21, 1994.

3. Preston Manning, "Broadening the Circle," audiocassette, March 4, 1994.

4. Steve Chase, "Stepping out of Preston's Shadow," *Alberta Report*, February 21, 1994.

5. Ross Howard, "Anderson's Resignation Demanded over Suit against Ottawa," *Globe and Mail*, January 12, 1994.

6. Edward Greenspon, "Tax Revolt Brewing, Manning Warns Ottawa," *Globe and Mail*, February 21, 1994.

7. Jim Sheppard, "Reformers Attack Delay in Changes," *Calgary Herald*, March 22, 1994.

8. Joan Bryden, "Grits Stop Debate on Redistribution," *Calgary Herald*, March 25, 1994.

9. "Play by the Rules," *Calgary Herald*, March 25, 1994; "Debasing the Franchise (II)," *Globe and Mail*, March 25, 1994.

10. David Roberts, "Reform, Indian Leaders Agree on Self-Rule," *Globe and Mail*, June 7, 1994.

11. *House of Commons Debates*, June 9, 1994, 5071; "Reformer Likens Natives to Overindulged Children," *Calgary Herald*, June 10, 1994.

12. Susan Delacourt, "Reformers Feel Seasick as Grubel Makes Waves," *Globe and Mail*, June 11, 1994.

13. Menno Boldt, *Surviving as Indians: The Challenge of Self-Government* (Toronto: University of Toronto Press, 1993), 172–74.

14. Susan Delacourt, "Reform Party Stalling MPs' Summer Recess," *Globe and Mail*, June 22, 1994.

15. Resolutions approved by the Reform Party caucus, December 8, 1993, in relation to MPs' pay, pension and perks; Geoffrey York, "What Reformers Will Renounce," *Globe and Mail*, December 18, 1993; Norm Ovenden, "'Ride on Gravy Train' Rapped," *Calgary Herald*, June 2, 1994.

16. Geoffrey York, "Party Asks Reform MPs to Give Up Part of Salary," *Globe and Mail*, December 10, 1993.

17. Jane Taber, "Manning Opts for the Back Seat in the House," *Calgary Herald*, January 5, 1994.

18. *The Reformer*, vol. 2, issue 1, January 1994.

19. "The Power in the House," *Hill Times*, January 20, 1994, 13.

20. Jane Taber, "Manning Opts for the Back Seat in the House," *Calgary Herald*, January 5, 1994.

21. *The Reformer*, vol. 2, issue 2, March 1994.

22. Larry Welch, "Talk Tough to Taxman, Manning Urges Canadians," *Calgary Herald*, March 10, 1994.

23. Sheldon Alberts, "Manning Seeking Input on Suicides," *Calgary Herald*, March 31, 1994.

24. Preston Manning, "Constituent Consensus Rules," *Calgary Herald*, May 1, 1994; letter to Charles O. Hudson, June 7, 1994.

25. Sheldon Alberts, "The Question Is, How Long Can Civility Last?" *Calgary Herald*, January 16, 1994; Anthony Wilson-Smith, "A Calming Presence," *Maclean's*, February 28, 1994, 17.

26. Sheldon Alberts, "Silent Majority," and Joan Bryden, "Chrétien's 'Honeymoon' Just Goes On and On," *Calgary Herald*, March 6, 1994.

27. Norm Ovenden, "Liberals Laughing at Reform's Ottawa Performance," *Edmonton Journal*, April 16, 1994.

28. "Manning Says He's in It for the Long Haul," *Calgary Herald*, March 13, 1994.

29. Mario Toneguzzi, "Reform to Refocus Efforts in House," *Calgary Herald*, June 23, 1994.

30. Edward Greenspon, "Loosening the Reins of Power," *Globe and Mail*, July 25, 1994.

31. Joan Crockatt, "Reform's Changes Do Little for Image," *Calgary Herald*, July 22, 1994; "Manning Assigns Team to Shadow Duty," *Globe and Mail*, July 22, 1994.

32. CFCN news broadcast, November 6, 1993.

33. Manning, *The New Canada*, 328.

34. Geoffrey York, "Planned Code of Conduct Sparks Criticism," *Globe and Mail*, March 17, 1994; Sheldon Alberts, "MP Resists Moral Regulation," *Calgary Herald*, March 17, 1994.

35. Norm Ovenden, "Reform Party: Formal Code Abandoned," *Calgary Herald*, March 25, 1994.

36. Manning, *The New Canada*, 155.

37. "Manning Wasn't Always Paid Well," *Globe and Mail*, April 6, 1994.

38. Reform Party of Canada, minutes of executive council meeting, February 11–12, 1994.

39. Reform Party of Canada, constitution, October 29, 1992, s. 9(d). Emphasis added.

40. Reform Party of Canada, minutes of executive council meeting, February 11–12, 1994, 9.

41. Announced in the Reform caucus the week of May 9–13, 1994.

42. Reform Party of Canada, minutes of executive council meeting, February 11–12, 1994, 9.

43. Lorne Gunther, "Reform's Rocky Intro to Ottawa," *Alberta Report*, April 25, 1994, 7.

44. Ibid.

45. Geoffrey York, "Party Asks Reform MPs to Give Up Part of Salary," *Globe and Mail*, December 10, 1993.

46. Reform Party, *Principles and Policies*, 1991, 23.

47. Pay, Perks, and Pensions Committee Recommendations, December 7, 1993, 3.

48. In a memo to caucus dated February 21, 1994, Manning informed them of the allowances.

49. Resolutions Approved by the Reform Party Caucus, December 8, 1993, in relation to MPs' Pay, Perks, and Pension.

50. Kenneth Whyte, "Sandra Manning Should Take an Active Role in Her

Husband's Work," *Globe and Mail*, March 19, 1994; Miro Cernetig, "Manning Collects $31,000 a Year from Party," *Globe and Mail*, March 26, 1994.

51. Miro Cernetig, "Manning Collects $31,000 a Year from Party," *Globe and Mail*, March 26, 1994.

52. Sean Durkan, "Reform MP Blasts Boss over Perks," *Calgary Sun*, April 6, 1994.

53. *Calgary Sun*, April 6, 1994.

54. Management and planning committee of executive council to members of Reform caucus, April 6, 1994.

55. Geoffrey York, "Reform MPs Snarl at Party Rebuke," *Globe and Mail*, April 8, 1994.

56. David Steinhart, "Manning Urges Unity in Reform Caucus," *Calgary Herald*, April 12, 1994.

57. David Steinhart, "Reform MPs Name Own Ethics Watchdogs," *Calgary Herald*, May 7, 1994.

58. Reform Party of Canada, minutes of executive council meeting, February 11 –12, 1994, 8.

59. Joan Crockatt, "Reformers Still Struggling with Learning Curve," *Calgary Herald*, June 24, 1994.

60. Mario Toneguzzi, "Reform to Refocus Efforts in House," *Calgary Herald*, June 23, 1994.

61. Preston Manning, "Countdown to Victory," audiocassette, December 2, 1993.

62. Preston Manning to constituency presidents, candidates, area organizers, memo, August 29, 1988.

63. James M. McPherson, *Ordeal by Fire: The Civil War and Reconstruction* (New York: Knopf, 1982), 125.

64. "The Blue Sheet," 6.

65. [1988] 2 S.C.R. 712.

66. Geoffrey York, "Hold the Steaks and Pass the Poutine," *Globe and Mail*, April 11, 1994; Sheldon Alberts, "Party Counting on Female Francophone," *Calgary Herald*, May 15, 1994.

67. David Steinhart, "Manning's Tour de Force," *Calgary Herald*, April 22, 1994.

68. "The Cross Canada Check In: Quebec Region," *The Reformer*, May, vol. 2, issue 3, 1994.

69. Preston Manning, "Broadening the Circle," audiocassette, March 4, 1994; "Reform Fund Canada Report," *The Reformer*, vol. 2, issue 3, May 1994.

70. Expansion committee personnel proposals, January 27, 1994.

71. Cliff Fryers, "Reform: On the Move!" *The Reformer*, vol. 2, issue 2, March 1994.

72. Preston Manning, "Broadening the Circle," audiocassette, March 4, 1994.

73. Ross Howard, "Manning, Labour Not a Perfect Union," *Globe and Mail*, May 6, 1994; David Steinhart, "Reform Party Leader Booed by Unionists," *Calgary Herald*, May 6, 1994.

74. Reform Party, *Principles and Policies*, 1991, 18–19.

75. Richard Nadeau and André Blais, "Explaining Election Outcomes in Canada: Economy and Politics," *Canadian Journal of Political Science* 26 (1993): 775–90.

76. Ibid., 782.

77. Ibid.

78. Susan Delacourt, "Focus on Bloc Worries Manning," *Globe and Mail*, January 21, 1994; Susan Delacourt, "'Tribal Politics' Riles Chrétien," *Globe and Mail*, April 14, 1994.

79. Geoffrey York and André Picard, "Irwin's Comments Erode Chrétien Strategy on Unity," *Globe and Mail*, May 19, 1994; "Manning Chastises Harcourt," *Calgary Herald*, May 20, 1994.

80. *House of Commons Debates*, May 24, 1994, 4343.

81. Ross Howard, "Manning Sounds Separatist Warning," *Globe and Mail*, May 26, 1994.

82. *House of Commons Debates*, July 7, 1994, 4908. The phrase "as one people" was omitted in the French version.

83. Ibid.

84. Ibid., 4910.

85. Preston Manning, "Manning: If Quebec Chooses Separation, What Then?" *Globe and Mail*, June 9, 1994.

86. Mario Toneguzzi, "Reform Will Push Separatism Woes," *Calgary Herald*, May 27, 1994.

87. *House of Commons Debates*, July 7, 1994, 4909.

88. Mario Toneguzzi, "Reform Jockeying for New Voice," *Calgary Herald*, June 9, 1994.

89. Hugh Winsor, "Referendum Question Arises," *Globe and Mail*, June 1, 1994.

90. Don McGillivray, "Manning Falling Prey to Ottawa Disease," *Calgary Herald*, June 6, 1994.

91. "Full Steam Ahead to Assembly '94," *The Reformer*, vol. 2, issue 4, June 1994.

CHAPTER 10

1. Sheldon Alberts, "Reformers Find Groove," *Calgary Herald*, August 20, 1994.

2. Sheldon Alberts, "Bloc Fires First Shot in 'War,'" *Calgary Herald*, October 1, 1994.

3. Sheldon Alberts, "Reform's Shots Hit Grits," *Calgary Herald*, October 29, 1994.

4. Anne Dawson, "Marching in Footsteps of Reform," *Calgary Sun*, October 30, 1994; Sheldon Alberts, "Hanger has no regrets," *Calgary Herald*, October 30, 1994.

5. Tu Thanh Ha, "Manning Plans Slow Approach in Unveiling Key Party Policies," *Globe and Mail*, October 26, 1994; Sheldon Alberts, "Reform Keeps Spending Plan under Wraps," *Calgary Herald*, October 26, 1994.

6. Information from Line Maheu, October 31, 1994.

7. Philip Gordon, to Tom Flanagan, letter, October 31, 1994.

8. Sheldon Alberts, "'Canada Wasn't Rejected,'" *Calgary Herald*, September 13, 1994.

9. Kim Lunman, "TV Poll Backs Reform Stand," *Calgary Herald*, October 4, 1994.

10. Preston Manning, "A New and Better Home for Canadians," October 15, 1994, 8.

11. Ibid., 9.

12. Jim Silye, "Separatists Threats in Parliament? You Bet I'm Angry!" *The Reformer*, September 1994, 1.

13. Reform Party of Canada, Assembly 1994, "Successful Policy Resolutions and Amendments to the Party Constitution" (draft).

14. Part I, Reform Party Policy Resolutions for Debate, Resolution #2.

15. Ibid., Resolution #8.

16. Hugh Winsor, "Reform's Ideological Purity Diluted," *Globe and Mail*, October 17, 1994.

17. Tu Thanh Ha, "Manning Spoiling for Fight on Unity," *Globe and Mail*, October 17, 1994.

18. *Alberta Report*, October 31, 1994.

19. CBC, "As It Happens," October 20, 1994.

20. Sheldon Alberts, "Reform Rejects Gay Families," *Calgary Herald*, October 14, 1994.

21. Sean Durkan, "Gay Policy Debate Upsets Calgary MP," *Calgary Sun*, October 14, 1994; Sheldon Alberts, "Second MP Breaks Ranks over Gays," *Calgary Herald*, October 16, 1994.

22. Sheldon Alberts, "Second MP Breaks Ranks over Gays," *Calgary Herald*, October 16, 1994.

CHAPTER 11

1. Stephen Harper and Tom Flanagan, "Our Benign Dictatorship," *The Next City* (January 1997), 35–40, 54–7; Flanagan and Harper, "Conservative Politics in Canada: Past, Present, and Future," in William Gairdner, ed., *After Liberalism* (Toronto: Stoddart, 1998), 168–92.

2. Preston Manning, *Think Big: My Adventures in Life and Democracy* (Toronto: McClelland and Stewart, 2002), 271–3.

3. Manning, *Think Big,* 271.

4. Ibid, 288.

5. Ibid, 298.

6. Ibid, 328.

7. Ibid, 333.

8. The Alliance raised $19.6 million in 2000, compare to $20.1 for the Liberals. Elections Canada website, www.elections.ca/ecFiscals/2000/table01_e.html.

9. Manning, *Think Big*, 343–5.

10. Faron Ellis, "The More Things Change…The Alliance Campaign," in Jon H. Pammett and Christopher Dornan, eds, *The Canadian General Election of 2000* (Toronto: Dundurn, 2000), 76.

11. Tom Flanagan, "Alliance Tax Policy: Getting It Right," *National Post*, 9 October 2000.

12. Mark O. Dickerson and Thomas Flanagan, *An Introduction to Government and Politics: A Conceptual Approach* (Toronto: Nelson, 2002; 6th ed.), 160.

13. Manning, *Think Big*, 346.

14. Ellis, "The More Things Change," 81.

15. Warren Kinsella, *The War Room: Political Strategies for Business, NGOs, and Anyone Who Wants to Win* (Toronto: Dundurn, 2007), 143.

16. Tom Flanagan, "Taking Stock: Making Choices," *National Post*, 29 November 2000.

17. Quoted in William Johnson, *Stephen Harper and the Future of Canada* (Toronto: McClelland and Stewart, 2005), 288.

18. Manning, *Think Big*, 394–7.

19. Deborah Grey, *Never Retreat, Never Explain, Never Apologize* (Toronto: Key Porter, 2004), 190–213.

20. Anthony Downs, *An Economic Theory of Democracy* (New York: Harper and Row, 1957), 131.

21. John Laschinger and Geoffrey Stevens, *Leaders and Lesser Mortals* (Toronto: KeyPorter, 1992), 168–70.

22. Tom Flanagan and Harold Jansen, "Election Campaigns under Canada's Party Finance Laws," in Jon H. Pammett and Christopher Dornan, eds, *The Canadian General Election of 2008* (Toronto: Dundurn, 2009), forthcoming.

23. *Recall and Initiative Act*, SBC 1994 c. 56.

24. Johnson, *Stephen Harper*, 254–5.

25. Bill C-341, s. 2, House of Commons, 1996–97, www2.parl.gc.ca/HousePublications/Publication.aspx?DocId=2329733&Language=e&Mode=1&File=16.

26. Johnson, *Stephen Harper*, 276.

27. In the first edition of *Waiting for the Wave*, 47, I wrongly attributed the slogan to Ted Byfield. The real creator was Ralph Hedlin, a columnist for Byfield's *Alberta Report* magazine.

28. Victory speech, 23 January 2006, posted at www.freerepublic.com/focus/f-news/1564396/posts.

29. Edward Greenspon and Anthony Wilson-Smith, *Double Vision: The Inside Story of the Liberals in Power* (Toronto: Doubleday Canada, 1996), 235–6.

30. Herb Grubel, *A Professor in Parliament* (Vancouver: self-published, 2000), 255.

31. www.arationaladvocate.com/worldofeconomics.htm.

32. Manning, *Think Big*, 276.

APPENDIX

1. Rein Taagepera and Matthew Soberg Shugart, *Seats and Votes: The Effects and Determinants of Electoral Systems* (New Haven: Yale University Press, 1989), 84.

2. Anthony Downs, *An Economic Theory of Democracy* (New York: Harper and Row, 1957), 128–29.

3. Arend Lijphart, *Democracies: Patterns of Majoritarian and Consensus Government in Twenty-One Countries* (New Haven: Yale University Press, 1984), 127–49; Richard Johnson et al., *Letting the People Decide: Dynamics of a Canadian Election* (Montreal and Kingston: McGill-Queen's University Press, 1992), 85–111.

4. Maurice Pinard, *The Rise of a Third Party: A Study in Crisis Politics* (Montreal: McGill-Queen's University Press, 1975/1971), 37.

5. Maurice Pinard, "The Independence Issue and the Polarization of the Electorate: The 1973 Quebec Election," *Canadian Journal of Political Science* 10 (1977): 215–59; Pinard, "The Parti Québécois Comes to Power: An Analysis of the 1976 Quebec Election," *Canadian Journal of Political Science* 11 (1978): 739–75.

6. Maurice Pinard, "Third Parties in Canada Revisited: A Rejoinder and Elaboration of One-Party Dominance," *Canadian Journal of Political Science* 6 (1973): 442. Emphasis in the original.

7. Alain G. Gagnon and A. Brian Tanguay, "Minor Parties of Protest in Canada: Origins, Impact, and Prospects," in Gagnon and Tanguay, eds., *Canadian Parties in Transition: Discourse, Organization, and Representation* (Scarborough: Nelson Canada, 1989), 239.

8. Stephen L. Fischer, *The Minor Parties of the Federal Republic of Germany: Toward a Comparative Theory of Minor Parties* (The Hague: Martinus Nijhoff, 1974), 26.

9. Steven J. Rosenstone, Roy L. Behr, and Edward H. Lazarus, *Third Parties in America: Citizen Response to Major Party Failure* (Princeton, N.J.: Princeton University Press, 1984), 181.

10. E.C. Manning, *Political Realignment: A Challenge to Thoughtful Canadians* (Toronto: McClelland and Stewart, 1967), 51.

11. Randall G. Holcombe, "Barriers to Entry and Political Competition," *Journal of Theoretical Politics* 3 (1991): 231–40; Filip Palda, *Election Finance Regulation in Canada* (Vancouver: Fraser Institute, 1991).

12. Anthony Downs, *An Economic Theory of Democracy*, 118.

13. Ibid., 259.

14. Patrick Donleavy, *Democracy, Bureaucracy and Public Choice* (New York: Prentice-Hall, 1991), 132–35.

15. Réjean Landry, "Incentives Created by the Institutions of Representative Democracy," in Herman Bakvis, ed., *Representation, Integration and Political Parties in Canada* (Toronto: Dundurn, 1991), 446–48; Steven J. Brams, *Rational Politics; Decisions, Games, and Strategy* (Boston: Academic Press, 1985), 32–36.

16. Ibid., Brams originally developed the model for American primaries. It works better there than for parties because, with the turnover of candidates, the factor of inertia is not so great.

17. Downs, *An Economic Theory of Democracy*, 131.

18. See Keith Archer and Alan Whitehorn, "Opinion Structure Among Party Activists: A Comparison of New Democrats, Liberals and Conservatives," In Hugh G. Thorburn, ed., *Party Politics in Canada* (Scarborough: Prentice-Hall Canada, 1991), 144–59.

19. Robert Mason Lee, *One Hundred Monkeys* (Toronto: Macfarlane Walter and Ross, 1989), 135–36.

20. Landry, "Incentives," 449–52; William H. Riker, *Liberalism Against Populism: A Confrontation between the Theory of Democracy and the Theory of Social Choice* (Prospect Heights, Ill.: Waveland Press, 1988), 185–88.

21. Donleavy, *Democracy, Bureaucracy and Public Choice*, 112–44.

22. Riker, *Liberalism Against Populism*, 197–232.

23. Lijphart, *Democracies*, 130.

Selected Bibliography

Archer, Keith, and Faron Ellis. "Opinion Structure of Reform Party Activists." Midwest Political Science Association, Chicago, April 1993.

Archer, Keith, and Alan Whitehorn. "Opinion Structure Among Party Activists: A Comparison of New Democrats, Liberals and Conservatives." In *Party Politics in Canada*, edited by Hugh G. Thorburn. Scarborough: Prentice-Hall Canada, 1991.

Barr, John J. *The Dynasty: The Rise and Fall of Social Credit in Alberta*. Toronto: McClelland and Stewart, 1974.

Barr, John J., and Owen Anderson. *The Unfinished Revolt: Some Views on Western Independence*. Toronto: McClelland and Stewart, 1971.

Baxter-Moore, N.J. "Ideology or Pragmatism? The Politics and Management of the Mulroney Government's Privatization Programme." *British Journal of Canadian Studies* 7 (1992).

Beck, Nuala. *Shifting Gears*. Toronto: HarperCollins, 1992.

Bell, Daniel. *The End of Ideology: On the Exhaustion of Political Ideas in the Fifties*. New York: Free Press, 1962.

Bersuson, David, J.L Granatstein, and W.R. Young. *Sacred Trust? Brian Mulroney and the Conservative Party in Power*. Toronto: Doubleday Canada, 1986.

Boldt, Menno. *Surviving as Indians: The Challenge of Self-Government*. Toronto: University of Toronto Press, 1993.

Brams, Steven J. *Rational Politics: Decisions, Games, and Strategy*. Boston: Academic Press, 1985.

Byfield, Ted., ed. *Act of Faith*. Vancouver: British Columbia Report Books, 1991.

Canovan, Margaret. *Populism*. London: Junction Books, 1981.

Dobbin, Murray. *Preston Manning and the Reform Party*. Toronto: James Lorimer, 1991.

Donleavy, Patrick. *Democracy, Bureaucracy and Public Choice*. New York: Prentice-Hall, 1991.

Downs, Anthony. *An Economic Theory of Democracy*. New York: Harper and Row, 1957.

Eagles, Monroe, James P. Bickerton, Alain G. Gagnon, and Patrick J. Smith. *The Almanac of Canadian Politics*. Peterborough: Broadview Press, 1991.

Fischer, Stephen I. *The Minor Parties of the Federal Republic of Germany: Toward a Comparative Theory of Minor Parties.* The Hague: Martinus Nijhoff, 1974.

Flanagan, Thomas, and Faron Ellis. "A Comparative Profile of the Reform Party of Canada." Canadian Political Science Association, Charlottetown, June 1992.

Fraser, Graham. *Playing for Keeps: The Making of the Prime Minister, 1988.* Toronto: McClelland and Stewart, 1989.

Gagnon, Alain G., and Brian A. Tanguay. "Minor Parties of Protest in Canada: Origins, Impact, and Prospects." In *Canadian Parties in Transition: Discourse, Organization, and Representation,* edited by Alain G. Gagnon and A. Brian Tanguay. Scarborough: Nelson Canada, 1989.

Henry, Shawn. "The Bases of Support for the Reform Party of Canada: Riding a Populist Wave or Providing a Conservative Alternative?" Master's thesis, University of Calgary, 1993.

Holcombe, Randall G. "Barriers to Entry and Political Competition." *Journal of Theoretical Politics* 3 (1991).

Hurtig, Mel. *A New and Better Canada: Principles and Policies of a New Canadian Political Party.* Toronto: Stoddart, 1992.

Johnston, Richard, et al. *Letting the People Decide: Dynamics of a Canadian Election.* Montreal and Kingston: McGill-Queen's University Press, 1992.

———. "The People and the Charlottetown Accord." In *Canada: The State of the Federation 1993,* edited by Ronald L. Watts and Douglas M. Brown. Kingston, Ont.: Institute of Intergovernmental Affairs, 1993.

Johnston, Richard, Neil Nevitte, and Henry R. Brady. "Campaign Dynamics in 1993: Liberals, Conservatives, and Reform." Canadian Political Science Association, Calgary, June 1994.

Landry, Réjean. "Incentives Created by the Institutions of Representative Democracy." In *Representation, Integration and Political Parties in Canada,* edited by Herman Bakvis. Toronto: Dundurn, 1991.

Laschinger, John, and Geoffrey Stevens. *Leaders and Lesser Mortals: Backroom Politics in Canada.* Toronto: Key Porter, 1992.

Laycock, David. "Institutions and Ideology in the Reform Party Project" Canadian Political Science Association, Ottawa, June 1993.

Laycock, David. *Populism and Democratic Thought in the Canadian Prairies, 1910–1945.* Toronto: University of Toronto Press, 1990.

Lee, Robert Mason. *One Hundred Monkeys.* Toronto: Macfarlane Walter and Ross, 1989.

Lijphart, Arend. *Democracies: Patterns of Majoritarian and Consensus Government in Twenty-One Countries.* New Haven: Yale University Press, 1984.

Luntz, Frank I. *Candidates, Consultants, and Campaigns: The Style and Substance of American Electioneering.* Oxford: Blackwell, 1988.

Machiavelli, Nicolo. *The Prince,* translated by George Bull. Harmondsworth: Penguin, 1961.

Magleby, David. "Opinion Formation and Opinion Change in Ballot Proposition Campaigns." In *Manipulating Public Opinion: Essays on Public Opinion as a Dependent Variable*, edited by Michael Margolis and Gary A. Mauser. Pacific Grove, Calif.: Brooks/Cole, 1989.

Manning, E. C. *Political Realignment: A Challenge to Thoughtful Canadians.* Toronto: McClelland and Stewart, 1967.

———. "The White Paper on Human Resources Development." Edmonton, 1967.

Manning, Preston. *The New Canada.* Toronto: Macmillan Canada, 1992.

———. "The Reconciliation of Parties In Conflict: The Theory and Application of a Model of Last Resort." In *With Heart, Mind and Strength: The Best of Crux 1979–1989*, edited by Donald M. Lewis. Langley, B.C.: CREDO Publishing, 1990.

McCall-Newman, Christina. *Grits: An Intimate Portrait of the Liberal Party.* Toronto: Macmillan Canada, 1982.

McPherson, James M. *Ordeal by Fire: The Civil War and Reconstruction.* New York: Knopf, 1982.

Melnyk, George. "Waiting for the Wave." *NeWest Review*, April/May 1989.

Nadeau, Richard, and André Blais. "Explaining Election Outcomes in Canada: Economy and Politics." *Canadian Journal of Political Science* 26 (1993).

Nesbitt-Larking, Paul. "Patterns of Protest in the 1992 Referendum and the 1993 Federal Election." Canadian Political Science Association, Calgary, June 1994.

Nevitte, Neil. "Electoral Discontinuity: The 1993 Canadian Federal Election." Jerusalem: Israel Association for Canadian Studies, May 1994.

Newman, Peter C. *The Distemper of Our Times: Canadian Politics in Transition.* Toronto: McClelland and Stewart, 1968.

Pal, Leslie A. "The Political Executive and Political Leadership in Alberta." In *Government and Politics in Alberta*, edited by Allan Tupper and Roger Gibbins. Edmonton: University of Alberta Press, 1992.

Palda, Filip. *Election Finance Regulation in Canada.* Vancouver: Fraser Institute, 1991.

Pinard Maurice. "The Independence Issue and the Polarization of the Electorate: The 1973 Quebec Election." *Canadian Journal of Political Science* 10 (1977).

———. "The Parti Québécois Comes to Power: An Analysis of the 1976 Quebec Election." *Canadian Journal of Political Science* 11 (1978).

———. *The Rise of a Third Party: A Study in Crisis Politics.* Montreal and Kingston: McGill-Queen's University Press, 1975.

———. "Third Parties in Canada Revisited: A Rejoinder and Elaboration of One-Party Dominance." *Canadian Journal of Political Science* 6 (1973).

Riker, William H. *Liberalism Against Populism: A Confrontation between the Theory of Democracy and the Theory of Social Choice.* Prospect Heights, Ill.: Waveland Press, 1988.

Rosenstone, Steven J., Roy I Behr, and Edward H. Lazarus. *Third Parties in America: Citizen Response to Major Party Failure.* Princeton, N.J.: Princeton University Press, 1984.

Sawatsky, John. *The Insiders: Government, Business, and the Lobbyists.* Toronto: McClelland and Stewart, 1987.

Sharpe, Sydney, and Don Braid. *Storming Babylon: Preston Manning and the Rise of the Reform Party.* Toronto: Key Porter, 1992.

Simpson, Jeffrey. *Faultlines: Struggling for a Canadian Vision.* Toronto: HarperCollins, 1993.

Sinclair, Peter R. "The Case of Western Canada." In *Riel to Reform: A History of Protest in Western Canada*, edited by George Melnyk. Saskatoon: Fifth House, 1992.

Taagepera, Rein, and Matthew Soberg Shugart. *Seats and Votes: The Effects and Determinants of Electoral Systems.* New Haven: Yale University Press, 1989.

Walker, Michael, and Isabella Horry. "March's Solution: How to Effectively Cut Federal Spending." *Fraser Forum*, March 1993.

Whyte, Kenneth. "Preston Manning: PM or Post Mortem?" *Saturday Night*, July/August 1993.

Wilson, James Q. *American Government: Institutions and Politcs*, 3rd ed. Lexington, Mass.: D.C. Heath, 1986.

Zwarun, Suzanne. "Women and the Reform Party." *Chatelaine*, March 1992.

Index